# What's In Your Backpack?

*Overcoming 7 Mistakes
That Can Steal God's Best For Your Life*

Russ Shinpoch

First published by Dog Ear Publishing
4010 W. 86th Street, Ste H
Indianapolis, IN 46268
www.dogearpublishing.net

ISBN: 978-1-4575-1192-9

This book is printed on acid-free paper.

Printed in the United States of America

*This book is dedicated to*

## My wife Carol,
## The Love of my Life

Because of her...
first kiss,
commitment to Christ,
uncommon dignity,
contagious laugh,
love for the beach and bikes on Hilton Head,
ability to listen to my dreams and failures without appearing bored,
dedication to rescuing children through speech therapy,
passion to travel from Alaska to Zambia,
gift of hospitality,
coupon cutting,
love for children and grandchildren,
sustained grace toward me through multiple life changes,
prayer over every my every step in leadership roles and writing this book,
AND homemade cinnamon rolls...

*God has given me an awesome life!*

# ACKNOWLEDGEMENTS

*My parents,* **John and Barb**, *have been huge encouragers through all my success and failures, always believing in what God was doing in my life.*
*They model the life I strive to live. I am thankful to be their son. I love them.*

*My children,* **Joanne, Joel, and Jonathan** *have adapted to multiple moves and lived in the public spotlight amazingly well.*
*Their respect and belief in me has been an undeserved lifeline.*
*I am thankful to be their father. I love them more than life.*
*Joanne's husband,* **Trey**, *and Joel's wife,* **Jennifer**,
*have offered consistent encouragement.*
*They are cherished family.*
*Most of all, laughter and balance comes to my life through the adventures of*
**Anna Kate, Abby, Emma, Callie, and Jessie.**

# CONTENTS

# The *BACK*story

Africa was our dream destination. It was July—dry season in southern Africa. Johannesburg, South Africa to Victoria Falls, Zimbabwe was the final leg of the 8,000-mile flight package that began in Atlanta, Georgia. Our African family safari and mission adventure started in Vic Falls with local cooks serving us an evening buffet of croc, antelope, hippo, wart hog, and a sampling of whatever other wildlife moved too slow that day. The barbequed zebra was amazing! Just kidding. It could have been python for all I know. An evening boat ride on the Zambezi River erased the stress-fatigue of crossing 7 time zones and capped months of anticipation. Panoramic views of elephants near the river banks silhouetted against a copper-colored sunset were deceptively innocent. Perfect Nikon moments. Nobody suspected it was a sign of the surreal danger that would unfold on week two of our journey. And I got a *once-in-a-lifetime* photo of it!

Fast forward past week one—an amazing, 6-day family safari and mission venture 100km deep into the bush *(see the story in Chapter 5 for more details)*. Excited but exhausted from time zone shifts, survival camping, intense encounters, and sleepless nights, our family and team retreated to Sikumi Tree Lodge at Hwange National Park, Zimbabwe (the largest game reserve in the country) for a 3-day recovery prior to the return flight. There were nightly debates around that campfire about what we appreciated most—a shower, a bed, or the buffet? We slept in Swiss Family Robinson-style tree houses overlooking a huge waterhole, listening nightly to the roar of black-maned Kalahari lions capturing prey just outside the perimeter of our compound. Game guides were on call for *tourist-style* jeep safaris, night or day, steering wide-eyed guests perilously close to giraffe, Cape buffalo, wart hog, gazelle, leopard, lion, rhino, elephant, and more. To experience it to the max, my family crowded into an open-top old jeep for another late afternoon safari drive and photoshoot. The guide didn't miss a hole on the jungle roads trying to reach a remote waterhole by sunset to capture the chaos of diverse game converging for an evening drink (or meal). Our first sign of impending danger was the guide's statement that he had his rifle beside the driver's seat.

Without warning, deep into a dense jungle area, the guide suddenly stopped the jeep in the middle of the trail and got serious: "Sit still. Do not move. Do not talk." It seemed like we were surrounded with sounds of something crashing through the trees and brush. It got confusing—sounding like something wild was coming at us from all directions. We were in the path but hopefully not in the way. The guide then looked back at us with a big smile as though he was taking credit—or wanting a tip—for creating an experience any normal tourists would die for (we almost did): "Elephants. A whole herd." I thought, "What's up with the smile? We're going to die!" Seconds later, massively-tusked bull and female elephants with their young close beside were knocking down trees and brush like it was grass, snorting and stomping their way around our jeep. I always thought you could see something that big coming a mile away. You can't. It was scary how quickly they burst out of the thick jungle growth. When you are only a few feet away, you realize how massive they really are. I knew I should have paid more attention to the charging elephant scene in *King Solomon's Mines*. Like the inexperienced English hunter in the movie, we just froze for a few seconds in disbelief. None of us could speak. Then somebody grabbed my arm with a death grip. I thought it was the guide because I didn't hear any shots. I wondered if my wife loved me enough to throw herself in front of the herd for me, but she didn't move. My sons quickly jumped to the back of the jeep (as if that would do any good), tossing the camera in the air toward me. While the guide said, "Don't worry. Just don't make sudden moves," I snapped a couple of random shots out of total fear, faster than a 4G download. One of those photos now hangs in our hallway like a trophy! In those milliseconds where everything seemed to shift into slow motion, I assumed we would be killed in the elephant stampede, but the photos of how we died would be discovered, so at least it would seem dramatic. It was the closest I've ever come to having something happen that might get me interviewed by Matt Lauer on the TODAY Show. It was a huge herd, spooked by lions or something, stampeding and gone in less than two minutes. We were so close to the elephants—*which means close to death*—that I could smell their armpits and see the plaque on those giant ivory tusks. That has become another unforgettable "near miss" life-moment that we serve up with laughter occasionally as a good memory at family gatherings…at least, several years later we laugh…nervously. I can show you my scars…uh, where the *camera* hit me. Here's my bridge analogy…

That whole African adventure thing—*the stampede, the sunsets, the choices, the smells, the scenes, the sounds, the sacrifices, the fatigue, the experiences, the emotions, the animals, the grass fires, the songs, the dances, the insects, the rivers, the diseases, the history, the languages, the tribes, the huts, the starvation, the idols, the wood carvings, the food, the heat, the people, and the reactions*—was all bundled, processed, and stuffed into my memory and spirit…sometimes selectively, sometimes indiscriminately. All of it shaping in some degree my emotions, attitudes, decisions, thinking, plans, and relationships forever. That God-created spirit—our mental/emotional/spiritual life-center—is what I label a **BACKPACK** for the purposes of the larger conversation of this book. Just think of it as a way to describe the inner person you really are that captures, contains, and controls all your experiences, reactions, memories, thoughts, emotions, and choices. Here's the downside. Because God created us to enjoy a relationship with Him in an awesome life, like a real **backpack**, your spirit has a limited capacity for negative emotions and destructive choices. If you don't manage those self-defeating emotions and choices in compliance with

God's instructions for your life-race, you will be weighed down and over-whelmed—like carrying an **overloaded backpack**. And what you pack inside—positive or negative—defines both your level of happiness and the direction of your life.

In that sense, our safaris were no different than any other ordinary moment, segment, or season of life. Every day we are moving forward in our life-journey toward some destination of our choice. We lock into situations by choice or get "stampeded" by circumstances that have the potential ultimately to shape who we are. Those life experiences often define us in ways we don't always stop to investigate. A lot of what we chase and some of what we get dumped on us is negative and toxic. And our natural reaction is to hold on to wrong or sinful reactions and desires—*that we can't explain, feel we didn't deserve, want to enjoy, can't defend, or suck us into addiction*—in order to stay in control. Pack enough of those self-defeating responses into your spirit—your **backpack**—that are connected with pain, disappointment, hurt, or rejection and they will own your life, overloading your ability to cope and live life the way God intended.

Result? You become vulnerable to making *7 frequently repeated mistakes that can steal God's best for your life.* In this book, we'll target, expose, and investigate these **7 MISTAKES** so you can get past them successfully and *embrace God's destiny for your life.* On the journey, we will also deal with more life-saving techniques than gadgets on a Leatherman Multi-Tool, as our trail takes some surprising twists and turns around big issues like a *60 Minutes*-style investigation into temptation, debunking myths about commitment, making 7 Right Choices to re-pack your backpack, taking the steps toward real confession that creates healthy relationships, capturing the secrets of endurance, researching the DNA of a choice, and even making sense of suffering.

You have a history like nobody else, full of positive and negative experiences. But you also have a heart hunger for something better…like everybody else. God is real and wants to help you process what happens to you in a way that moves you forward toward His destiny for you. There is an awesome life planned for you. It's more than a journey. It's a race—a competitive race with huge stakes. Threats are coming at you from every direction. And you can't survive it if your **backpack** is overloaded with the weight of really bad emotions and experiences that God never intended for you to carry…or, more scary…to own you!

If you want something better…if you are willing to risk allowing God into your conversation, debate, or investigation…if you get the fact that every choice matters and you don't have forever to make a decision and you are really not in control…then take on this book. Please finish the book. It may not come together for you until the last chapter. You don't have to agree with everything I put on the table, but I do think you have to deal with the big issues. Thanks. Hope it makes sense. That's my prayer—that God would speak to you in these pages—and your life would be radically changed.  Oh, and by the way…that you would be free of that stuff in your **backpack** that's killing you right now!

**So, what's in your backpack?**

# PART ONE:

# The Backpack

## Chapter 1

# The Backpack

**Today is your only reality.** You've got a past. The future is a question mark...and life can't be paused...or reversed.

### A 13-year-old, an Officer and a McDonald's Surveillance Camera

"I asked him for 10 cents....for cookies." That simple request by Davian Tinsley, 13, started the last conversation of 36-year-old Police Officer Jeremy Henwood's life. Davian approached Officer Henwood at a San Diego McDonald's counter on Sunday, August 7, 2011. Speaking about Officer Henwood's reaction to Davian, NBC News reporter Lee Cowan memorialized his last act: "Rarely do surveillance cameras capture the good in people....he opened his wallet and his heart to a kid he'd never met." [1] Officer Henwood paid for the cookies, picked up his order, filled his drink, and walked out of that McDonalds restaurant. Minutes later he was dead, gunned down by a fleeing robbery suspect while just sitting in his patrol car. A life ended too soon.

A hero. A Marine captain and combat veteran. Remembered and respected by peers as a generous and upbeat leader. A fellow Marine officer friend even called him "Motivator". He flew planes, skied, scuba-dived, and hated writing reports. And now we've all lost him. Cowan didn't just capture the tragedy—he nailed it: "A crime made even more incomprehensible by the fact that he had just returned from Afghanistan and served two tours in Iraq as a U.S. Marine....It was the last thing he did that summed up the way he lived....Kindness can go a long way, but life isn't always fair." [2]

Can you explain what happened? I can't. It's not right. You know it and I know it. It's way too random. And unexplained tragedies are all too frequent. But neither his family nor those who now know his story can escape being a part of that reality. My heart broke for them. No matter how much we want to believe that tragedy isn't real, or wish that it never happened, it is reality. That moment can't be reversed. Just like neuroscience

Ph.D. candidate James Holmes firing 4 guns of ammo into a packed premier of *Dark Knight Rises* at the Century Theater in Aurora, Colorado on July 20, 2012, killing 12 and wounding 58, is all too real. Life is a series of moments...some chosen...some chosen for us...that link to create a mosaic of an amazing, mysterious, a sometimes boring, a sometimes *take-all-the-oxygen-out-of-the-room* journey. All of us are on a unique life-journey. Your journey is simultaneously in motion and under construction right now. And you are not doing it alone, even if you want it that way. God is in the mix. And choices matter for now and for eternity. That's my position. That's reality too. And reality actually matters in doing life.

Life is brief. Trials are universal. Disappointment is epidemic. With almost zero choice, we are routinely forced to absorb *Mt. Everest-size* pain and *9-11-size* questions that imprint our spirit. Our spirit is the God-designed processing center of emotions, attitudes, memories, and decisions. All life events are captured in our spirit, and how we manage what happens to us shapes our capacity for happiness, responsiveness to God, and ability to make choices and build relationships.

Negative experiences happen. Nobody can rewind 9-11, change the outcome of the 2012 SuperBowl, wish Down syndrome away, or pretend divorce doesn't exist. Those and more are downloaded on the hard drive of your memory...stories shaping your life journey.

And all of us have stories. Lots of them. Embedded in those stories, like strata on the walls of the Grand Canyon, are layers of changes. And all of us face changes—*planned, positive, painful, perplexing, or permanent*—with results that are often unexpected and unwanted. What we do with the changes—how we manage life's intersections and interruptions—shapes our stories and determines the ultimate destiny of our journeys. It's a familiar choice to either *process* or *pack* the bad stuff. Whether you know it or not, you are right now either dealing with routine and predictable hurt or denying it by cramming the raw stress deeper into your spirit. Deal with it...or it will eventually own you.

That's why I've chosen the **backpack** image. Your spirit is like a backpack in the sense that your mind and emotions capture and carry everything that happens to you—*a lot of it negative and destructive.* Unless you follow God's instructions for your life-race, those unprocessed emotions and choices become overwhelming and weigh you down—like an **overloaded backpack**. All your choices and reactions to every single situation on your life journey are dumped into the mix and must be managed. A backpack is typically used to carry personal items or gear essential for everything from family trips, business deals, sports events, hiking, emergency medical response, soldiers on patrol, and travel, to classes at school. So I'm using a backpack to represent your spirit and whatever unfiltered emotions and choices you choose to carry in your spirit. My plan? To help you avoid and/or get rid of the sinful experiences, negative reactions, killer emotions, destructive thinking, defeating relation-ships, and bad choices that you are packing by: (1) challenging you to take responsibility for your individual, non-reversible, irreplaceable, God-designed journey of life; and, (2) creating some momentum to manage your own "emo-tional and spiritual backpack" by looking at how you make choices.

So this book is about survival…and purpose…and meaning…and some *unpacking*…and maybe some *re-packing*. It's about how and why we make choices…how we interpret and deal with what happens to us—the mostly negative reactions we carry around with us every day, all crammed into our memories, emotions, and spirit like an **overloaded backpack**. Fact: Nobody wants to be owned by anything. So why are you? Everybody wants freedom. Why aren't you free? Everybody wants peace. What's taken it from you? Everybody wants a purpose. Why can't you figure it out?

**What's in your backpack?** What are you carrying around? Why? What are going to do with it? The hurt and disappointment is real. What you choose to pack and carry influences what you will achieve and how you impact others. Let's bundle it: *(1) You ARE what you carry; and, (2) What you keep gets carried into the next relationship.*

So, let's talk about how it feels to carry around *your* backpack.

## Tim McGraw's Next 30 Years

**It's complicated.** At least that's how it feels. You could never have imagined you would be where you are. You can't explain what's happened to you. There were expectations…dreams…plans. Things weren't supposed to be this crazy…this painful. Maybe you didn't ask for it, don't want it, didn't expect it, or can't explain it, but mentally you have voted—you can't go on like this! Sometimes it feels like a crime scene investigation with no clue as to who's guilty. You've tried to work through the issues on your plate and it's not getting better. It's not work-ing, and you aren't sure why. But…you are covering it up well…or at least *you* think you are. Not many people would guess at what you've got underground in your emotions, but you just are not *where* you want to be…or not *what* you thought you could be. You want answers. You want solutions. You want closure. Things need to be fixed. Changes are needed and you are trying to deal with it, move on and just do life. Antonio Curtis of Vallejo, California got that kind of a message when he dialed a wrong number:

> *"I am not available right now, but I thank you for caring enough to call. I am making some changes in my life. Please leave a message after the beep. If I do not return your call, you are one of the changes."*

Possibly you feel like you were destined to achieve more, have more, or experience more, but it's always just out of reach. Just when you thought you got what you wanted and everybody else said you had to experience, it wasn't what you thought. You've climbed one mountain peak only to discover a sign that says: "This is not it. Go back. Take a left at the last mountain trail and try again." You are sick and tired of the junk at home, work, school, and on your Facebook page. You know you can't keep lying to yourself by arguing that the next date, marriage, class, sale, championship, post, job, degree, sale, vacation, drink, home, par, getaway, baby, party, promotion or election will be the answer.

Conclusion? Something's not right. An error message has popped up. But no officer has had to arrest you. The paparazzi are probably not chasing you to capture that one embarrassing moment. Friends haven't done an intervention. The boss has not called you in. *60 Minutes* is not requesting an interview. When you're alone late at night, just you, a pizza, movie channel…and God…it's all too real. Or you feel trapped in this bubble of confusion when you're in the car, in traffic, on the trip, in seat 19B for the long flight, after the game, when the party's over, the morning after, during the test, with ear buds in, all alone in the locker room or at the office, or even zoning out while your friend is talking. Your thoughts drift and this familiar inner voice whispers again that you KNOW that you are simply not the person you want to be…and should be! You want to do it better but you haven't got the answer. Country music mega-star, Tim McGraw, hit on it in his song, "My Next Thirty Years":

*I think I'll take a moment, celebrate my age*
*The ending of an era and the turning of a page*
*Now it's time to focus in on where I go from here*
*Lord have mercy on my next thirty years*

*Hey, my next thirty years I'm gonna have some fun*
*Try to forget about all the crazy things I've done*
*Maybe now I've conquered all my adolescent fears*
*And I'll do it better in my next thirty years*

*My next thirty years I'm gonna settle all the scores*
*Cry a little less, laugh a little more*
*Find a world of happiness without the hate and fear*
*Figure out just what I'm doing here*
*In my next thirty years*

*Oh my next thirty years, I'm gonna watch my weight*
*Eat a few more salads and not stay up so late*
*Drink a little lemonade and not so many beers*
*Maybe I'll remember my next thirty years*

*My next thirty years will be the best years of my life*
*Raise a little family and hang out with my wife*
*Spend precious moments with the ones that I hold dear*
*Make up for lost time here, in my next thirty years*
*In my next thirty years*

Like the song, maybe you thought you would be doing life differently by now. Life is multiple-choice. You've picked *"d. All of the above"* to cover your bases, but what you've chosen is not working for you. You are tired, really sick of trying to maintain whatever image you think everybody else wants from you. Sustaining the impression of being successful and satisfied is taking more energy every day. There's this sense of feeling like a hypocrite to your family and closest friends. More than that, you might be ready to give up—feeling empty, frustrated, or discontent, lacking passion and energy, maybe losing it with anger, and definitely confused. It's bizarre, but those are just symptoms of bigger issues.

## Shrimp in the Curtain Rods

Here's the deal. You've been hurt…rejected…disappointed. We all have. Life changed when it happened. You know you haven't totally been in control since. Like being harnessed into one of those inflatable bungee runs, you feel like you are pulling against huge resistance, and when you weaken you'll be jerked back to the beginning. Everything you do and feel seems linked to that moment when hurt violated you. The hurt is re-shaping you and you aren't happy or comfortable. And it's not going away. Sometimes you obsess with questions like, "Why did this happen? When will the pain go away? How do I quit thinking about this? When is this going to make sense? Is anybody listening?" And, even though it's incriminating to admit, you have secretly wanted God, or Tin Tin, Jason Bourne, Manny or Sid the Sloth from *Ice Age*, a TRANSFORMER, Alex the lion from *Madagascar*, Harry Potter, Jack Sparrow from *Pirates of the Caribbean*, comedian Dennis Miller, Marine Jake Sully from *Avatar*, a Colombian drug cartel, an NFL defensive lineman, Indiana Jones, the Washington press corps, and/or a red-meat lawyer to put some hurt on the person(s) you think is responsible for your misery.

Sort of like the woman, in the infamous internet story that follows, whose life had become so complicated that she chose a simple solution.

After 17 years of marriage, a man dumped his wife for a younger woman. The upscale downtown condo was in his name, and he wanted to remain there with his new love, so he asked the wife to move out, promising to buy her another place. The wife agreed but negotiated for three final days alone there to pack up and move her things.

She spent the first day packing her belongings into boxes, crates and suitcases. The next day movers came and loaded the stuff. On day three, she sat down for the last time at their beautiful dining room table by candlelight, put on some soft background music, and feasted on a pound of shrimp. When she had finished, she walked into each room, deposited a few shrimp shells into the hollow of the curtain rods, cleaned up the kitchen, and left.

When the husband returned with his new girlfriend, it was awesome for the first few days. Then slowly, the condo was overtaken by a strong odor. They tried everything to eliminate the awful smell. Vents were checked for dead rodents, and carpets were steam cleaned. Air fresheners were hung everywhere. Exterminators were brought in to set off gas canisters, during which time they had to move out for a few days. In the end they even paid to replace the expensive carpeting. Nothing worked. People stopped coming over to visit. Repairmen refused to work in the house. Even the housekeeper quit.

When they could not take the stench any longer, they decided to move. A month later, even though they had cut their price in half, they couldn't find a buyer for their stinky apartment. Word got out, and eventually even the local realtors refused to return their calls. In desperation, the couple had to borrow a huge sum of money from the bank to purchase a new place.

The ex-wife called her former husband and asked how things were going. He gave her the full drama of the "stinking condo". She listened politely and said that she desperately missed her old home, and would be willing to reduce her divorce settlement in exchange for getting the condo back. Knowing his ex-wife had no idea how bad the smell was, he agreed on a price that was about 1/10th of what the condo had been worth, but only if she were to sign the papers that very day. She agreed and within the hour his lawyers delivered the paperwork. A week later, the man and his new girlfriend stood smirking as they watched the moving company pack everything to take to their new home…including the curtain rods!

When you've had your life flipped, a little "shrimp in the curtain rods" feels **really** good, doesn't it?

Problem: you *still* don't have the life you wanted…or answers…or control…or confidence…or peace.

You've pushed back…but that's not the same as dealing with it!

Ask LeBron.

## LeBron James and the REAL Heat

According to my totally unscientific and most recent "man-on-the-street" interviews, 10 out of 10 people battle resentment and believe that God, their parents, a coach, a boss, Bill Gates, the media, Mark Zuckerberg of Facebook, President Obama or President Bush, McDonald's, a travel agent, customer service, the car wash attendant, and other random guilt-transference targets could have treated them better. Yes, you are the proud owner of some very real issues and infamous moments that give an aroma to your life like "shrimp in the curtain rods". Your mind and spirit have been loaded up, filled to capacity, and jammed with open cases. You've got a **backpack**. It's really yours...and it's overloaded! Admit it. Come clean about how insanely crammed full it is as well as how obsessed you are about defending and protecting the stuff you've accumulated. It's not invisible. It doesn't cease to exist just because you pretend there's no obese backpack with embedded straps. You know what I'm talking about.

The only career goal 27-year-old, 3-time NBA MVP LeBron James didn't own until June 21, 2012, was a championship ring. Sports analysts agreed that defeating the Oklahoma City Thunder to capture his first NBA Championship, the Miami Heat mega-star would silence his critics and overcome his personal demons. He made a statement, averaging 30 points and nearly 10 rebounds and 6 assists per game! But LeBron confessed that losing the 2011 NBA Finals to the Dallas Mavericks with a sub-par performance was the best thing that could have happened: "It humbled me. I knew what it was going to have to take, and I was going to have to change as a basketball player, and...as a person to get what I wanted."[3] And he did change. What drove his obsession? By his own admission, it was the stuff in his overcrowded emotional backpack.

In a December 6, 2011 interview with ESPN's Rachel Nichols, NBA superstar LeBron James opened up for a personal moment. After enduring a year of being boo-ed and labeled as the "villain" for leaving the Cleveland Cavaliers for the Miami Heat, climaxing in losing the 2011 NBA Championship to the Dallas Mavericks, he collapsed from the stuff that had piled up in his backpack: "I just know I didn't play well. I didn't have enough game-changing plays....Probably one of the hardest times of my life. After the finals, I sat in my room for 2 weeks...did absolutely nothing...talked to absolutely nobody..." He admitted that his dreams were destroyed and those events were just the most recent to dramatically force him to re-think his life. James quietly repeated his private list of negative moments in the backpack he has had to reconcile: "Growing up without a father...not knowing sometimes if my mom would come home, my junior year when I lost the state championship, and then the finals, gave me an opportunity to learn who I was as a person, and now go forward." Wow. That's powerful.

But we've all been there. You can just be driving down the road and some random thought about a hurt or failure will pop-up, and tempts you to re-live the incident, re-try the characters in the courtroom of your emotions, or re-invent a new way to get even, compensate, or cover-up. Why? Because you are carrying around extra weight—*bad times, negative feelings, sins, mistakes, stupid decisions, scars from hurt and disappointment, garbage dumped and inflicted on you by others, explosive emotional undercurrents from your past*—that pulls you down and wears you out...AND...you haven't completely dealt with it.

Why not? Actually, there are at least 2 reasons.

## GIVE ME 2!

**Reason #1** that we don't deal with the negative experiences and emotions is this—**Life is busy.** We've all got goals. Obligations buzz around us like mosquitoes. Commitments are all over the map. With extreme schedules, it's really easy, it even feels necessary, to file the unresolved issues deep in your spirit and move forward. Suck it up. Board the plane. Prepare for the next meeting. Rehearse the speech for the next rally. Bills have to be paid. Sales have to trend up. Deliveries don't stop. ER rooms fill up, so physicians and nurses have to show up. Scripts have to be written. Cases have to be researched for court. Lyrics need to be memorized for the next tour. A sermon has to be ready for the next worship. Fat chance of your boss giving you a day off because you can't figure out why your boyfriend dumped you. There's a 24/7 news cycle. Cars keep lining up in the drive-thru lane. Your competition doesn't care if you and your wife and kids argued this morning. Life doesn't stop. Sub-contractors are showing up. Clients keep calling to buy and sell stocks. Your teacher is not going to postpone the exam until you figure out who you are. Don't expect the other team to call a time-out just because you don't know what play to run next. You can't quit being a mom or resign from being a dad just because your co-worker is a jerk or your ex has turned into a Transformer creature over visitation issues. And there are kids at home who need diaper changes, meals, carpools, video games, and homework checks. So, you bury whatever the emotions are and take care of the kids. The President has to move on to the next issue. So do you. Makes sense, right?

**Reason #2** we don't deal with the bad moments from the past is that— **We think we can multi-task,** i.e., manage to haul it around with us and maintain a "normal" existence. Today's culture is really deceptive in that sense. Most people get applauded—some even get promoted, get endorsement deals, or win elections—all for maintaining the image of being able to carry more and more stuff in their backpack and still perform...or party...well. The expectation is that facing issues, admitting mistakes, or re-thinking life's purpose, is a tragic waste when you can just move on to the next relationship, marriage, job, or experience. Things are disposable. They can be used and tossed as quickly as a young dad releases a dirty diaper—milliseconds! And nobody in Washington, D.C., at your school, or in the media seems to blink.

The bad stuff from the past is not easily surrendered. It interferes with what God has designed for your life, but you still defend it, sometimes unconsciously, like a new BMW. On top of that, if you leave the bad experiences and choices untouched long enough, you'll also begin to see everything through a very distorted grid .... AND you are actually headed for something unexpected ....

*Chapter 2*

# Carrying A 3rd Grader?

Image is *almost* everything. In American culture, image rules. At least for politicians, CEO's, actors, and sports icons. And sometimes, for ordinary people like you and me. With the 24/7 news cycle and media feeding frenzies, image can now be created or crashed in milliseconds. Tiger was a big casualty. Grossing $90 million or more annually in endorsements alone, his image was so powerful that I only needed to mention his first name.

"The image" took its first hit when a then 33-year-old Tiger drove over a fire hydrant, crashed his black Cadillac Escalade into a neighbor's tree, and was found lying barefoot and bleeding on the pavement in that bizarre incident in front of his home near Orlando about 2:30am, November 27, 2009. Although Tiger rebounded to win 3 tournaments by July, 2012, what happened was huge. An empire and an image started crumbling. Sponsors bailed out or created distance. Statements and interviews from mistresses, tantalizing denials, suggestive text messages, recorded phone calls full of panic and strategy, witnesses, and photos…PLUS his ex-wife Elin getting $750M and the kids in the 2010 divorce settlement…PLUS…declining performance in golf tournaments, all combined to reveal a more accurate image of Tiger the man, not the athlete.

**Lo Que Paso, Paso**

Simple translation? "What happened, happened!" The reason we were so disappointed and shocked is because we so desperately wanted to believe in "the image". In ESPN sports analyst Rick Reilly's *Go Fish* blog, he called Tiger the "first superstar athlete chased down by a digital posse" and believes whenever the crisis is over, "Woods will still be the most successful and willful and talented athlete alive, but he will be a much different person than he was—chastened, humbled and, at long last, human….The man won a U.S. Open on a broken leg. He's the first athlete to make a billion dollars. He is on pace to swoop past Jack Nicklaus' record of 18 majors before he's got a gray hair.

Maybe when you can make little dimpled golf balls go 340 yards and land in a target the size of a throw rug, you start to believe you can do anything in life and get away with it."[1]

We all believed. We all bought in. So did Tiger. He said so. The conspiracy of denial is both convenient and accessible to all of us. The universal lie? *Our past will never be exposed, and doesn't have to be explained if it is. Just manage it. Carry the bad stuff around until it owns you and eats your life in big bites, and then you can deal with it.*

## The Crash

So it wasn't just Tiger's Cadillac that crashed that night. It was his image. We ALL have carefully crafted images held together by our belief that we can manage two lifestyles, be two different people, and be bullet-proof. Everybody is there at some point. We're all control freaks at heart. But whether you take the Bible seriously or only heard it mentioned in a Jim Carrey movie, the Bible says that we can actually deceive ourselves (see 1 John 1:8). Some argue, by lifestyle, that it's totally possible to believe in God, have a "no-boundaries" self-serving life, *and* never accumulate any excess baggage. Or at least that's the belief system that celebs like Charlie Sheen, politicians like Congressman Anthony Weiner, and Christian leaders like Ted Haggard, and millions of others have apparently subscribed to. To gen up a controversy, recall Jesus' statement that you can't simultaneously navigate two opposing life-value systems: *"No one can serve two masters. Either he will hate the one and love the other, or he will be devoted to the one and despise the other" (Matthew 6:24, NIV).* Agree or disagree, Jesus couldn't be misunderstood on this point. He actually said that trying to divide your loyalties between two competing commitments will never be successful. Want ultimate meaning? Then think first about ultimate chaos. Try believing you can love God and chase prosperity with equal passion or the same level of devotion. That's real failure. Two girlfriends will force you to choose also. Two competing gods, idols, priorities, lifestyles, or whatever, cannot co-exist. Not just that it's *challenging* to manage…it's *impossible.*

The crash—and we've all had our own "crashes"—also pointed to a routinely voiced belief that a person can casually violate God's laws and never get caught or pay a price. God is still here. He's still God. He is still in control. Tiger's tree just stands as a natural monument to reveal both a husband who reached the limits of his ability to self-manage, and a God who called a quick and merciful time-out. God refused to be ignored any longer. God effectively said, "That's enough. Keep living this way and you self-destruct. It's time to back-up the image industry and look at the real person." Tiger has now taken responsibility and faced both the consequences and his personal spiritual issues. But God is still a sidebar for American culture rounding the curve into 2013. Nobody seems to believe they can collapse…or crash.

## Tree-Moments

Everybody has a "TREE-moment", when the self-constructed image crashes and you are shaken to the core. It's a moment, normally not scheduled, when you are forced to deal with the life and character created not by one really stupid decision but years of selfish pursuits and self-deception. Every person ignoring God will eventually have it. God sets it up if we don't. Few change. Everybody needs to. America won't ultimately go down because our troops have to fight terrorists in Afghanistan or Iraq. We're weakening from the inside-out. It's an epidemic more scary than H1N1. Our character is suspect. More people are "crashing into trees" and nobody cares why. Media circles like vultures. Talk show hosts joke. Corporate sponsors pull contracts. Life goes on.

Oh, by the way, there was another historic "TREE-moment" when a man's image seemingly crashed. Jesus, labeled as Messiah, was nailed to a wooden cross. The state-controlled media of his era believed they succeeded in putting Him on it, but He was there by choice to pay for the tragic, destructive choices we've all made and don't want to own. Because He loved randomly and recklessly with no prejudice against anyone of us, He took the blame for every one of our indiscretions and all of our public and private evil, and went down for it. The only perfect and innocent Person ever to live, died for heart crimes He did not commit, and then rose from the dead to offer forgiveness and real life.

Maybe you need to know about that OTHER tree. That's where I believe Jesus gave His life so you could have a life. Jesus is Lord over everything…including start-overs and second chances.

## Carrying A 3rd Grader?

Starting over…getting it right this time…begins with dumping the image and dealing with what you have imported. All of that stuff you put on hold so you could sort through it later doesn't magically disappear. It's like throwing dirty laundry into a pile hoping it mysteriously becomes clean on its own. Things pile up. Eventually it's easier to buy new clothes than deal with dirty laundry. But it's still there. Tossed into your emotional/spiritual backpack mix indiscriminately…the pile is growing.

Overloaded with emotional leftovers from some really stupid choices, and XL-regret from what you think were missed opportunities that can never be replaced, you don't know where to go next with your family, relationships, investments, team, career, ministry, marriage, kids, or faith. ***You are carrying around excess weight.***

Here's a visual for you. Trying to carry all that stuff around with you is like **carrying a 3rd grade boy** all day just to protect him. Health experts estimate that an average third-grader should weigh about 75 pounds. Imagine carrying that kid around all day—no breaks. He gets tired, hungry, thirsty, bored, whines, and constantly talks or argues with you. He wants things you don't have time for, and sometimes physically struggles with you. There is no comfortable way to carry him all day, but you are determined to adjust, turning sideways to get through doors, pushing back the car seat to have room to drive, or explaining to strangers who stare. You can't have lunch with a friend without being interrupted by this kid, shifting everything from your body posture to your attitude to keep him quiet. But people around you notice the conversational inferences and references to the boy, your fatigue or anger from trying to cope and compensate, the schedule and lifestyle adjustments, and the ridiculous strategy of protecting the child this way. You can't do it forever. And it's not like the child gets smaller. He keeps growing. The weight increases and life becomes more difficult.

## Johnny Cash, San Quentin, Merle Haggard, "Tweeter" and the Missing Song

In a similar way, every one of us carries unresolved issues and leftover consequences from the past. And, according to the Bible, we haul around tons of other *spiritually disabling* junk and infectious, decomposing, stinking *emotional* garbage. Take the story of the Samaritan woman who admitted to Jesus in a private noonday conversation that she had five failed marriages, was living with a guy, and was *still* miserable and searching (see John 4:18). Fast forward that idea.

January 1, 1958. When the late country music hall of famer, Johnny Cash, performed that day at San Quentin Prison in what was to become a classic moment of country music history, he was not aware that his rebel style inspired an inmate who was searching for identity. That 20-year-old— Depression-era, California-born of Oklahoma dust-bowl migrants in an old railroad boxcar-outlaw who was serving his 5th prison sentence since age 11— became a fan. Soon he would tell the world he was "proud to be an Okie from Muskogee" (near my family town). He's a lung cancer survivor and former convict who's lived hard and played hard, now in his fifth marriage and is most comfortable writing lyrics on box tops. He once reflected, "Willie Nelson's the one who told me the reason it costs so much to get divorced is because it's worth it."[2] He piled up 13,000 followers on Twitter (he calls it "Tweeter") the first day he gave in to messing with social media. In the first 9 years of his 50+year career, after completing his sentence in San Quentin prison, Merle Haggard recorded 30 albums, on his way to becoming a country music legend and one of the most influential singer/songwriters in the business with 38 No. 1 hits. At 75 years of age in 2012, the seemingly ageless Haggard was on tour again, keeping the story-telling magic alive to sold-out venues. Jenna Bush Hager tagged along on his tour to capture a taste of the magic, stating, "It seems like music is just a lot of who you are." Haggard: "That's about all I am. That's what I'm for. That's what I do. I eat, sleep, and breathe it. And, uh, people around me, if they can't handle it, they just have to get away. This is how it is."[3] With nothing to prove or lose, that iconic voice stated what his identity was tied to, and his non-negotiable terms for knowing him—family included. Son Ben, who performs with his dad to great reviews, acknowledged those terms don't change, confessing, "He's really critical. It's good criticism, though. I cherish every minute of it." Most revealing about The Hag's life? It's in his response to Jenna Bush-Hager: "I still feel like I'm one song missing, that there's one song I ought to write that will give me the most satisfaction of any. I'm still chasing that."[4] A life incomplete? A soul still searching? A hunger never satisfied? All of that and more.

With the huge, unnecessary weight on our mind and in our spirit, we get worn out trying to manage life with the bad things from the past, when in fact, life is intended by God to be lived **FREE** from that piled-up trash. You may have mistakenly believed that you have to carry that trash—because everybody you know is packing it—and just learn how to adapt. But it will eventually kill you emotionally, spiritually, and maybe even physically.

### Kim Phuc, the Photo, and Coffee

Journalist Greg Hardesty said, "For years, Kim Phuc had been running away from the famous photograph. It defined her, trapped her, [and] preserved her in an unforgiving world of pain, anger, and sadness."[5] Nick Ut, the Pulitzer Prize winning AP photographer, captured her moment of horror in the iconic photo that became one of the most recognizable and haunting images of the Vietnam War, symbolizing the collateral damage of civilian suffering. On June 8, 1972, a napalm bomb was dropped on her Vietnamese village, Trang Bang, by the order of an American attempting to bomb enemy strongholds, who had been twice assured that no civilians were present. Nine-year-old Kim ran naked and crying down the road from her hiding place in the village temple, "arms outstretched in terror and pain, and skin is flapping from her legs as she cries, 'Nong qua! Nong qua!'" ('Too hot! Too hot!').[6] After getting the photo, Ut transported Kim and other injured children to a Saigon hospital, where doctors concluded that the third-degree burns covering over half her body were so severe, survival was questionable.[7] Yet, 17 surgical procedures and a 14-month hospital rehab later, she returned home![8] However, despite positive physical recovery, Kim was rarely free from pain, nightmares and anger: "The anger inside me was like a hatred high as a mountain, and **my bitterness was black as old coffee** [emphasis mine]. I hated my life. I hated all people who were normal, because I was not normal. I wanted to die many times. Doctors helped heal my wounds, but they couldn't heal my heart."[9] Prohibited from completing medical school by the Vietnamese government so she could be used for media propaganda, Kim spent time in a library where she discovered a Bible and began to investigate Christianity with the help of a relative and friend. After 10 years of questions and pain, Kim said, "I could not wait to trust the Lord," Kim said. "[Jesus] helped me learn to forgive my enemies, and I finally had some peace in my heart." [10] Kim compared the darkness that had consumed her heart to a black cup of coffee which had to be poured out and replaced with God's love: "Even though I still have so many scars, my heart is cleansed. It's not easy to change, but **I had to pour out that coffee in my heart a little bit every day until God could fill it with his love** [*emphasis mine*]." [11] In 1996, Kim spoke at the Vietnam Veterans Memorial in Washington, D.C. to honor American troops and express that forgiveness.

Let's use Kim's image. Managing all the bad stuff from the past we have packed into our spirit is also like carrying around a large coffee mug. The mug is filled to maximum capacity, but the people you meet all day are constantly pouring more in (symbolizing the latest, freshest difficulties you've faced and can't avoid). It is risky and relentless. And because the mug is like your spirit—limited in size and capacity, unable to hold any more once it has reached its limits—it will logically overflow and spill, damaging whatever it stains. You can't cope with more stuff if you don't have any more room inside. God designed us with spiritual and emotional limits. Push them and bad things happen.

Another reality is that with the hot coffee right at the edge of the rim, it only takes a slight bump for it to spill out and hurt you or someone else. Interestingly, whatever is in that mug is what comes out. If it's filled with coffee, then coffee not Coke, splashes out on whoever is closest. Similarly, when you are "bumped" (i.e., experience more hurt, loss, disappointment, or crushed expectations than what you can handle), whatever is in your spirit comes out. Jesus actually focused on the issues when He explained that when your words spill out, they expose what is going on inside of you: *"Your words show what is in your hearts"* (Matthew 12:34, CEV). You do have a limit. You can only handle so much before what's in you drives everything you do.

That's explains why you hear and see what you hear and see from some people—inappropriate anger, authority issues, refusal to trust, constant whining or criticism, withholding love, avoiding forgiveness, selfishness, addictive desires, competitiveness, jealousy, gossip, running from commitments, obsessing, compulsive behavior, or control issues. It's sourced in what they carry inside, in their hearts. It's who they really are. Words reveal what's going on deep inside. Words define them at that moment. Resentment or bitterness from an unresolved hurt creates hyper-sensitivity to every comment and choice because it has to be passed through the distorted grid of, "Everybody tries to hurt me". That damaged-heart condition makes them hold out the insane and unrealistic expectation...the *impossible* standard...that's it's *your* job to keep them happy (i.e., so they don't have to take responsibility for the junk in their own backpack).

### Are Pop-Tarts Food?

So the convenient…maybe classic…image that came to my mind was an **overloaded backpack**. They *are* the visual landscape on college campuses, airport terminals, city streets, and coffee shops. Every kid seems to have a backpack. Students fill them with laptops, iPods, books, food *(yes, Doritos and Pop-Tarts qualify as food)*, clothes, water bottles, cell phones, movie ticket stubs, notes, keys, IDs, makeup, money, and probably small reptiles for all we know. Moms obsess with worry about spinal curvature with overloaded backpacks. Ask any mother. She'll tell you the kids' backpacks should not be overloaded and should be cleaned out at least annually. But mom doesn't have to courage to go in there to do it, and the kids don't care. Even with those ridiculously tight food-prep rubber gloves, TSA (Transportation Security Administration) people at airports are probably terrified to search inside a student's backpack without back-up. There could be something alive and growing out of a week old, half-eaten burrito, *Eggo*, McD's fries, or Pop-Tart. Just for the record, how long does a Pop-Tart have to be buried under books before it officially becomes a fossil? It's just easier to stuff the backpacks full and overloaded than it is not to carry a backpack that weighs more than your sister. It's just what the backpack generation does now. By the way, here are some obvious good instructions from eHow.com on "How To Wear A School Backpack" with my translation in parentheses: [12]

> **Step 1:** Pack your backpack with the weight distributed evenly. Make sure crushable, soft items are on the outside and the top of the pack *(put the Twinkies on top of the books, not between them)*.
> **Step 2:** Wait until you are completely dressed, including your jacket, before you put your pack on *(or you need a 3XL jacket and look like the Hunchback of Notre Dame)*.
> **Step 3:** Hoist the backpack onto your shoulders by slipping your arms into the armholes. Adjust the shoulder straps so that they are evenly placed in the middle of each shoulder *(as opposed to the other option of placing the straps around your neck which limits breathing)*.
> **Step 4:** Walk with your body weight leaning forward just slightly to avoid being pulled over backward by the pack *(if not, you are on your back like an upside-down turtle with your friends standing over you texting about it)*.
> **Step 5:** Be mindful of the extra width of your body when trying to move through narrow passageways *(either get used to knocking people down or just bring 2 friends & a rope to pull you and your backpack out through the car window)*.

### TIPS & WARNINGS

✓ Remove your backpack before sitting back against any hard surfaces, like the school bus seat or your chair *(or risk falling forward on your face and licking a dirty floor)*.

✓ Never put your backpack on unless it is completely zipped, or you may lose something out of the open zipper *(laptops do not bounce—well, maybe a Mac does)*.

It's just as tricky when your emotional and spiritual backpack is overloaded.

So, here's the premise of this book: ***We all have bad stuff in our backpack that must be emptied to be free to live the purpose-filled life God designed.***

And the process taught by this book: ***We not only have to eliminate the bad choices that have made our journey miserable, but we have to replace them with the best choices to experience life as God intended.*** It's not enough, therefore, to brag that you don't do certain stupid or sinful things. To run the life-race that God has custom pre-designed for you, *His race* (that's right, it's HIS race ultimately, not yours!), you have to intentionally and strategically abandon, denounce, separate from, withdraw from, discard, and generally leave behind all the junk you've collected—sometimes from years of unguarded and unfiltered choices. Then you have to discipline your life by replacing those with consistently good choices.

We all carry around negative emotions, self-defeating beliefs, commitments that compete with the right goals, or relationships that drain rather than energize us—all that stuff from past hurtful and confusing experiences, and sinful choices that ultimately limit potential and create discouragement.

Actually, it's more threatening than that. Here's the bigger issue: what we're all carrying around ***competes*** with God's plan for our lives. Substituting your plan for God's plan is like boarding a plane going the wrong direction, away from your intended destination. You're going to be really disappointed when you land.

**Your backpack is full. Put down the backpack. Step away. Assume the position.** It's time to take it off and unload the negative stuff that is wearing you out and pulling you down, and discover God's awesome plan.

The basic map for this incredible journey of chasing your God-designed life-plan is already a matter of open, accessible public record in the Bible. Specifically, it's detailed in Hebrews 12:1-3. We'll explore some related trails, but the original map, with instructions, is there:

> *1 Therefore, since we are surrounded by such a huge crowd of
> witnesses to the life of faith, let us strip off every weight that
> slows us down, especially the sin that so easily trips us up. And
> let us run with endurance the race God has set before us. 2 We
> do this by keeping our eyes on Jesus, the champion who initi-
> ates and perfects our faith. Because of the joy awaiting Him,
> He endured the cross, disregarding its shame. Now He is seated
> in the place of honor beside God's throne. 3 Think of all the
> hostility He endured from sinful people; then you won't become
> weary and give up.* (NLT)

The Greek word translated "run" (*trecho*) in verse 1 above literally refers to moving forward and doing it quickly!  *Trecho* means to go forward without restrictions, in total freedom.  The idea is to spend your strength and energy in performing or achieving something, not on the crazy sins that ultimately mess up your life.

What's the takeaway?  The goal is to unload the negative choices that are making a purposeful life difficult to the point of being impossible, and start making the right choices.  A runner minus excess weight equals a winner!  The formula, a sort of basic *life-math* type principle, looks like this:

Runner (Backpacker)

– <u>Excess Weight</u> (Negative experiences)

= Winner!

My prayer is that God will give you something from this book that will set you free to run the *life-race* God has custom-designed for you, without regret . . . AND . . . with huge impact!

# PART TWO:

# The Race

*Chapter 3*

# It's About Direction...
# Not Perfection!

*"I went into a McDonald's yesterday and said, "I'd like some fries."*
*The girl at the counter said, "Would you like some fries with that?""*
–Jay Leno, The Tonight Show

Someone said you know it's time to start running again when . . .
- ✓ *You try to do a few pushups and discover that certain body parts refuse to leave the floor.*
- ✓ *Your children look through your wedding album and want to know who mom's first husband was.*
- ✓ *You get winded just saying the words "10 kilometer run".*
- ✓ *You come to the conclusion that, if God really wanted you to touch your toes each morning, He would have put them somewhere around your knees.*
- ✓ *You step on a talking scale and it says, "Come back when you are alone!"*

Or think about this person's responses to exercise:
- ✓ *For every mile you jog, you add one minute to your life. This enables you, at the age of 85, to spend an additional five months in a nursing home at $5,000/month.*
- ✓ *I joined a health club last year, spending $400 in the process. I haven't lost a pound. Apparently you have to show up.*
- ✓ *I have to exercise early in the morning, before my brain figures out what I'm doing.*
- ✓ *I like long walks, especially when they are taken by people who annoy me.*

✓ *The advantage to exercising every day is that you die healthier.*

✓ *I have flabby thighs but fortunately my stomach covers them.*

✓ *If you are going to take up cross-country skiing, it helps to start with a small country.*

✓ *I don't jog—it makes me spill my milk shake.*

Somehow, running just doesn't come natural for most of us. It's not what we think about all day. Eating out? Now that's a passion. We network with friends for restaurant reviews, click on Groupon offers, "like" places on Facebook, strategize for reservations, and schedule childbirth around a night out. Running? No, it doesn't make the average American's calendar reminder. One day I was feeling really guilty that my exercise routine had fallen off. Fear of high cholesterol and tight clothes was a small factor. So I put on my cool Nike running outfit, jumped in the car...and drove around until the guilt went away! Then I pulled back in the driveway, changed clothes, and went to get a sausage and egg biscuit on the way to the office!

Most of our culture resists disciplining the daily schedule for serious, "*get-in-shape-and-avoid-the-annual-physician-weight-lecture*" kind of workout. Yet, for those who commit to being a lifetime, devoted follower of Jesus, running your God-designed, custom life-race in a disciplined way is part of the package. When you commit your life to Jesus, it's more than just asking forgiveness for sins. You are in effect agreeing to a life-long race—a high risk, wildly competitive adventure. Every stride, curve, and segment is supposed to be—and to survive intact, has to be—guided personally by Jesus. The commitment is to complete your course the right way, and enjoy the adventure. Here again is the challenge:

> *1 Therefore, since we are surrounded by such a huge crowd of witnesses to the life of faith, let us strip off every weight that slows us down, especially the sin that so easily trips us up. And let us run with endurance the race God has set before us. 2 We do this by keeping our eyes on Jesus, the champion who initiates and perfects our faith. Because of the joy awaiting Him, He endured the cross, disregarding its shame. Now He is seated in the place of honor beside God's throne. 3 Think of all the hostility He endured from sinful people; then you won't become weary and give up. (NLT)*

## MULTIPLE CHOICE?

In those key verses, the race instructions are clear. Running the race doesn't happen without an up-front commitment. The commitment is assumed and expected. It's part of your new life in Jesus, your spiritual DNA. An initial, lifetime surrender to Jesus includes a surrender to His daily purpose, AND assumes a commitment to the disciplined choices required to run the race. No way to separate "becoming a believer" from "running the race". God doesn't give you multiple choice options, like choosing "e" below:

    a.  I want forgiveness of my sins

    b.  I want to go to heaven

    c.  I want the extra value life with fries. Hold the pain—and Supersize it!

    d.  I will run God's life-race for me by God's rules

    e.  a, b, and c only

What makes the commitment real is how we choose to run the race. In fact, it's how believers make Jesus visible and relevant to the world. If we say that Jesus is the Savior, it is a definitive statement that He alone can change a life. Real change. At the core. Radical. Unexplainable, but undeniable to the people who know you best. Becoming a believer is actually the importing of a new life—Jesus' life inserted into you. It really is "downloaded" in the sense that His Spirit instantaneously creates a new life inside you (see John 3:6).

In one of Jesus' most publicized "private" conversations with a skeptical religion professor named Nicodemus, Jesus educated the professional by explaining that knowing God required a spiritual experience he couldn't initi-ate, control or intellectually explain: *"So don't be surprised when I say, 'You must be born again.' The wind blows wherever it wants. Just as you can hear the wind but can't tell where it comes from or where it is going, so you can't explain how peo-ple are born of the Spirit."* (John 3:7-8, NLT). It was an intentionally con-frontational manifesto. New life…salvation…a relationship with God, is all part of the moment of exchange when you surrender to Jesus for a lifetime. Your desires change, shifting immediately to pleasing Jesus—first and exclu-sively (see 2 Corinthians 5:17).

So, if you identify with Jesus, claiming that He has made you into a new person, and then you avoid the race or abuse the rules, you are not credible and Jesus doesn't seem believable. After all, if Jesus isn't worth your best effort or discipline, if your life isn't elevated to something better that what the rest of the culture lives, then why should that friend of yours—your husband, a co-worker, the teammate, boss, or serious skeptic—consider buying in?

### Shaun White and Perfection

So, running your life-race is a not-so-thinly-disguised commitment. The Greek word used here, *"trecho"*, is actually a firm challenge to a lifetime race. Translation? God's expectation is that you "keep on running". It's more of a marathon-style approach required than a short-distance sprint. Believers don't run their life-race to earn points with God in order to get to heaven, but to achieve everything God gives us opportunity to do in this lifetime. In that sense, performance is less the issue than passionate perseverance. In other words, it's not about **perfection**, but **direction**. Everybody who knows you, already knows you aren't perfect, but have they seen change…or a serious effort to change? Just committing to Jesus and His plan for your life doesn't make you perfect, but it re-orients your life direction. People know if it's real *and* if you are real. But perfect isn't overrated for Shaun White!

January 29, 2012. Intense! Perfect! Pro snowboarder and extreme athlete, Shaun White, soared to a record-breaking perfect score of 100 to win his 5th consecutive Snowboard SuperPipe gold at the Winter X Games in Aspen. He's the first to win five consecutive SuperPipe gold medals, bringing his total Winter X Games medal count to 17 (12 gold). "It's unreal, I have wanted that 100 forever," White said. "For me, it wasn't complete until I landed that run. I have been to so many X Games now, and I will forever remember this. Getting…the perfect score. It is crazy."[1] It's even more crazy when you realize Shaun was born with a congenital heart defect and had two cardiac surgeries before age five. Shaun refused to let the physical problems define him or limit him. They were quickly overcome by an early commitment. Shaun started snowboarding *and* signed his first sponsorship at age six! His mother had to order him to slow down by telling him he could only board backwards, or switch, a skill that would develop his career.[2]

So, if the issue is to "keep on running" the race, then it makes sense to settle the whole commitment thing immediately. Either get on the bus or get off the bus. To run your life-race for Jesus half-heartedly is a loser's approach. It will be a disaster. There's no fulfillment in it. You will get boo-ed by the skeptics and swallowed by the temptations. Neither is there a part-time option. Runners don't start a race, stop for lunch, shopping and a few texts or calls, and then return to do the next segment. It's impossible to successfully finish if a runner goes off course to chase other things along the way. If you believe you can commit to Jesus' purpose for your life, plan to party a while, and then slide back into the race, you're gonna get killed spiritually.

Here's why. *First, that kind of thinking assumes God is casual about the whole commitment thing and won't enforce the boundaries.* God will discipline you by shaking things up to get your attention or shut you down in order to protect you from stupid choices (see Hebrews 12:5-12). To think that God isn't sensitive about violations of His commands and insults to His holy character is the original high-risk behavior. The first couple, Adam and Eve, actually believed they could hide from God after eating off-limits fruit (see Genesis 3:6-8).

*Second, it's like believing you will be the same person—at the same level of passion for God and wisdom—whenever it is you decide to come back and get serious.* God removed strength from the original "Iron Man" guy, an Israeli military hero named Samson, because he thought he could mess around with women and still have God's favor when He needed it (see Judges 16:15-21). *Third, you underestimate the power of sin if you think you can jump in and out of the race without damage.* Wrong choices lead to more disastrous choices. You only get weaker the more you cheat on the race rules.

You are more vulnerable to the bad stuff. Check out the shamed Christian leader, Demas, who walked away from ministry (see 2 Timothy 4:10). Your inconsistency becomes the excuse for non-believers to cancel their plans to investigate Christianity. Being a hindrance to a person believing on Jesus has big-time, eternal consequences. ***Fourth, if you define commitment as 50% party and 50% playing by the rules, then it's really not biblical commitment in the first place.*** God sees through that. Most people quickly and ultimately realize that God is really hard to deceive. Commitment is just what you think it is—a stand-alone, single, narrow, sacred, eternal kind of choice. Not a whim, fling, fad, membership you can cancel if it doesn't work for you, or product you can return if you are dissatisfied. Radical truth? By definition, choosing Christ means saying NO to all other alternatives for life: *"Then Jesus said to his disciples, 'If any of you wants to be my follower, you must turn from your selfish ways [deny himself], take up your cross, and follow **Me**'"* (Matthew 16:24, NLT, **emphasis** mine).

### "Kind of Pregnant?"

Everybody does it. Some do it multiple times a day. Some do it and walk away. It's controversial. It's relevant to every relationship and ideology. What is it? Commitment. And definition matters. Clarity is important. By definition, commitment means you have surrendered to something or someone. There is something or someone that you have elevated to become the most important priority. In effect, you have sorted through the options, compared values, and made a specific choice about what is non-negotiable, a core value that will own your time, energy, worship, or focus.

The reason that people sometimes struggle with running the race God's way is *NOT* because they get tired or face obstacles. Hitting a wall is just part of everything from *Man v. Food* to marriage. It's because they are *NOT* committed.

Once, when a 20-something girl asked me to help her resolve some conflict with a guy, I asked her if she was married. Her answer was as ridiculous and goofy as it was revealing: "Uh, sort of." That was a weak way of saying to me, *"Here's my updated version of commitment: I've had lots of relationships with guys that didn't work out, and I'm taking the easy way out, not dealing with my issues, so now I'm just having sex with one guy because that's what it will take to keep him, and this is a good guy because he is splitting the bills and giving me enough space so if I get unhappy I can try something else anytime, but I really love this guy, at least that's what I feel this morning, and hope it will work out, but doubt if it will because we can't get along and I don't know why but he makes me crazier than I already am."*

How can you expect success, or even more basic still—stability—if you have never settled the commitment question? God's expectation to get rid of the negative stuff we have piled up in our lives, and avoid destructive sinful choices that can put a runner on the ground quickly, is an impossible task without commitment. On the flip-side, if you sell-out to the entire race, and do it on the front-end, it's more difficult to quit and you are less vulnerable to discouragement.

My friend and former college pastor at an Atlanta church I served as Pastor, Kevin Pounds, left there in a missionary-type entrepreneurial spirit, to follow a specific God-call and created a church near Rutgers University in New Jersey. Following that success, in 2011, he relocated to the spiritually diverse community of Burlington, Vermont to run a non-profit community service organization called **Serve Burlington** (e.g., with projects like resettling refugees), and develop a church. In an initial blog, Kevin wrestled with the core issue for all believers who are sorting through the commitment question:

> *Following Jesus requires having an open hand with everything in our lives: our desires, our feelings, our convictions, our comfort zones, our security, our insecurity, our self confidence, our dreams, our fears, our plans, our relationships, and even our identity. Telling culturally conditioned consumers that we must deny ourselves is not an easy message, but it's always a big first step to follow Jesus. Sometimes we compromise by offering incremental obedience (i.e. moving towards obedience in small incremental steps), but Jesus' challenge was always all or nothing-either you're in or you're out.*[3]

He's right! There's no middle ground. Nobody is "kind of pregnant". You can't straddle the center line on the interstate with your car and survive. Nobody is "sort of President" or "occasionally Jewish". Nor is a bill "almost paid".

Within 48 hours after the 8th deadliest tornado in U.S. history swept through Joplin, Missouri on May 22, 2011, taking 116 lives and wreaking havoc with millions of dollars in damage, community leaders vowed to re-open schools on schedule by August 17. Not vague. Not half-hearted. Not conditional. And they did it! Schools re-opened on time and students returned to some normalcy. Their commitment was real. You *can* do this commitment thing you know!

But…either you're in or you're out!

## INVESTMENT OPTIONS

Everybody invests in something. We all make choices about values, schedules, relationships, beliefs, or finances. Something or someone rises to the top to dominate our time, direct our spending, and shape our decisions. And the truth is that, whatever we value the most, is what owns us and is what we worship. People invest in what they value the most. Jesus nailed it with a simple, raw truth: *"Your heart will always be where your treasure is"* (Matthew 6:21, CEV).

Basically then, the way to prevent confusion about choices later and the guilt that can result from making unwise choices, is to **invest early and invest big**—in the stuff Jesus says will give meaning and purpose to your life, of course. When you have processed your commitment, there's no confusion about direction. Figuring out what competes with pursuing what Jesus wants for your life is simple.

At a leadership event, pastor and best-selling author Dr. David Jeremiah told the story of a young man who confided in him that he had some inappropriate desires for a woman at work, and knew that if he didn't correct course, it would lead to a big mistake. Knowing what was at stake, Dr. Jeremiah told him it was an easy fix—QUIT! The young man replied, "I can't do that!" David said, "Which do you love more, your wife or your job? You have to choose. If you choose your job, you are going to lose your wife."[4] To his credit, the young man realized this was a big life-intersection about commitment, took the counsel, immediately asked for a transfer, and got it.

The explanation is simple. He had made a long-term commitment to his marriage because of his bigger commitment to Jesus. A relationship with another woman would violate both commitments, and he knew he was too weak to survive the temptation for much longer. With the conflict, he was forced to make a decision. He not only honored his commitment to Jesus and his wife, but he added strength to it.

If a man keeps a daily lunch appointment with a female client, friend, or co-worker, and comes home to his wife at night, he will eventually choose his lunch partner over his wife because he can't be committed to both at the same time, and his date doesn't require as much commitment. And, like Jesus said, you can't serve two masters! Deal with this reality: **The temptation is always to downsize your commitment, never to upgrade it or protect it.**

So, a commitment to run the race is a lifetime pursuit of Jesus' specific plan for your life. Don't commit to it if you don't intend to run it right. This is serious stuff: *"Each one of us will give a personal account to God"* (Romans 14:12, NKJV). If you are struggling, it could be because you made an emotional response to Jesus instead of a heart-surrender. Without the *"I'll-not-only-die-for-Jesus-but-live-for-Him"* commitment, you will continue to be miserable, doubting where you stand with God, wondering why happiness seems so elusive, feeling like you were destined for more, and beating yourself up for every misstep in the race.

## It's Your Race

The 1981 movie, *Chariots of Fire,* won 4 Academy Awards, including the Oscar for Best Picture as it reproduced the true-life drama of two athletes in the 1924 Olympics: Eric Liddell, a devout Scottish Christian who saw competitive running as a way of glorifying God before returning to China as a missionary, and Harold Abrahams, an English Jew who competed to overcome prejudice.[5] Liddell's passion for God and running was inspiring: "I believe

God made me for a purpose, but he also made me fast. And when I run I feel His pleasure." As he boarded the ship to Paris for the Olympics, Liddell learned that the heat for his 100-meter race was scheduled on a Sunday. He promptly refused to run the race despite strong pressure from the Prince of Wales and the British Olympic committee, because his Christian convictions prevented him from running on the Sabbath. Having already won a silver medal in the 400-meter hurdles, Lord Andrew Lindsay offered to trade his place in the 400-meter race on the following Thursday to Liddell, who gratefully agreed. Refusing to compromise his religious convictions in the face of national athletic pride made him a global celebrity. Winning the gold medal in the 100-meter race was a satisfying victory over racial prejudice for Abrahams. Liddell amazingly defeated the heavily favored U.S. athletes and won the gold in the 400-meter race, bringing the British team home in victory. Liddell kept his commitment and returned as a missionary to China. It is said that all of Scotland mourned his death in 1945 in Japanese-occupied China.

Following a victory in a race, Liddell spoke to the crowd, comparing life to a race, which is the theme of this book:

> *You came to see a race today. To see someone win. It happened to be me. But I want you to do more than just watch a race. I want you to take part in it. I want to compare faith to running in a race. It's hard. It requires concentration of will, energy of soul. You experience elation when the winner breaks the tape, especially if you've got a bet on it. But how long does that last? You go home. Maybe your dinner's burnt. Maybe you haven't got a job. So who am I to say, "Believe, have faith," in the face of life's realities? I would like to give you something more permanent, but I can only point the way. I have no formula for winning the race. Everyone runs in her own way, or his own way. And where does the power come from, to see the race to its end? From within. Jesus said, "Behold, the Kingdom of God is within you. If with all your hearts, you truly seek me, you shall ever surely find me." If you commit yourself to the love of Christ, then that is how you run a straight race.[6]*

"Everyone runs in her own way, or his own way." Everybody has their own unique life-race. The issue is first whether you will commit to run the race for Jesus. There is a cost to running for Him. There is also an opportunity cost.

What is the trade-off?

What happens if you don't take it seriously?

What happens if you don't run the race right?

Let's take a look.

## Chapter 4

# Life without McDonalds?

It was 1954. A fifty-two-year-old charismatic Chicago milk-shake machine salesman visited a restaurant client in San Bernardino, California. The salesman's annual salary from his company that was about to be eaten alive by competition? A whopping $12,000. Later, history would prove he wanted more. The fast-talking salesman arrived at his client's restaurant only to see huge crowds lined up under giant golden arches for 15-cent hamburgers and 60-second delivery in a squeaky-clean place run by the McDonald brothers. In his autobiography, Ray Kroc said, "That night in my motel room I did a lot of heavy thinking about what I'd seen during the day. Visions of McDonald's restaurants dotting crossroads all over the country paraded through my brain."[1]

He knew this was his moment of destiny. Two generations later, the late Ray Kroc is an entrepreneurial icon. The cultural and business landscape of the planet changed because the future multi-millionaire made a personal, individual, private decision to do something bigger with his life. Yes, he's the same Ray Kroc whose success-obsession led him to comment, "If you see your competitor drowning, stick a hose in his mouth!"

Imagine that moment though. He's alone in his motel room that night trying to process what he's seen. The McDonald brothers had obviously discovered something that worked. Would he be willing to set aside everything else he was doing that was less important—that didn't fit his new dream and could hold him back—and focus all his energy and resources on creating something that had never been done before? It was a real opportunity...and a real risk.

Called "America's Greatest Marketer" by American Way Magazine, author of 13 books, and creator of *Squidoo.com*, Seth Godin might describe Kroc's ultimate decision as "living near the edge of the box" versus staying in the box or getting out of the box.[2] Kroc saw it. If he didn't do it, life would go on, and somebody else would get it. America was not debating why there were no hamburger chains dotting the landscape near interstates and suburbs. The McDonald brothers weren't waiting on Ray Kroc to get an idea, get his life together, show up, or cut a deal. They were good with their life and business and $100K annual income. They resisted Kroc's franchise idea because they had tried it before and failed. Typical, huh? Kroc's opportunity surfaced only when he evaluated his life and choices.

> *Too old to start again from scratch, the middle-aged salesman believed the comfortable existence he and his wife, Ethel, led in suburban Arlington Heights, Illinois, would vanish if this venture failed. "If I lost out on McDonald's, I'd have no place to go," he said.*[3]

The cost? Kroc knew he had a destiny bigger than his current company. He knew his life was not supposed to be defined by his past or his role. He knew there was a real trade-off for irreplaceable moments. Of course, not everybody shares Kroc's core values and his obsession, nor agrees with his decisions and his personal trade-offs.

> *"I believe in God, family, and McDonald's—and in the office, that order is reversed," he liked to say. But it seemed McDonald's always came first. Kroc's sales experience taught him that business was a Darwinian proposition, in which those least fit and adaptable would go the way of the dinosaur. Ethel didn't share her husband's visceral feel for the restaurant business, and angered by Ray's late-life gamble, she resented the way the new company had taken over her husband's life....[Kroc wrote]"It closed the door between us." The thirty-nine-year marriage would finally end in divorce in 1961.*[4]

1954 will never happen again. Kroc only had 1 shot at 1954. You and I have a spiritual-based life-race to run and neither do we get a second chance at first opportunities. There are trade-offs if we are unwilling to focus on the bigger purpose.

As a trivial and fascinating sidebar, I heard that Willow Creek Church Pastor, Bill Hybels, once revealed his father passed up an opportunity to write a check for $1,000 as initial investor when Kroc approached him and his buddies at their country club in Chicago not long after the incident in that opening story. Yeah. For real. That really happened. Anybody can misjudge a moment. Anybody can be too comfortable. We all make mistakes. Let's reduce them!

## 7-PACK

What are the risks? What do you stand to lose? What do you swap for your future? What happens if you don't take God's expectation to "run the race" seriously, and you don't run your race right? There really is an opportunity cost. Sometimes you don't get a second chance. It's easy for believers to assume that we won't get caught up in anything that takes away our love for Jesus, our passion for worship, the ambition to have a successful career and a meaningful life, the energy to invest in the needs of hurting people, our vision to help the nations, or the desire to lead our family the right way. After awhile we become overconfident—in effect, *deceived*—believing we can live two lives simultaneously, that we can handle the questionable stuff and still do everything God has put in our heart.

Let's prepare for a successful life-race by investigating *7 frequently repeated mistakes*—the **7 MISTAKES**. They are real...AND avoidable...AND when you get their *down-side risks*, it can motivate you to go for God's best!

> **Mistake No. 1: Wasting your potential.**
> **Mistake No. 2: Repeating bad choices.**
> **Mistake No. 3: Allowing bitterness to drive choices.**
> **Mistake No. 4: Thinking quitting is a good option.**
> **Mistake No. 5: Neglecting worship.**
> **Mistake No. 6: Avoiding commitment.**
> **Mistake No. 7: Mislabeling God's character.**

## MISTAKE No. 1: Wasting your potential.

If you don't run the race right, you will miss God's best. What you are really giving up is unused potential. You compromise the person you could become. Every time you race in another direction you are shrinking your options. It's like trying to put a SMALL t-shirt on a XXL guy! Nobody can imagine what God could do with a life that is totally sold out to His purpose. There are awesome people, exciting adventures, and unique experiences you are throwing away if you fail to follow God's expectations. It's like God has already planned for you to achieve great things, booked those moments on His calendar, and by not getting free from the negative stuff and sins that are pulling you down, you are cancelling appointments daily!

### Is 18-27-36-43-59 Your Lottery Number?

You are better than that! You are more than that! Don't let the bad stuff define who you are! Don't be captured by things that keep you from God's best! Suck it up. Have the guts to do a life-scan and be honest about the results. If you are choosing to enjoy the unhealthy lifestyle, it means you have rejected superior options offered by God. The longer you choose to live in "Loserville", the more it costs you, and the more you realize you have surren-

dered time that can never be recaptured. You will never be 18...27...
36...43...or 59 again. Impossible to get those moments back. Your kids grow
up. They are only 3 years old once. They are only freshman once. Not even
billionaires or Congress or a stimulus bill can buy back missed opportunities.

"Georgia is a very lucky state," bragged Georgia Lottery spokeswoman
Tandi Reddick. "There have been quite a few repeat Georgia Lottery winners
who have Lady Luck on their side. It's fantastic for our players."[5] There are 15
repeat Georgia Lottery winners. Three people have won multiple times just in
the past year. Jennifer Hauser, 29, of Atlanta, is the latest two-time success
story. Playing an instant scratch off game on February 13, 2012, called *50X
The Money*, Hauser banked a check for $1 million, less than three months fol-
lowing claiming a $100,000 prize on another state lotto game, Georgia Lot-
tery Black.[6] "I was a little numb," Hauser told the Atlanta Journal
Constitution. "I didn't know what to think."[7] Hauser used the first prize to
purchase a new car and pay off bills and may use some of the $1 million to buy
her Mom a car. The odds of winning any lottery are insane (1 in 2,400,000
in Jennifer's case[8]), but the odds of the same person winning even bigger the
second time are astronomical.[9] Playing the lottery is a ridiculous life strategy.
But risking your God-given potential is a bigger gamble. When you assume
you know how to play without God—you lose!

So, if you are going the opposite direction from God's pre-designed life
race, you have to be honest and admit that there are some **rewards you will
forfeit** and **experiences you will never access**. Why? Again, it's because you
are packing things God has warned will hold you back. Drop all the sin and
the things that are pulling you down and you're going to realize there is **so
much more** you can do!

## ANGIE'S LIST?

There's more. There's more to what's happening to you than what you
think. We routinely underestimate God—focus on our setbacks and scars and
forget God has destined us for greater things—AND MISS THE GOOD
STUFF!

Angie gets it. She is a primary dental assistant for the lead dentist and
founding owner of a successful dental office in my city. Rather than go negative about the financial challenges in her own family due to her husband's job
layoff, Angie made the intentional choice to do whatever it takes to pursue God's
dream for her life. Not in the sense of chasing God so He would let her win the
lottery, but in a personal determination to believe God would help her overcome
her circumstances. And she didn't commit the frequent mistake of waiting for
some magic bullet or major breakthrough. Instead, she did the right thing.
Angie let God be God...in the moment...despite the risk...without hesitation
or fear. That's how you know what happened was real...and how God is real.
Oh, and the results back it up too. It happened on her second job which she

took on to push through their financial challenges. It happened when she
needed every dollar she could save to take her daughter on a critical trip the
upcoming weekend. In her own words in an email to her boss...

> Dr. _____,
>
> I had an awesome thing happen over the weekend that I
> wanted to share with you. I have always believed that you
> always treat others the way you want to be treated and it will
> come back to you many times over! I was working at *[a local
> grocery store]* on Friday and had a gentleman come through
> my line to check out. Before I could scan the first item he
> stated I needed to wait. While he was looking for his wallet I
> asked if he had left it in the car. He stated worse than that, "I
> left it a home." I then asked if he lived close by. He said he
> was from *[a town about 30 minutes away]*. *[I was]* thinking
> to myself that is too far to drive back and get his wallet. He
> asked if I could put the items aside and he would come back
> with his money. Before he could say anything I had rang up
> his few items. I said, "I will just take care of this for you
> today. It's on me. That's too far to come back." He was
> taken back and stated, "You can't do that". I politely stated
> it was okay and that I wanted to help him. I believe the items
> *[totaled]* $13.53. He seemed stunned that anyone today
> would share that kind of kindness. Just before I went on
> break, one of the team members at *[our store]* that bags for us
> handed me $20. I just thought that the gentleman had come
> back in and handed it to her to give to me, paying me back.
> I really didn't think much of it. Then as I was leaving for the
> day, my team leader said she needed to talk with me before I
> left. Thinking to myself "What have I done now?" She then
> went to get our General Manager. Now I am thinking I had
> done something I shouldn't have! She asked me if I had paid
> for a customer's groceries. I of course told her and *[the Gen-
> eral Manager]* the story. She then tells me that the gentleman
> not only went back *[home]* but came back to the store to give
> me $100! I was so caught off guard and began to cry because
> I was leaving to go out of town for the weekend and could
> have really used the extra money. The General Manager
> looked at me and said that was awesome customer service
> and proceeded to give me a $50 gift card! At this point I
> didn't know what to say. So my $13.53 gift was multiplied
> many times over into $170!!! Talk about blessings from God!
> I thought to myself this is what life is about! Helping others

when they need it most, expecting nothing in return! Just knowing that you did the right thing; because it always comes back to you in blessings whether you know it or not! Hope this touches you as much as it did me! [10]

Not only will that store have a customer for life, but God will too! Angie's faith was increased and her focus was shifted from her needs to living bigger for God.

Hebrews 12:1 starts with a little pre-race perspective: *"Therefore we also, since we are surrounded by so great a cloud of witnesses"* (NKJV). It's like a coach getting in the face of an elite Olympic athlete, just before the medal round of their event, to both challenge them and calm them. It's a classic motivational statement.

No matter what level of awareness you have as a believer, it's good to be reminded of what's at stake. We're not always living at maximum desire or intensity.

The race is real. It won't be repeated. The competition is intense. Your race can be won. It can be completed and done right. A huge crowd of witnesses have already paid a price. They played their role successfully to move God's purpose forward until His Son returns for us. But this is the generation that may get to wrap it up!

So, it's on!

## HISTORY 101

Traditional interpretation of our focus verse (Hebrews 12:1), says that it is a reference to the lives of biblical role models from Hebrews chapter 11. The record of their adventures is punctuated with a common phrase: "by faith." Ordinary people did extraordinary things simply through raw trust in the character and wisdom of a sovereign, loving, and holy God they couldn't even see. Abel, Enoch, Noah, Abraham, Sarah, Isaac, Jacob, Esau, Joseph, Moses, Rahab, Gideon, Samson, Samuel, David, and a massive list of anonymous believers made their mark on history. God expected them to do some ridiculous stuff. This "crowd of crazies" in the world's opinion (see Hebrews 11:38-39), left a legacy, not just of scary faith, but of well-managed lives.

Not one was perfect. In fact, some of their worst choices have become classic biblical models of what NOT to do. God would never want us to repeat the drunkenness of Noah, the deception of Jacob, the anger of Moses, or the adultery of David. But that's not the point.

Imperfect people were rewarded when they set aside, not their intellect, heart passion, or ambitions, but their fears, questions, traditions, and schedules—to unhesitatingly obey a perfect God. Normally, what God expects will never make sense to the rest of the non-believing world anyway. Build a giant ark on dry land? A slave turns down the sexual advances of his boss' wife and becomes Prince of Egypt? A prostitute leads covert operations to save a new nation called Israel? An enemy nation engaged and taken over with only 300 soldiers? A teenage boy believes he could do what the entire national military couldn't get done, by putting down a 9-foot cursing-machine—an enemy giant—with only a small rock?

## LINSANITY!

The 2012 New York Knicks basketball team was 8-15 before Coach Mike D'Antoni put an untested, unknown player in the starting lineup. The Knicks then won 8 of their next 9 games. Celebrities packed the seats behind the Knicks bench. Crowd were on their feet. Ticket prices soared. They got the hottest selling NBA jersey—No. 17.

Harvard grad Jeremy Lin is only 6'3", small by NBA lineups, but averaged 25 points and 9 assists in his first 9 starts as the Knicks point guard. In the *Bleacher Report*, Peter Emerick gave his explanation for the phenom: "In only nine games in the NBA as a starter, Jeremy Lin has hit more big-time shots and game winners than most players do in their entire career, and he's done so by simply being the most fearless player on the court. When his team needs him the most, Lin doesn't back off, he attacks. He doesn't do that because he's the biggest or best player on the court. He does so because he's not afraid to fail, and that's what makes him such a solid player and teammate….Humility is the one word that aptly describes the kind of player that Jeremy Lin is, and it's one of the reasons why the New York Knicks have rallied around him."[11]

It's the attitude behind the amazing game-winning shots, crazy assists, and routine turnovers that captured NYC and unleashed "Linsanity". He's inspiring. He's fearless. He takes risks and makes mistakes—proven by averaging 5.9 turnovers per game. Emerick is right: "A lot of players in the NBA play the game afraid to make mistakes, which holds them back from achieving their potential…. Leadership is something that the Knicks lacked early on in the season, and little did they know their best leader was sitting on the bench the whole time. Fearless leadership is what wins NBA Championships, and that's exactly what Lin brings to New York."[12] He's a leader. He's real. Listen to Lin's transparency: "Last year I was trying not to make mistakes. I was trying to fit in. This year I said, you know what, I've given everything I can to this year. I'm going to make sure I do it my way, and if it doesn't get me where I want to go, I can live with that. One thing I know is that if I go down, I'm going to go down fighting."[13] That conviction has kept him from quitting after going undrafted in the 2010 NBA Draft, riding the bench with the Golden State Warriors, surviving only two weeks with the Houston Rockets, and sitting on the sidelines even after being picked up by the Knicks. When the Knicks were ready to release Lin from his contract before it became guaranteed, an injury to the starting point guard prompted Coach Mike D'Antoni to give Lin a chance. You know what's happened. LINSANITY!

Jeremy Lin is not mistake-free. He's pride-free about it. Because of that, he is **not wasting his potential**.

But others have. Buried in the Hebrews 11 Hall of Fame is the reference to the crazy story of a *prince-turned murderer-turned shepherd-turned speaker-turned national leader*. Moses **wasted his potential** but became one of the greatest comeback stories ever. His undrafted success story began as the definition of a classic failure and under-performer when he substituted his plan to become Israel's national hero and deliverer by killing an Egyptian to save one of his own race—a Hebrew slave. Substitute plans always fail because they are premature end-runs around God. God's timing is always perfect. We're not. God's leadership validation track for Moses was *miracles* (Exodus 5-12)— Moses used *murder*. After 40 years in desert hiding and a burning bush confrontation with Yahweh God, he got better at obeying just in time. The direction God gave for Moses as he led hundreds of thousands of former slaves out of Egypt (see Exodus 13-14) was to camp at the edge of the desert near the Red Sea. With 600 chariots and an elite military force, an enraged Pharaoh pursued that flash mob of a nation. When the Israelites realized Pharaoh was about to pin them against the Red Sea, they assumed it was a death trap and screamed accusations back at God and Moses. It was a "We're gonna DIE!" moment, blaming God for putting them in a crisis with no visible way out— even using a ridiculous lie that they had a better life as slaves in Egypt. Fear says "Talk back." Despair says, "Look back." Impatience says, "Go back." Pride says, "Fight back." Faith says, "Come back...to God." God just wanted faith—exclusive and immediate trust. Moses stood strong before the people that time and God miraculously parted the Red Sea. They ran across despite their fear and weakness. Point?

**It's not about perfection. It's about direction.** That's worth repeating! Are you moving forward, making progress, changing, ditching the sins and heavy weights, and adding the right choices? The faith-heroes of Hebrews 11 were a mix of disappointing weaknesses and amazing risk-taking. But that's what's so motivating. Despite their doubts, fears, lusts, and failures, they pursued God. Their heart was to live for something bigger (see Hebrews 11:13-16), like God's approval and heaven, even though it was invisible (see Hebrews 11:1). And usually that meant rewards and recognition and relief were postponed.

What our faith ancestors achieved is legendary, but not out of reach for us. That's the point. Their success should inspire already fully-devoted followers of Jesus. In fact, it should even motivate semi-devoted, half-hearted, distracted, *"I-don't-know-if-I-can-make-it-through-with-all-my-issues"*-big-sin-entangled believers.

This was *not* a challenge exclusively targeting the elite, already hyper-successful believers, but a command for the whole dysfunctional group of followers that Jesus is still changing. So get over it! You can't create an excuse that exempts you from accountability for running the life-course God has designed for you. Why? Because it's not about your take—whether you think you'll do well, how stressful it appears, whether you will still get to do what you want or have to give up something, or even about your hope that God *might* unleash some amazing chain of miracles for you. God intends that you start the race—NOW—and do it right. He's big enough to develop you and get past any confusion, fear, hesitation, or sin. Since when has your sin ever prevented God from ultimately accomplishing His purpose, anyway?

God is sovereign, in control, totally directing all circumstances. To even intellectually opt for another view will put you over the edge and pervert His biblical identity. Think about it. A sin-saturated world did not prevent God from implementing and completing His plan of making salvation available to us by sending Jesus. Jesus defeated that sin through His death on a cross, crying in victory, *"It is finished!"* (John 19:30, NLT). Nothing incomplete. No second guessing. No doubt about whether the Savior could remove sin and bring life. Unbelief from people amazingly dogged Jesus even post-resurrection. But He unleashed an uninterrupted stream of belief as well.

### More Than There Are Starbucks or McDonalds?

At the moment I'm writing this, worldwide there are 16,635 Starbucks locations, and more than 30,000 McDonald's restaurants (making it the leading global foodservice retailer). And for my analogy, there are probably more hindrances to getting into the race than there are Starbucks or McDonalds. But it's important to think about what might interfere with your initial motivation. If you know your weaknesses, maybe you can deal with them. What is it that keeps even experienced, they-should-know-better, believers from simply committing 100% to the process of improving?

### 10 Commitment-Killers

Here's a short list of commitment-killers:

1. **A divided heart.** *Simple choice. You've got to love Jesus more than the other stuff.*
2. **A short-term perspective.** *Nothing worthwhile is easy or gained quickly. Nobody develops strength of character, resolve, boldness, or wisdom in a drive-thru lane. Discipline is always about doing what's right now for reward later. Mike Krzyzewski, Duke University Head Basketball Coach and record-holder for the most NCAA Division 1 wins, commented: "Discipline is doing what you are supposed to do in the best possible manner at the time you are supposed to do it."*
3. **Waiting for perfection before trying.** *If you waited until you or conditions were perfect, you'd never start college, get married, have kids, invest your money, try out for a team, start a business, or go public with*

*your faith. That's the point. The difference between believers and non-believers is not that believers do not sin, but believers are held to a higher standard of being honest about our imperfections and hopefully consistently take action to eliminate them.*

4. **A performance mentality.** *Nobody has to earn God's love or approval. It's about you loving Him back through your worship and obedience. You will fail. He will not. Keep going.*

5. **A false image of God and the believer's life.** *If you view God as judge, CEO, distant Creator, unpredictable dictator, or stiff monarch, it steals motivation to obey because you expect to get beat up for any mess up. So, the tendency in your attitude is to do the minimum. You will be competing against Him, not committing to Him without conditions. When you understand and embrace God as your Savior, Leader, Healer, Deliverer, and Comforter, you get it—that the believer's life is a "love kick-back" to God!*

6. **Getting over the brand of your past life.** *Jesus forgives sin and removes guilt. It's Satan and your enemies that keep resurfacing your past. The miracle of new life in Jesus is that He intentionally uses those who have been the most messed up (e.g., John 4:17-18, 8:11, 21:17). If Jesus doesn't have an issue with your past, why are you still in bondage? You are only limited by the sin you have not yet confessed. A forgiven past is a fresh platform! Past failures do not predict future results. Swap out the shame. Bury it by creating a new pattern of obedience—brutal confession and passionate worship—until the voices die!*

7. **Looking for inspiration from the wrong crowd.** *The reason a confident, clean, committed life looks so bizarre to skeptics and so appealing to seekers is because it is tragically so rare. The majority of people will tell you that living for Jesus in a spiritually dark generation can't be done and shouldn't be attempted. Hang out with those who have a passion for God. Listen to those who are getting it done. Learn from people who have changed. Your friends, frat brothers, sorority sisters, co-workers, teammates, or golf buddies either make you want more of God or more of the culture. Choose your relationships carefully. Don't align with people who have tried and quit and are angry with God. Break away from negative people. Avoid compromised people. Say "no" to the party crowd that wants to pull you down to their level. Spend the minimum time around those who are content, and maximum time with those who are courageous.*

8. **Being a high-maintenance person.** *If you are easily hurt, emotionally fragile, expecting other people to cater to you, wanting explanations for everything that happens to you, or constantly struggling to find energy, it will be hard to commit to a disciplined race-lifestyle. Get over it. This is not ultimately about you. You're going to take some hits for*

*following Jesus. He did it first for you! Why should you be exempt? (see John 15:20).*

9. **Fear and trust issues.** *Were you betrayed or abused in the past? Did you grow up in a family where dad wasn't believable, mom wasn't accessible, promises weren't credible, or forgiveness wasn't possible? If so, you might lean toward being less motivated to trust what God says works. Fear of being hurt again can keep you in bondage to the wrong way of life, and less likely to risk anything.*

10. **Getting lazy.** *One woman said that a man's idea of helping with housework is lifting his leg so his wife can vacuum. People trend toward laziness in relationships. Nobody is naturally aggressive about abandoning the pleasures of sin either. Our fleshly human nature is like a powerful vacuum suction force, without an OFF-switch, pulling us downward toward sin. Putting out an effort to change takes huge energy and focus, especially if you've been negligent, sloppy, careless, indulgent, or developed sin-tolerating patterns.*

These commitment-killers can be avoided.

It is possible to get free...to get moving forward...when you know the secrets to obedience.

## Chapter 5

# Nothing Spreads Like Fear

*"The average person touches their face 3 to 5 times per minute.*
*In between, we're touching door knobs, water fountains, and each other."*
–From the 2011 movie, **Contagion**

"The truth is being kept from the world....No one is immune....Nothing spreads like fear." Those riveting lines are from the 2011 movie, ***Contagion***, starring Matt Damon and Gwyneth Paltrow, which imagines the scenario of death, panic, and misinformation from the spread of a mysterious virus in the U.S. Their realities also fit the premise we've been pushing—you can't allow fear to kill what God started doing in your life. Many people talk about their life in past tense, like "I knew God once" or "I was on the right track for a while" or "I used to be into God". Fear can keep you from moving forward with God to reverse the bad choices and replace them with the best choices.

### 7 Secrets of Obedience

Using just one premier example from the Hebrews 11 list of "Faith Hall-of-Famers", Abraham, we can learn key secrets to getting started right.

> *8 It was by faith that Abraham obeyed when God called him*
> *to leave home and go to another land that God would give him*
> *as his inheritance. He went without knowing where he was*
> *going. 9 And even when he reached the land God promised*
> *him, he lived there by faith—for he was like a foreigner, living*
> *in tents. And so did Isaac and Jacob, who inherited the same*
> *promise. 10 Abraham was confidently looking forward to a city*
> *with eternal foundations, a city designed and built by God.*
> (Hebrews 11:8-10, NLT)

1. **Timing is everything.** *First, Abraham obeyed **when** he was called. God expects us to respond to Him immediately with hesitation or debate.*

2. **Motives must be pure.** *He also obeyed **because** he was called. People who have surrendered their lives to Jesus are concerned about pleasing Him.*

3. **Pursue only God's plan.** *Abraham obeyed a **call**. His responsiveness was to God's custom, pre-designed life-race alone, not a substitute plan.*

4. **Don't wait for others—LEAD!** *Abraham obeyed **first**. He did not wait upon others to respond. He followed what he understood God expected and others would follow later.*

5. **Chase something bigger than you.** *Abraham obeyed **to go out**. He was willing to separate from his family and homeland and start over to see God do something that had never been done before.*

6. **Expect God to reward what you do.** *He obeyed **to receive** whatever reward God had designated. His obedience was sourced in a conviction that God rewards those who obey.*

7. **Get started. Ask questions later.** *Finally, he took a huge risk—he went out **not knowing** where he was going. There was no demand that all of his questions be resolved before trusting God in the next step.*

The lyrics of "Moving Forward" (by Ricardo Sanchez & Israel Houghton from Free Chapel), reflect that kind of resolve.

*I'm not going back*
*I'm moving ahead*
*I'm here to declare to You*
*My past is over*
*In You things are made new*
*Surrender my life to Christ*
*I'm moving, moving forward*
*Forward, forward, forward, forward*

*What a moment*
*You have brought me to*
*Such a freedom*
*I have found in You*
*What a Healer*

*You make all things new*
*Yeah, Yeah, Yeah*

*You have risen*
*With all power in Your Hands*
*You have given me*
*A second chance*
*Hallelujah, Hallelujah*

*You make all things new*
*You make all things new*
*I will follow You, forward*
*Anywhere You go, I will follow*

## Kim Jong-il and Secrets

One of the dirty little secrets among the believing crowd is that we have bought into a frequently repeated lie about being bullet-proof. What's the lie? Just this. Sometimes we convince ourselves that refusing to obey, protecting the very sins and encumbrances that weaken us, will NOT hold us back spiritually. The truth is 180-degrees the opposite. You don't stay in the same place spiritually. You are either moving forward or backward. Your confidence in a big God is either increasing or decreasing. You are either conquering sin or it's conquering you! Maintaining the same level of passion for worship, prayer, or generosity is impossible. One *in-your-face* statement is from the missionary-preacher-author Paul, to the highly dysfunctional and immature group of believers in the ancient city of Corinth in Greece. To this crowd that was still struggling to break away from issues like exclusivism, celebrity worship (maybe the original *American Idol* crowd), weird beliefs, casual sex, homosexuality, adultery, drinking, partying, greed, and white-collar theft, Paul spoke to eliminate any confusion: *"The message of the cross is foolish to those who are headed for destruction! But we who are being saved know it is the very power of God"* (1 Corinthians 1:18, NLT).

Those who have rejected belief in Jesus are not at a spiritual standstill, just hanging out in the category of non-belief or staying open with a positive attitude until they reach a final decision. It is clear biblical teaching that non-believers continue to slide deeper into rebellion, their lives stretched closer to a breaking point, and their hearts are harder today than yesterday.

One day, every person will stand before God to give account of how we managed the exact number of days God planned for us, and how we responded to the truth we received (see Romans 1:18-21; 14:12). And, because God gives every person a unique set of gifts, talents, abilities, and attributes, we all will be individually judged by Him on the basis of whether we have managed those talents and opportunities to bring honor to His name. Translation? That inviolable truth applies to every person on the planet, but it's understandable with large-scale examples like pop-music icons, the late Michael Jackson and Whitney Houston. Their deaths were a huge loss to millions. Whether Michael Jackson or Whitney Houston were true believers in Jesus or not, they will be judged on whether they used their talents and success—the voice, dancing skills, crowd charisma, ability to fill arenas, collect Grammys, and sell albums—to promote, not themselves, but the one true living God. If those *once-in-a-generation* gifts were not exclusively devoted to making Jesus known, there is a corresponding accountability.

Specifically, every person will be evaluated on their response to Jesus. Ultimately, *"every knee should bow…and every tongue confess that Jesus Christ is Lord"* (Philippians 2:10-11, NLT). But for the purposes of this section, the reality framed by God is that nobody will be able to use *ignorance* as a defense (see Romans 3:19). Insanity? Maybe. Ha. But only in the sense that it's crazy to think we could oppose God all our lives and escape judgment. Literally, everybody will shut up in God's presence because He has both the truth on us and the final word on our lives and eternal destination. All will be BUSTED!

Know as the "Supreme Leader", North Korean dictator Kim Jong-Il died in December, 2011 after 17 years in power. According to a 2004 *Human Rights Watch* report, the North Korean government under Kim was "among the world's most repressive governments", holding up to 200,000 political prisoners according to U.S. and South Korean officials,[1] with zero freedom of the press or religion, no political opposition or equal education.[2] Kim Jong-il has already faced Jesus. So has Osama bin Laden. Everybody, from world leaders to ordinary people, will bow and confess that Jesus is Lord seconds after they die. God will judge our secrets by the standard of Jesus (see Romans 2:16). *"Each one of us will give a personal account to God"* (Romans 14:12, NLT). Did you know that every sin we commit is fully visible to God? Everything we do is like performing it right in front of Him! *"Nothing in all the world can be hidden from God. Everything is clear and lies open before him, and to him we must explain the way we have lived"* (Hebrews 4:13, NCV).

## CAUGHT ON VIDEO

Several years ago, my wife and I attended a 50th wedding anniversary party for some close friends. As we entered the room where the reception was being held, we realized that we were totally surrounded by people we did not know and faced a long program with speeches from friends and family honoring them. We loved the couple but didn't want to get stuck in a boring program. So to do the right thing socially, we introduced ourselves to a few people and smiled, strategically working our way to a corner of the room near the exit so we could leave discreetly after a few minutes. While standing at the back, listening to the beginning of the memory list, we casually whispered to each other in the way husbands and wives do when they believe they are alone and cannot be heard. We made some funny remarks about how people looked and acted, that we didn't know anybody, and how we wanted to get out quickly. Just before our slick exit, I turned around and almost knocked over a video camera on a tripod, set up right behind us to record the event without anybody at the party realizing they were being recorded. Yes, the red light was on! No, we didn't ever ask if the family watched the video! I bought the video from the photographer for $1,000 and destroyed it! Just kidding...I didn't pay that much. Seriously, God knows every secret.

In that sense, Romans 1:18-19 is like getting caught on secret video with its crushing reality: *"For the wrath of God is revealed from heaven against all ungodliness and unrighteousness of men, who* **suppress the truth** *[emphasis mine] in unrighteousness, because what may be known of God is manifest in them, for God has shown it to them"* (NKJV). The word imagery here is like God is constantly speaking to you, making you aware that He is showing up everywhere you are, and you keep shoving away those moments, pretending they didn't happen, that God isn't real, and that your push-back is good enough to stop God from coming after you again. But He doesn't. He just keeps coming—showing up. Pursuing you relentlessly. In that sense, you are being stalked!

Constant suppression of the truth requires a lot of energy and focus. Anger and fatigue take over in a prolonged battle with God and His inescapable truth. When you see people with higher than normal levels of frustration, inappropriate anger, irritation that doesn't match the situation, or emotions that are out of proportion, it's because they are engaged in an internal spiritual war with God. Suppression creates casualties. Not victims, casualties. Without realizing it, you will become obsessed with getting rid of or separated from any person, situation, or location that has even a remote chance of turning into hearing something about God again. Rejecting God's truth will keep you slammed. It's like trying to hold 50 ping pong balls underwater, simultaneously, without any help. His truth just keeps popping up, surfacing at awkward times and awful times for every non-believer. It's universal. Deal with it.

But more critical, is that, whether anybody admits it or agrees with it, truth cannot be altered, ignored, or removed. Further, it teaches that God's judgment is totally justified because every person who has ever lived has intentionally, deliberately, consciously, and consistently suppressed the truth they know about God.

## Atheists and Dinosaurs

Wow. Those verses are unambiguous. Not that atheists are like dinosaurs that have become extinct. The Bible clearly says that no such critter, like an atheist, has ever existed in any period of history! According to those verses, God has revealed Himself to every person. In fact, there's a large pile of condemning evidence out there—and it's irrefutable according to this biblical report. **God has revealed Himself in 3 ways to every inhabitant of the planet in history.**

First, God makes Himself obvious and real through **creation**. God's existence, and "invisible attributes" like wisdom, beauty, power and authority as Creator, are on sharp and vivid display daily in nature—the created world (see Romans 1:20, NIV). Nature so obviously displays and points to God that the verse says we are *"without excuse"* in front of any landscape, horizon, sunset, ocean, tree or mountain range. The complexity of our planet and even the human eye, the existence of water and tides, the mysterious laws of gravity and nature that hold our universe together, and the human instruction code called DNA, all logically demand an Intelligent Designer. Check out my real-life evidence that follows.

### DELTA + 8,000 miles + Land Rovers + Siankwakwani + SPAM + *The Lion King* = A Doctor?

It was our first family safari…and mission venture. After the longest non-stop Delta flight in the world at that time from the States, crossing 7 time zones and over 8,000 miles, we finally worked our way from Johannesburg, South Africa to Victoria Falls, Zimbabwe. The following day, way overstuffed backpacks and gear were loaded into two trail-worn Land Rovers, to travel more than 100km down jungle trails, past villages ( like Siankwakwani), over mountains, and through wild grass fires that landed us at our destination in a remote valley of the Zambezi River in Zambia. With the masterful help of a constantly smiling guide and translator named "Friday" (whose birth language was *Tonga*, a Bantu dialect), and a veteran missionary a world away from his home in Arkansas, we set up our tent camp for the 6-day adventure, cooking rice and Chai tea over open fires. But as spoiled Americans, we couldn't have survived without dozens of cans of SPAM and Vienna Sausage, jars of peanut butter, and boxes of crackers. Our days were spent meeting villagers wandering through the jungles into the valley, who had heard rumors of white people in the valley and were telling the story of a God who not only created the world but visited it. Though we drank unpurified water from a local well that was carried for hundreds of yards in old 5-gallon military gas cans, and were visited at night by animals, we survived! Nobody was bitten by a malaria mosquito, suffered from diarrhea, contracted and disease or fever, was attacked by snakes, or cowered in fear in the tents when hyenas laughed. We were too focused on what was happening. Villagers gathered nightly around our giant campfire, singing with amazing vocal tones, harmonies, and rhythms. It was like finding King Solomon's Mines AND the original vocalists for *The Lion King!* Our guide Friday provided the only instrument—his most prized possession—a vintage 1940's accordion, given to him decades ago by a missionary and held together only by used duct tape. Those voices echoing across the valley, the smiles lighted through a crackling fire, and a respectful silence when listening to bible stories—exposing an unrestrained raw hunger to discover God—are some of my most treasured and enduring memories.

But the biggest life-moment started when a young Zambian mother walked slowly into our campsite perimeter with a very small boy struggling to walk and stand beside her. Both dignity and desperation emerged through the mother's demeanor. Worn clothing told a story of intense poverty or suffering. His distended stomach, blank stare, skin and hair discolorations, and mouth infections were obvious signs of severe malnutrition and possibly symptomatic of other unknown diseases. With over 70 dialects and languages spoken in Zambia, our multi-lingual translator Friday was the lifeline. He explained the sadness behind her words as he translated her tribal language. She had heard rumors of white people staying in the valley who were speaking of a God who created the world. Believing for some time that the vast grandeur she saw in nature must have been designed by a wonderful God, she had walked miles over mountains and through jungles in hopes that we would explain this powerful Creator and ask Him to save her dying son. Our team shed tears as we surrounded them. I placed my hands on the frail little 5-year-old boy, praying…actually *begging* God to miraculously heal this boy—to save his life and show his mother that God was real and loved them. Nothing immediately or visibly changed—*including* our faith that God would answer. We placed the little boy on a log by the campfire. My 19-year-old daughter sat near him, watching him with intense compassion and trying to get him to sip some hot tea simmering in a tin pan. It didn't end there. There's more.

At the campfire worship time the night before we left, we presented the final piece of the biblical story of God's Son, Jesus Christ, dying on the cross to purchase forgiveness of sin and eternal life for all who would believe. With only small, flickering flames left, we asked all who wanted to become followers of Jesus to stand. There was total silence. No movement. A couple of minutes passed. Then I realized the adults and children alike were taking time to consider the seriousness of that commitment. The first to stand was a young blind man. One by one, people of all ages responded, until twenty-five unashamedly stood in front of their families and friends to express belief in Jesus. As far as I was concerned it was the most important thing happening in the world at that moment. A million stars in that clear nighttime sky were the only witnesses. Early morning sun warmed the emotional scene of good-byes, hugs, and packing the Land Rovers to return. Oddly enough, the only bible we had left was handed to the blind man, standing with that small group of new believers gathered under a giant acacia tree to hear our departing prayer. Holding the bible tightly to his chest like it was a million dollar check, he accepted our challenge to take on the impossible role of being "teacher" for them.

**A can of Spam? $2.50. A round-trip ticket from Atlanta to Johannesburg, South Africa? $2,500. Used Bible for a blind man? Maybe $2.00. Bag of rice and Chai tea? Pennies. The *After*story of that campfire moment? Priceless.** There are 4 follow-ups you have to hear. First, after returning to our home in Atlanta, Georgia, I would learn that God spoke to my daughter in that scene, confirming her sense of call to a career in medicine. She is now a successful physician, known for giftedness in diagnosis and compassion. It started in a jungle with a dying boy. Second, without anybody in the camp being aware, a friend secretly captured that scene between my daughter and the boy in a photo. That photo has been proudly displayed in my office as a reminder of unexpected moments when a loving God multi-tasks to meet needs. Third, the boy was healed and lived! Fourth, none of the "acacia tree people" could read, but just one year later, over 200 people were worshiping Jesus together under a large, open, grass-hut shelter on the plain near the tree.

Do NOT limit God. There's so much you can't explain in life, including that story, without admitting both the existence of God and your desire to experience Him. Unless God is in the mix, your story doesn't survive. God has revealed Himself through creation—the spectacular network of nature with billions of pixels and delicate balance. God loved the Zambian mother and boy so much that He decided before time began to reveal Himself to her through the beauty of the African landscape, and send us for follow-up to explain His plan and demonstrate His power. Without our prompting, without any exposure to academia or media, she knew God existed. God is there. He is real. You know it.

Second, God has revealed Himself—His holiness...morality...right and wrong—through the **commandments** that were first distributed through the Jewish nation (see Romans 2:6-12, 17-24). Those who are aware of the laws are totally accountable. Laws simply expose the sin and sinful motives in our hearts, because nobody can perfectly keep all the rules. Romans 3:19-23 explains that nobody is really good enough to meet the standards of God's perfection and holiness. We have all sinned, and know it! In fact, when we know what God commands us to avoid, our sin nature gets stirred up and we can't help investigating it: *"I would not have known what it means to want something that belongs to someone else, unless the Law had told me not to do that. It was sin that used this command as a way of making me have all kinds of desires"* (Romans 7:7-8, CEV). It's like somebody asked, "Why is it that when we are told there are billions of stars in the universe we accept it without question, but when we see a sign that says WET PAINT, we immediately want to touch it?"

Third, God has imprinted an awareness of His existence on the **conscience** of every person (see Romans 2:14-16). Your conscience accuses or excuses your thoughts and choices, depending upon the situation, but it is still an immoveable moral compass. The conscience can be good (Hebrews 13:18 / 1 Peter 3:16), be pure if a believer makes the right choices (1 Timothy 3:9), or be weak (1 Corinthians 8:7) and unreliable if there is slippage. However, your conscience can also be fried with lies (1 Timothy 4:2 / Ephesians 4:19), evil (Hebrews 10:22), or perverted with constant bad choices so that it no longer works right in all situations (Titus 1:15). But it still exists in every person.

It's described like a "law written on the heart". In effect, even if you weren't raised in a religious or faith-based home, village, or culture; even if you have been totally surrounded with secular, post-Christian intellectual processes and political correctness all the way through the university system or political food chain; even if you have made your life and career in skeptical media; and even if you have existed on the streets and in the bars with addicts and pimps, you KNOW who God is, and you know right from wrong, because of that pre-programmed conscience. It's like software that can't be uninstalled. That unmistakable check in your thinking that makes you hesitate—that voice that can't be silenced—keeps you painfully aware of God's presence and His knowledge of all secrets. According to this text, you really know down deep inside that you are going to be judged for the secrets of the heart. You'll stand before God and give an account.

So, the biblical truth is unavoidable. We KNOW God is real, sin is real, and a final accounting is real. And yet...we still hold out. Those who die and spend an eternity without Jesus simply just became professionals at avoiding God and truth. I know. I was a angry, professional skeptic...a really good one. Not much different than this famous Jewish guy.

## The Original Road Rage

The most famous bible example both of resisting an irresistible truth and God's ability to interrupt a life at will, is the dramatic conversion of Saul (Acts 9:1-9). At the peak of his rage, believing he was winning points in his personal jihad by destroying the lives of Christians, this Jewish religious extremist, legalist, and Pharisee, was struck blind. While carrying legal documents that would expand his campaign against the ever-encroaching threat of those Jesus-followers, the resurrected, glorified Jesus appeared and physically shut down his road trip to Damascus...and his sight.

In their brief conversation, Jesus accused Saul of persecuting Him personally, not just attacking believers. Actually, Jesus wanted Saul to explain why Saul hated Him so intensely. Why was Saul so obsessed with removing the name and influence of Jesus? It was personal and it was bigger than what Saul ever admitted. His hatred was not primarily about real ideological conflict. Saul was not taking Christians to court, prison, and execution because he was primarily consumed with theological purity, preserving power for the Temple elite, or correcting misconceptions. Maintaining religious identity and integrity was just a convenient and believable cover. It never was about preserving Jewish tradition and interpretation. Saul's core issue was his refusal to believe that he was accountable to God. So, by his own *mea culpa* years later, he admitted he plunged deeper into personal guilt, bitterness, and obsession when he rejected the option that Jesus could be the Jewish Messiah (see Acts 22:4-5 and 1 Timothy 1:13).

**Truth does not evaporate, cease to exist, fall apart, or disappear simply because you might choose to reject it.** Jesus said He Himself was *"the way, the truth, and the life. No one comes to the Father except through Me"* (John 14:6, NKJV). So, to dismiss Jesus is to reject ultimate truth, and to reject truth is to dismiss Jesus. This was a huge battle of wills and Saul was losing. Worse. He was totally typical of every non-believer. He knew he was losing and wouldn't surrender to the truth he knew about Jesus that was accurate.

And the most interesting comment emerges when Jesus exposes Saul's well-disguised spiritual tension: *"It is hard for you to kick against the goads"* (Acts 9:5, NKJV). That's insider-trading information. There had been uncountable moments of conviction that Jesus labeled as "goads". "Goads" were long, pointed sticks used to poke and move livestock in a specific direction. In effect, Jesus reminded Saul that He had been poking him with truth for a long time through a variety of events and it had been an all-consuming, violent, fierce, energy-draining, anger-creating conflict. Saul wasn't going to surrender. Witnessing the death of an articulate speaker for Christianity named Stephen was arguably the most crushing conviction Saul endured, and yet it didn't create belief in his heart. Saul stood by while his peers, radical Pharisees intent on destroying any threat to their religious power system, stoned Stephen. Stephen's dying words, that he saw Jesus and chose to forgive his assassins (see Acts 7:54-60), must have caused countless sleepless nights, because nobody but Jesus can create forgiveness for the worst terrorism imaginable. The most powerful man had to be shut down by something more powerful. So Saul had to be stopped—unexpectedly, abruptly, completely—or he self-destructs.

Maybe you are consumed with the same invisible, internal war. You know, it doesn't have to be like that. Jesus died to remove your sins and pour His life into you. Life under His control, protection, and direction is unbelievable on the good side. That's why Saul, later known as Paul, spent the rest of his life telling his story to anybody who would listen and to some who refused to listen. As an itinerant preacher and prolific author, the new story consumed him and is unfolded in 13 of the 27 books of the New Testament in the Bible. Jesus' love and forgiveness was so revolutionary and central to his core existence that he ultimately chose to be martyred rather than abandon the Savior who extended radical forgiveness to him.

### Is it Smart?

Just as non-believers can't remain spiritually locked-in to the same status, neither can believers. It's just as crazy to think that because we have the Holy Spirit, or "the forgotten God" as Francis Chan calls Him, living inside us, that there is some invisible momentum that keeps us moving forward with greater discipline and passion for the things of God. The guarantees given believers revolve around a gift-list of essentials like irrevocable forgiveness, the Spirit's inseparable presence, and a certain future in heaven (Ephesians 1:7, 13-14). Beyond that, there is no spiritual immunity for believers. Trials pressure us to the breaking point (1 Peter 1:6, 4:12 / 2 Corinthians 4:8-11). Temptation is real (James 1:2). Deception takes over (1 John 1:8). We lie if we say that we don't sin. Again, as Paul explained to a really messed up Corinthian church, freedom in Christ brings its own unique tension: *"All things are lawful for me, but all things are not helpful. All things are lawful for me, but I will not be brought under the power of any"* (1 Corinthians 6:12, NKJV).

What's the take away? Just this. It's really possible to become entangled or pulled down even with good stuff. The good can become the enemy of the best. Lots of legitimate and fun stuff competes with and crowds out what God is begging us to do. So, obviously, our life-race suffers. Nothing wrong with a Smartphone. Unless you are live-streaming a game while on a date with your wife at a restaurant.

You are free to do anything. Biggest question? **Is it smart?** Freedom for the believer is not an entitlement to sin. ***Reckless behavior***, even if you have opportunity and permission, does not equate to ***right behavior***. The decision-principle here is whether *you* rule the choices, or *unwise choices* begin to run your life. What's permissible is not always helpful. So, progress can be reversed. Without boundaries for our freedom—some fences, rules, or restraints—we can fall right back into previous sins that nearly killed us.

The setbacks cost us precious momentum. Confidence is lost. Guilt sneaks in like a thief to steal our joy. We start to question our love for God, and wonder how we walked into that really stupid decision. To make an important reconnection here, we also put a dent in our dreams and call "strike one" as we fall short of what we were really capable of doing. When we are embarrassingly short of living up to potential, it hurts.

### Storms, Seizures, Struggles and John Maxwell

On multiple occasions, Jesus made that point to His underperforming disciples. First, there was the panic in the disciples' boat caught in a massive storm (Matthew 8:26). Then, that embarrassing moment when they failed to heal the little boy with seizures and demons in front of a crowd (Matthew 17:17). When the disciples struggled to forgive, they actually asked Jesus to *"increase"* their faith (Luke 17:5, NIV). Jesus not only knew they had greater potential, but He set them up to own that untapped excellence.

Just like those ordinary men, called "disciples", who were trying to emulate Jesus, you have unused potential. Leadership coach John Maxwell states simply, "We are unchanged because we are unchallenged." That's why Jesus' comeback to them was couched in extreme confrontation. He asked them why they were fearful, called their faith "small", linked them to a faithless generation, and demanded they chase forgiveness as a lifestyle, not a list.

## Carpe Diem is NOT a dead fish!

Frankly, we're all underperforming! Look at the stuff competing for your God-passion, and see it as a "potential-killer". If you really think you could do better, have more to give, more to experience, then run the race right. God's expectation to "run the race" means there is more He believes you can accomplish.

Commitment creates confidence. Surrounded by "the great cloud of witnesses" is the visual we must focus on as we begin our race. Other people have done it, and done it well. So can you! There are role models, solid examples, and winners who have achieved incredible things. Their life-records survive in places like Hebrews 11 to inspire us never to underestimate our potential. Better yet. Those mini-biographies collectively create the equivalent of a spiritual "Declaration of Independence" so that we would never underestimate the size or sovereignty of our God! Confidence in God, unlike people, is never wasted or misplaced. God is faithful to whatever He has promised. You can be too. Don't toss away the most amazing life—YOURS!

*The Dead Poets Society* is an old movie starring Robin Williams as Professor Keating, a teacher at an exclusive prep school for boys in 1959. To teach them a love of poetry and inspire them to chase their dreams, he involves them in some bizarre experiences. From ripping out pages in their textbook to courtyard drills and standing on a desk, the Professor exposes them to different viewpoints, and employs radical methods as he confronts them repeatedly with the challenge "carpe diem", or "seize the day". The movie plot tracks the giddy freedom found by his class as each student makes gut-wrenching decisions about breaking away from the oppressive expectations of rigid parents and the inflexible traditions of the school. Many students decide to follow the desires of their heart, knowing time is limited. One young man risks losing the career his father designed and demanded for him by pursuing a role in a theater production. Conflicted because his father refused to support him and his success, he ends his life. That moment of suicide, tragic and totally preventable, overtakes the film, probably purposely, because it is the ultimate reminder we only get one chance! Professor Keating is blamed for pushing the student to the brink and suffers an immediate and controversial dismissal from the school he loves. The movie poignantly ends in a scene with students standing on their classroom desks in honor of the accused and recently dismissed Professor Keating, and in silent protest of a return to traditional roles.

Yes, if we don't run the race right, we lose potential. You may lose precious life. You may lose eternity. Worse. You might even keep somebody else from finding it.

Seize the day!

## Chapter 6

# Once Upon A Night In A Hotel

March 1, 2010. Conan O'Brien got a $33 million severance package and Jay Leno got the *Tonight Show* back. After hosting it for 17 years and surviving a 9-month tour of duty in prime time TV, Leno returned to his old show with a comedy take-off on *The Wizard of Oz*, like Dorothy waking up after a weird dream. It took him all of 3 days to take over the ratings lead in American late night programming. One new comedy segment was called, "What Did You Think Was Gonna happen?" Sort of like *America's Funniest Videos*, in this IPO (Initial Public Offering), Jay showed a video of a guy straddling two cars, one foot on each bumper, while his buddy lighted a bottle rocket underneath him. Yeah. I know. It's unbelievable. Can people actually be that dumb? You know what's coming. The bottle rocket ignites, lands in his pants, and he jumps really high. And it wasn't the first time this guy had done this!

It's funny. Really funny if you were actually watching. Mostly because Americans believe stupidity needs to be...and *will be*...rewarded—usually with fire, flips, brief fame, an ER visit—and sometimes political office. Just kidding. You and I know better, and they knew better too. But that's not the point. The "bottle rocket guys" knew better, but either couldn't get dates, couldn't get jobs, or couldn't resist the experience, the thrill, the You Tube fame, or something. Who knows? Sometimes, even when you know you will lose in a trade-off, you still crazily do it. Anyway, our next step is taking on some more trade-offs if you choose not to run your life-race by God's rules.

So what's the next potential mistake mentioned in Hebrews 12:1?

Check it out: *"Let us lay aside every weight, and the sin which so easily ensnares us, and let us run with endurance the race that is set before us"* (NKJV).

### MISTAKE No. 2: Repeating bad choices.

Even if you aren't into Jay Leno the comedian, he's become the icon for strategic humor and quotable observations: "The Supreme Court has ruled that they cannot have a nativity scene in Washington, D.C. This wasn't for any religious reasons. They couldn't find three wise men and a virgin." It's a joke, people! But Jay did surface an "inconvenient truth". Everybody has some definition or standard of right and wrong. People innately—and usually quickly—make judgments that categorize choices as good or bad, smart or stupid, beneficial or harmful, righteous or sinful. And even non-believers normally laugh at or dismiss people who keep doing unwise things, repeating bad or stupid choices.

According to our focus verse, that doesn't have to happen! Specifically, the challenge for a person serious about honoring their lifetime relationship with Jesus is unmistakable—not impossible. It's not even unreasonable. Here's the core. If a person commits to a relationship, then you would expect them to honor the meaning of that relationship. If commitment to another person means anything, it's to prove how much you value them by doing what is right in that relationship.

Truth is important. Morals are valuable. Trust is indispensible. Wisdom is essential. Any and all of those values are like airbags in your car. When an accident triggers the airbag, it becomes an automatic safety buffer. Without things like truth, morals, trust, or wisdom, relationships are going to suffer some serious damage when mistakes are made. Husbands and wives shouldn't commit adultery. Employees shouldn't steal. Employers shouldn't lie. Parents should explain boundaries. Kids shouldn't lie to their parents. Students shouldn't cheat on tests. Teachers should be creative. Coaches should be fair. Athletes should give 100% effort. Judges should enforce law. That's normal. And we expect normal.

What's NOT normal is to believe that commitment doesn't have to be maintained. Like your teeth never need cleaning and your car never needs an oil change.? What's NOT normal is to think that commitment requires no tough choices. The value of something is reflected in the level of sacrificial commitment required to possess it or preserve it.

### You Can't SPIN Bill O'Reilly!

In relationships, the issue is not, "Are you going to live up to the other person's expectations?" That will *never* happen. You and I can't even please our moms, Democrats, Republicans, Independents, Bill O'Reilly, Jon Stewart, churches, Michelle Obama, Sean Hannity, or the IRS forever. Besides, the expectations of a mate, boss, friend, coach, the media, or American Idol judges, are a shifting target. Meet them once? Good, because tomorrow the expectations change and you've got to start guessing all over again! Someone has said, "A woman marries a man expecting he will change, but he doesn't. A man marries a woman expecting that she won't change, and she does."

Reaching the end of a job interview, a Human Resources person asked a young engineer fresh out of college, "And what starting salary were you looking for?" The engineer said, "Maybe $125,000 a year, depending on the benefits package." The interviewer said, "Well, what would you say to a package of 5 weeks' vacation, 14 paid holidays, full medical and dental, company matching retirement fund to 50% of salary, and a company car leased every 2 years—say, a red Corvette?" The engineer sat up straight, much energized, "Wow! Are you kidding?" The interviewer replied, "Yeah, but you started it." Unrealistic expectations will come back to bite you!

Stand-up comic Vanessa Hollingshead confessed, "I think I've discovered the key to life—lowered expectations. You know, whatever dreams you have, hopes you have, goals…lower them. And you can apply it to anything. I used to want to meet a guy that was kind, warm, loving. Now I'm happy if the guy has ears."

There's no lowered expectations in this verse, but instead, for long-term survival this verse packs a *higher* expectation for the lifetime Christ-follower. And you won't get worn out just trying to guess daily what it is. The expectation is fixed and simple: **Stop repeating bad choices!** Quit making excuses about why you make really bad choices that are just cover-ups for sinful behavior! Dump the self-defeating excesses that protect entangling sins. If you drive home drunk once and don't get caught or killed or crash, even though it was just a few beers at the game and only your kids were in the SUV, it was still wrong. If you do it again and get a DUI or wreck your car, then you've got a problem.

And while you're thinking about the consequences, don't cheapen that warning by going selfish or legalistic. The reason you should make the right choices to separate from sin and dump the things that wear you out and pull you down spiritually and emotionally, is not just to avoid looking stupid, improve your character, increase your confidence, or brag about your spiritual fitness. Yes, you end the bad-choice cycle in order to run the best race possible for you! Assuming, of course, you get the ultimate goal in Hebrews 12:2, *"looking unto Jesus, the author and finisher of our faith"* (NKJV). Whatever we do in this abbreviated existence has got to please Jesus and hold up at judgment.

Ray Stedman observed:

> *The race of the Christian life is not fought well or run well by asking, "What's wrong with this or that?" but by asking, "Is it in the way of greater faith and greater love and greater purity and greater courage and greater humility and greater patience and greater self-control? Not; is it a sin? But: Does it help me run? Is it in the way? Don't ask about your music, your movies, your parties, and your habits: What's wrong with it? Ask: Does it help me RUN the race!? Does it help me RUN - for Jesus?*[1]

## The Original Desperate Housewife?

A story has been circulated that as the army of Alexander the Great was advancing on Persia, at one critical point it appeared his troops might be defeated. The soldiers had taken so much plunder from their previous campaigns that they had become weighted down and were losing their effectiveness in combat. Alexander immediately commanded that all the spoils be thrown into a heap and burned. The men complained bitterly but soon came to see the wisdom of the order.

We accumulate STUFF! *Small, unguarded, bad choices* PILE UP TO CREATE BIG MISTAKES and lots of negative emotional and spiritual weight to carry around. One military training source targeted the effect of backpack weight on a soldier's combat readiness with a simple statement: "carrying too much weight accelerates exhaustion."[2] Military personnel are coldly precise, choosing only the essential items for survival, counting those items, and calculating the weight placed in a soldier's rucksack and assault pack. American Iraq War veterans say in combat they carried about 65 lbs. fully loaded, not including body armor and ammo. They know the smallest unnecessary weight in their backpack could impact their movement and reaction time, costing their life or their buddy's life in combat.

Contrast that with the epidemic of really lame thinking about routine choices. Like the following stuff that wouldn't hold up on a witness stand:

> ✓ *Nobody gets fat by eating just one extra bite of dessert.*
> ✓ *One drink normally doesn't impair judgment.*
> ✓ *Sharing frustration about your wife with a hot, sympathetic female co-worker isn't yet adultery, just friendship.*
> ✓ *Failing to study for one test probably won't mean flunking the course.*
> ✓ *Exceeding the speed limit by 20 miles per hour doesn't mean you'll get a ticket.*

When there's no immediate negative consequences, when nobody seems to get hurt, when it feels good and you get away with something—what's so bad? But...**bad choices don't just go away.** Really stupid behavior doesn't magically disappear after the first bite of cheesecake, the first drink, the first flirt, the first bad test, or the first driving mistake. As I told a college student over coffee at Chick-fil-A when he confessed an addiction to porn—hating himself for lying to his girlfriend that he was clean but then going right back to the computer almost unconsciously: "Habits can be killed. Desires survive." In fact, you better choose the "remove and replace" strategy for sinful habits, or you'll be killed. It's about more than pleasing your girlfriend. It's about pleasing your God.

Choice after choice to chase the wrong attitudes, emotions, commitments, relationships, or beliefs over time, fills the empty sections of your heart attitudes (i.e., your *"backpack"*), until it slows you down or shuts you down. The damage is invisible at first. Your spirit takes a hit. That part of you that communicates with God gets progressively weaker, like a dying battery. Soon, you become deaf to God's voice and arrogantly believe you are exempt from the consequences. God doesn't go anywhere. You pushback on Him! Repeated sin increases the distance between you and God and the further away you get as you wade deeper into sin, the harder it is to hear His voice.

The premier, extreme example of spiritual irresponsibility is the Old Testament story of the tragic loss of the career, home, and family of a rising entrepreneur and politician named Lot. I call it out because Jesus Himself isolated Lot's wife as the worst case scenario of spiritual deception from tolerating sexual immorality (Luke 17:32—*"Remember Lot's wife"*, NKJV). Lot, the nephew of Jewish patriarch Abraham, is the poster boy for this reality, an irrefutable truth—*small compromises always lead to big collapses.* Living in the cities of Sodom and Gomorrah for years (c. 2,000 B.C.) to build his fortune and advance his political career, Lot subtly lost his spiritual edge. He surrendered his convictions *one phrase, one conversation, one invitation, one commitment, one party, and one argument at a time*, giving them away to the lowest bidder in their culture. As a result, according to Genesis 19, when God's angels came to rescue Lot, his wife, two daughters and their husbands, from the corruption so they would not be killed in God's judgment upon the city, the sons-in-law laughed it off, and Lot briefly *"lingered"*, torn between two worlds (Genesis 19:26, KJV).

The hesitation indicated his heart was compromised. Ignoring God's specific warning not to look back when escaping the city, Lot's wife paid the ultimate price, turning into a pillar of salt (i.e., either a direct, immediate act of divine judgment, or getting covered with the explosion of fire and brimstone). She obviously had crossed over from protesting the community lifestyle to promoting it—maybe *the original desperate housewife?* Later, Lot's own daughters, who had lost any sense of moral boundaries growing up in that culture, got their father drunk in order to have sex with him (see Genesis 19:30-38).

So the next dirty little secret is that the most intimidating competition is not against the temptations that are so easily accessible, or your crazy friends that have zero restraint. Your most intense competition for sanity, stability, and spirituality? **YOU.** Details of Lot's short biography in scripture reveal the disaster was the result of little choices that chipped away at his conscience daily:

> *7 But God also rescued Lot out of Sodom because he was a*
> *righteous man who was sick of the shameful immorality of the*
> *wicked people around him. 8 Yes, Lot was a righteous man*

*who was tormented in his soul by the wickedness he saw and heard day after day. 9 So you see, the Lord knows how to rescue godly people from their trials, even while keeping the wicked under punishment until the day of final judgment.*
(2 Peter 2:7-9, NLT)

### Dave Ramsey, *60 Minutes*, Oprah, & Formulas

When *60 Minutes* and the *Oprah* show both booked Dave Ramsey for segments just 10 days apart, giving his financial consulting business even more national fame, he decided it was time to sit down with his leaders and teach them a life and marketing lesson. He labeled it *The Momentum Theorem*.[3] Arguing that momentum is not random but created, he developed a formula: *focused intensity over time multiplied by the influence of God equals unstoppable momentum*.[4] More than three decades of experience has proven to Dave Ramsey that breakthroughs are NO ACCIDENT. Success is the result of long-term, laser-focused commitment.

Michael Hyatt, Chairman of Thomas Nelson Publishers, was so energized by Ramsey's concept that he blogged about it on his Intentional Leadership site, and vowed to carry a copy with him. His summary? With the average NFL player's career lasting only 3.7 years (Ramsey says NFL stands for "not for long"), big moments are limited: "Why is it that football players who are paid millions of dollars to do one thing—catch a football—often drop it under pressure? Because they lose focus. They hear footsteps (fear) or get ahead of themselves (greed), rather than focusing on doing the one thing that is important (execution)."[5] They start thinking about a defensive player the size of a SUV trying to end their career or start planning their post-touchdown end zone dance before they ever catch the ball. The survival instinct and the success impulse are natural, but can still cause game-killing mistakes.

Competing requires focused intensity, i.e., discipline. Discipline is practical. For example, want your kids to know who you are when they are 13? You can't overload your schedule with competing commitments, and things that don't matter in the long run. Overall, the challenge is to create a pattern—**a habit of disposing of the excess weight of competing commitments and destructive potential of sinful lifestyle choices.** Whether it's dieting or paying down debt, most people lack persistence in developing the habits that make the difference in losing weight and getting healthy or reaching a financial finish line. AND YET...WE STILL REGULARLY DENY HAVING A BACKPACK (a spirit full of the consequences of negative choices)! Or deny that the backpack is bulging and stuffed beyond capacity.

The battle is whether or not we will embrace permanent change. Just like it's dangerous to lose weight, gain it back, and lose weight again and again in a vicious, depressing cycle, if you don't play by God's rules, you will repeat bad choices. By the way, did you know some experts say that it takes 21 days to build a habit? If you're going to dump the bad habits and create a good habit, stick with it for at least 21 days. Most of the people I've personally counseled that were dealing with consistency issues, would get serious about prayer, purity, positive thinking, or conquering some trial, BUT fell backwards to the old lifestyle and addictive habits within 72 hours. Then they wondered why God disappointed them and the Pastor misled them!

Biblical scholars tell us that the word in the Greek that is translated as "lay aside" describes actions like "stripping off clothes, ceasing what you are doing, changing what you have been doing, throwing it away, being done with it, putting it away." Translation? The cover-up has to end. There should be no **delay, distinction, or distance** issues tolerated. Meaning, for example, that there is no language in this "legislation" (i.e., the verse we are discussing), that permits you to hang on to some destructive indulgence that you enjoy for a little longer, to get rid of some sinful things but not others, or push some dangerous desire aside but keep it close enough to pick it back up again. If you commit to the race, and you've got any thought or any hidden strategy about hanging on to junk that's bad for you—cheating on your diet, spouse, boss, term paper, or anything that compromises what you know is truth—you're going down! That risky behavior has to be history!

## That Stubborn Belly Fat

The "weight" mentioned in Hebrews 12:1 describes a real load, literally referring to a bulk or a mass that will impact your ability to function or perform. It either influences or totally dominates your decisions and perseverance. Used only this one time in the entire Bible to metaphorically cover anything that hinders or prevents a specific action, it includes whatever holds you back. In the Greek, it represented a mass or excess body weight that athletes would try to get rid of during training so they could maximize their competitiveness in a race. It reminds me of non-ending infomercials and internet ads that advertise plans or products promising to help you get rid of "that stubborn belly fat". That stubborn belly fat is the hardest, and usually, the last weight to lose.

Another comparison is like carrying excess baggage, not just when you check-in for your flight, but packing it 24/7. Even Southwest Airlines would throw a yellow penalty flag at you, like their employees do in the popular television commercials attacking excess baggage fees by competing airlines. So our analogy of dealing with the unnecessary stuff in a backpack really fits. The more weight you pack, the more difficulty you have in mobility and energy. You can't move quickly when you're carrying extra pounds. Being a fully-devoted follower of Jesus requires big choices and serious endurance, continually rejecting anything that decreases your ability to live life in the way expected by your Lord. Breaking training regimes and race rules, including ignoring the pleas of their coach, will normally guarantee that a runner becomes a loser.

Even if a certain "weight" might be independently harmless, not a negative, or not wrong under normal circumstances, the disciplined runner is wise to separate from the limitations. A smart runner values a great performance over protecting an indulgence. Owning a home is a good thing, but becomes a "weight" when you are *underwater*,[6] owing a monster mortgage that ruins your finances and threatens your marriage. Achieving your career goal is commendable, but it becomes a "weight" when you miss your wedding anniversary date or can't make it to your kid's ball game or recital. Building a relationship with that awesome guy is great, but it can become a "weight" if that relationship decreases your passion to worship or serve God. If you start making cutbacks in your giving commitments to a ministry to feed hungry children because you shifted that money to buying a new car, that car can become a "weight" that limits the number of people you can help.

### Don Imus, Megyn Kelly, and Happiness

Under friendly pressure in an interview with radio personality Don Imus to explain her current happiness, Megyn Kelly, anchor of "America Live" on FOX News, confessed that after she graduated from law school she wanted to be successful, but found herself in a job that wasn't fulfilling and an unhappy marriage: "I made some bold changes, and here I am 10 years later."[7] She obviously got rid of whatever she believed was holding her back from personal happiness. Big decisions, but she removed her excess "weight" so she could live the life she desired.

What do you need to strip off so that you can run at maximum speed, do your best, reach your potential, and finish your race successfully? The word picture in the verse implies a definite break or separation from the wrong stuff that previously took over your life. The idea is that you should "PUT SOME DISTANCE BETWEEN" you and those things that hinder you from GIVING YOUR BEST.

There is a great, universal life principle in this concept that is missed by most people: **Separation brings freedom.** When you walk away from stuff that is defeating or depressing you, it gives you more time, a better attitude, a clear conscience, and greater wisdom. Like Olympic runners, who are willing to gain any legitimate, legal advantage in order to win, Jesus-followers should lay aside anything that pulls us down or takes away our desire, passion, & energy to know Jesus and make Him known.

### The Word Tiger Didn't Use

"I was unfaithful. I had affairs. I cheated. What I did was not acceptable and I am the only person to blame." February 19, 2010. In an uber-controlled setting far removed from the chaos of the scandal, standing behind a podium in business casual attire with a presidential-blue curtain in the background, Tiger Woods read those words from a statement that lasted 13½ minutes. No details were given to the 40 people in the room, or the global audience, to explain his serial adultery, the future of his marriage, or plans to renew his golf career. To his credit, he did what few celebrities have dared to risk by going public, focusing solely upon assuming all responsibility for his actions and a sincere resolve to rescue his marriage. The confession was right even if it didn't ultimately save the marriage or a mansion. Shane Bacon, Devil Ball Golf, reported: "There are times when divorce forces people to do strange things. Burn sheets. Throw out clothes. Toss rings into the ocean. But when you get $100 million in your divorce, you can trump just about anything and that's what happened with Tiger Woods' ex-wife [Elin Nordegren] when she bought a $12 million home and bulldozed the whole thing."[8]

Although Tiger offered an apology—which was totally right and commendable—and an explanation of the forces that exposed his weaknesses and choices and which was necessary—he stopped short of using the word "sin". Even with a direct reference to violating the tenets of his boyhood religious training in Buddhism, the word "sin" didn't make the cut:

> *"I have made you question who I am and how I could have done the things I did. I am embarrassed that I have put you in this position. For all that I have done, I am so sorry....I thought I could get away with whatever I wanted to. I felt that I had worked hard my entire life and deserved to enjoy all the temptations around me. I felt I was entitled. Thanks to money and fame, I didn't have to go far to find them."[9]*

It's a word none of us like to use. Sin is not a disease and you are not a victim. Sin is broader than just some extreme moral collapse like adultery. Sin is deeper than just a bad attitude or poor judgment as the result of great pressure or convenient temptations. Sin is bigger than a personal weakness. Nor is it just a failure to live up to your potential. Even an obvious crime like embezzlement, lying, or murder doesn't fully capture the biblical definition.

Without an accurate working definition, your life-race will be a total disaster. To run your race right, to avoid repeating those bad choices, it's necessary to be able to identify what qualifies as sin, to come clean and disclose it, and ultimately to break away from it. Just admitting you've messed up and hurt or disappointed people, describing the circumstances, trying to map the journey of your fall, setting goals to keep your family and professional life in balance, even confessing that you've done wrong, is . . . incomplete.

Sin is anything—from a lustful thought to drunk driving to skipping worship—that violates or even fails to fully perform the laws of God (I John 3:4— *"Everyone who sins breaks God's law, because sin is the same as breaking God's law"*, CEV), offends His holy character (Leviticus 11:45— *"For I am the LORD who brings you up out of the land of Egypt, to be your God. You shall therefore be holy, for*

*I am holy"*, NKJV), conflicts with His will (Romans 12:2—*"Don't copy the behavior and customs of this world, but let God transform you into a new person by changing the way you think. Then you will learn to know God's will for you, which is good and pleasing and perfect"*, NCV), or prevents you from doing something good (James 4:17—*"Therefore, to him who knows to do good and does not do it, to him it is sin"*, NKJV). In that final sense, passing up an opportunity to forgive someone, pray for someone, to serve in a ministry, or even give groceries to an out-of-work single mom can meet the definition of sin!

### Once Upon A Night In A Hotel

In fact, sin is not limited to your actions, whether you just did something out of total ignorance, impulsively, or intentionally. Jesus gave heaven's sweeping, far-reaching definition of sin in a familiar "guy-moment" illustration that really has universal application: *"anyone who even looks at a woman with lust has already committed adultery with her in his heart"* (Matthew 5:28, NLT). Assuming we agree that Jesus, who died for our sins, has the authority to define what meets God's ultimate test of selfishness, pride, or rebellion—then, bottom-line, sin is sourced in a heart attitude. Life, from God's perspective, is all about heart issues. Point? It's possible to indulge in thoughts and desires that qualify as sin and still look good on the surface. Since nothing escapes God's view, including your innermost secret thoughts and motives (Hebrews 4:13—*"Nothing in all creation is hidden from God. Everything is naked and exposed before his eyes, and he is the one to whom we are accountable"*, NLT), **we're all guilty** (Romans 3:23—*"For all have sinned and fallen short of the glory of God"*, KJV). By the way, it's impossible to successfully hide sin or avoid getting chased down by God's Spirit—being haunted with a sense of guilt, violation, emptiness, or tension. The Bible word for it is "conviction". You will be busted. There's no place to hide. You can't escape.

Dr. Ed Young, Sr., long-time Pastor of the Houston, Texas Second Baptist Church, told the story of his conversation with a deeply disturbed and confused college student. Home from college for a few days, the student met with Dr. Young in his office to explain his spiritual dilemma and emotional trauma. The student reminded him that he had been raised in church, was the son of a church leader, and had tried to live a God-honoring life through high school. However, he explained that when he landed on the college campus he started hanging out with the wrong crowd, did lots of things he was ashamed of, and ultimately found himself spending the night in a hotel room with a girl he barely knew. In desperation, obviously drowning with guilt, the young man confessed, "Dr. Young, ever since that night, I can't find God!" With great wisdom, Dr. Young picked up his Bible, opened it to Psalm 139, handed it across the desk to the young man, and asked him to begin reading the chapter aloud. He read slowly and deliberately through each verse as follows:

*1 O LORD, You have searched me and known me.*
*2 You know my sitting down and my rising up;*
*You understand my thought afar off.*
*3 You comprehend my path and my lying down,*
*And are acquainted with all my ways.*
*4 For there is not a word on my tongue,*
*But behold, O LORD, You know it altogether.*
*5 You have hedged me behind and before,*
*And laid Your hand upon me.*
*6 Such knowledge is too wonderful for me;*
*It is high, I cannot attain it.*
*7 Where can I go from Your Spirit?*
*Or where can I flee from Your presence?*
*8 If I ascend into heaven, You are there;*
*If I . . .*

And suddenly he stopped. Twice more the broken college student tried to finish the last line in Psalm 139:8 and choked. He couldn't get it out: "If I . . . If I . . .". Dr. Young took back his Bible and finished the verse out loud for him: "…If I…make my bed in hell, behold, You are there." Then Dr. Young cleared up his confusion with a simple observation, "Young man, your problem is NOT that you can't find God. It's that you can't get away from Him!"[10]

So, how do you actually delete those moments from your memory and restore serious intimacy with God? How do you get back to being honest with God and believable to people who know you? It's called **confession**…and it leads to repentance.

Wow. When did this get personal? Keep going. Don't laugh…and don't let **confession** intimidate you. Game on. Let's do the **confession** chapter right now!

# PART THREE:

# The Entanglements

## Chapter 7

# Confession is Cool!

Confession is suddenly cool…and convenient. Terry Raymond—you know him as Usher, maybe the greatest R&B artist in history—released an album called *Confessions*, which sold 20 million copies worldwide! His lyrics for *Confessions Part I* include:

*"Everything that I've been doing is all bad*
*I got a chick on the side with a crib and a ride*
*I've been telling you so many lies*
*ain't nothing good it's all bad*
*And I just wanna confess*
*'cause it's been going on so long*
*Girl I've been doing you so wrong*
*and I want you to know that."*

There is an explosion of need-specific websites promoting confessions for such diverse groups as moms, homeschoolers, shopaholics, and husbands. On August 8, 2011, Dr. Phil hosted a show called *Mommy Confessions*, complete with video that revealed an on-the-brink mom named Jessica in Alaska whose discipline struggles with her 7-year-old adopted son, Kristoff, included screaming at the boy, putting hot sauce in his mouth and placing him in a cold shower when he acted up. Jessica said she tried other disciplinary methods but nothing worked, and she didn't know what to do. She was later convicted of child abuse.

At *GroupHug.us*, you can post an anonymous confession. *Confessions.net* offers you space to confess or to read somebody else's confession. The *experienceproject.com*, a free social-networking site of online communities that has collected about 7 million life experiences to connect people, claims to be the largest online confessions site, soliciting both confessions and secrets. iTunes has introduced "Confession: A Roman Catholic App". It's advertised to offer a customized exam of your conscience based on age, sex, and vocation, password protected profiles, a step-by-step guide to the sacrament, ability to add sins not on their list and choose from 7 different acts of contrition, and interface capability for the iPad! If you want to confess, just click or touch, there's a way…and it's trendy.

## DEBT and DOUBT

With 11.1 million USA households "underwater" in their home mortgages (23% of all mortgaged homes) at the end of 2010 according to housing data issued by CoreLogic,[1] even in personal finances normal people eventually have to face their choices and the issue of confession. Life from God's perspective is all about heart issues, so confession is big with God. Like the debt restructuring companies that offer plans to get you out of debt, the Bible also offers a *structured* solution for fixing bad choices that even Dave Ramsey would appreciate, so you will never doubt where you stand with God. Some families, overwhelmed by the thought of financial bankruptcy and being in a permanent prison of debt, have chosen to "walk away" from their home mortgages. They just let the bank or lender take back the property, knowing they have lost equity, irreplaceable years, and good credit ratings. It's just too much to face. The monthly payment disappears, but the attitudes toward God and life and family *that created the choices…that created the cycle…that put them in the pit…*tragically can just get ignored like an overweight middle school student with acne.

When it comes to confession, don't "walk away" from your choices! Face them. Deal with them. Suck it up. Get real. Act like an adult! Grow up! So let's check out some truth that will set you free from doubt, and fix the guilt thing.

### Messin' with Sasquatch

The classic Jack Links' Beef Jerky TV ad campaign, with hilarious imitation-Bigfoot videos called "Messin' with Sasquatch", showed hikers getting brutal payback for pranking Bigfoot. The message was clear: respect Sasquatch or challenge him at your own risk. Whether you believe Bigfoot is real or not, in a counter direction, our culture has been "Messin' with Confession". Original biblical encounters with confession have been pranked as well. The definition and practice of confession has been twisted and distorted like a pretzel. But if you don't play by God's rules for confession, nothing changes in your heart.

Confession is owning—*as in* taking responsibility without making excuses or explaining why you did it—a specific sin, calling it an offense to God, and desiring to end it. If it's wrong, say it's wrong! Using qualifying phrases like "if I had known" or "when he did that" or "because she said", means you are clueless about either the damage you caused or the direction you should go. Start creating a positive outcome—just admit you screwed up. Period. If you've sinned, you deserve whatever happens. Real ownership of the sin will lead you to an unexpected, radical emotion. It's labeled *"godly sorrow"* when you realize the pain your sin caused Jesus (2 Corinthians 7:10, NIV). God desires real, deep-down truth (see Psalm 51:6). Repentance is a totally separate response. It is the next step, involving a change of thinking that moves you toward actual turning away or separating from sin.

In 1 John 1:9, the word "confess" means "to agree" with God about a specific sin, to speak out freely about it, without any denial or rationalization. Sin is never general. It is always connected to some specific person or incident (2 Samuel 24:10— *"But after he had taken the census, David's conscience began to bother him. And he said to the Lord, 'I have sinned greatly by taking this census. Please forgive my guilt, Lord, for doing this foolish thing'"*, NLT). For example, if you lied, you actually lied to someone specifically. Every sin is ultimately committed against God (see Psalm 51:4), and the Bible consistently repeats our need to confess our sins to Him first (see Psalm 41:4; 130:4 / Acts 8:22 / 1 John 1:9). The Bible also gives examples of confession to other people, such as Joseph's brothers asking for his forgiveness (Genesis 50:17-18), or the rebellious son confessing to his father (Luke 15:18; see also, Luke 17:3-4 / Ephesians 4:32 / Colossians 3:13).

To summarize, confession is a verbal statement to God first and any victim second. Go to God in prayer, name the sin for what it is, take full responsibility and blame nobody else, remind yourself of what sin did to Jesus, talk about God's holiness and faithfulness, and ask God for forgiveness...basically, just read Psalm 51 back to God out loud, inserting your name!

## Johnny Depp's Cover-Up

An internationally recognizable A-list actor had a secret. Johnny Depp, (of *Pirates of the Caribbean* movie fame), got a tattoo on his right arm years ago that read, "Winona Forever." It was tribute art for his then eternal love, Winona Ryder. Since that relationship didn't last for eternity, he chose a cover-up tattoo that now reads, "Wino Forever."

Cover-up tattoos are now a popular design solution to unwanted body art. One website service explains that if you woke up after a night of heavy drinking and found the ink had appeared out of nowhere, the odds of that tattoo-based love enduring are small. So they offer the cover-up option instead of expensive and inconvenient removal surgery, or simply wearing baggy jumpers for the rest of your life.[2] Cover-up may work for tattoos, but not the guilt or regret underneath them.

The exact opposite of confession is cover-up—concealing or hiding sin—not just hesitating to talk about it. Cover-up as a strategy has been tried since the Garden of Eden without any success. In political jargon, it's a "failed strategy." The sins you cover, God uncovers. The sins you uncover with confession, God covers with His forgiveness (see Proverbs 28:13). Confession is your step toward God to resolve the mess created by your sin. Confession is NOT an explanation of what happened, what you felt, blaming someone else, or just listing the offenses.

Confession is critical to spiritual health and survival for many reasons. How's this list for overkill? It's only slightly better than a doctor's exam:

1) *Confession releases you from the power of guilt and restores you to intimacy with God (Psalm 51:10);*

2) *Confession simplifies complicated stuff. Things look difficult or impossible until you start revealing and getting honest about what's happening in your heart (Genesis 50:15);*

3) *Confession is all about God changing the way you think and how you relate. It has to be done from a new position—a surrendered, broken, and submissive heart (Psalm 51:17);*

4) *Confession affects how useable you are for God's purposes. If you are carrying around TRASH—in an overstuffed backpack—you don't generate the right questions for God from non-believers! Instead of asking to know more about Jesus, they're wondering why you are carrying around sin and guilt! (2 Timothy 2:21—"If you keep yourself pure, you will be a special utensil for honorable use. Your life will be clean, and you will be ready for the Master to use you for every good work", NLT);*

5) *Without confession of sin, God will not answer your prayers (Psalm 66:18 / 1 Peter 3:7);*

6) *We don't really know what's in our heart and can be deceived (Psalm 19:12 / 1 John 1:8);*

7) *There's no cleansing or lasting change without it (1 John 1:9);*

8) *With confession, Satan cannot accuse us or access our hearts (Ephesians 4:26-27 / Revelation 12:10);*

9) *Hidden sin is a rejection of the Holy Spirit and you lose power to witness (1 Thessalonians 5:19 / Acts 4:31; 5:3 / John 16:13 / 1 Corinthians 5:10);*

10) *God is holy and has rules for how He is approached, worshiped, and respected (2 Timothy 1:9 / Psalm 24:3-4);*

11) *Unconfessed sin increases the desire to hide things from God and others (Genesis 3:10 / 2 Samuel 11:6 / Joshua 7:11);*

12) *Unconfessed sin makes you feel more comfortable with sin and creates strongholds (2 Samuel 11:6);*

13) *We can't function or think right when we carry guilt (Psalm 19:13; 51:2-3);*

14) *Unconfessed sin steals confidence about your relationship with God (Psalm 51:11);*

15) *Sin is against God, not just others (Acts 5:4);*

16) *Because integrity begins privately with God (Psalm 51:4);*

17) *We cannot give grace or compassion unless we have experienced it (Ephesians 4:32 / Psalm 51:1);*

18) *There is no relationship without trust and truth (Psalm 51:10);*

19) *Worship and sin can't co-exist (1 Samuel 15:24-25);*

20) *Unconfessed sin creates fear which distorts our view of God (Genesis 3:10); and, most important to believers...*

21) *Refusing to confess sin profanes the blood sacrifice of Jesus (Hebrews 10:29);*

## If I Die Young

Kimberly Perry, of *The Band Perry*, explained the story behind the lyrics of their hit No. 1 country song from their debut album, *If I Die Young*. It was written on a cloudy day in East Tennessee where she and her two brothers live. The family trio's message in the song is to make the most of whatever time you are given, whether it's two or twenty years: "We really have gotten to live and love at our young ages. *If I Die Young*, for us, is about if it all ends at this moment, look at what we've gotten to do. Whatever time we're given will be absolutely enough as long as we make the most of it."[3] They phrased it, "the sharp knife of a short life", as the lyrics reference the unexpected death of a young lover.

That's an awesome truth! Life is short. Cram it full of the right stuff. Their song is also a statement about doing life right. And you can't do life right without confession at some point.

Confession guarantees forgiveness, but it does not remove consequences. Confession done God's way triggers the promise of forgiveness and cleansing located in 1 John 1:9, but didn't apply to a traitor named Judas who confessed but never received forgiveness (see Matthew 27:3-5). His suicide speech was just a lot of regret over betraying Jesus to the Jewish and Roman authorities for execution. There may be forgiveness, but if confession is not done quickly there can be larger consequences.

Why do people avoid confession then? There are multiple reasons. Confession...

1) *Can be humiliating, embarrassing, and hurtful;*

2) *Puts you on record as having actually done wrong;*

3) *Makes you face what is really in your heart;*

4) *Forces you to take responsibility for your choices and not blame other people or God;*

5) *Can change someone's perception of who you are, making you unable to project and protect a certain image of yourself as better than you really are;*

6) *Introduces reality and you may think you cannot cope with it;*

7) *Causes fear that it's the beginning of the end—that you will lose everything if you admit failure (sometimes we actually do lose stuff like positions, respect, friends, finances, etc., in order to get right with God because it costs us something);*

8) *Is the first step in a long journey to getting things right, that sometimes tempts you to rationalize that there is so much stuff to "undo" that it is impossible, so why try or why even start by confessing?;*

9) *Is that crushing moment with God that you may run from because you believe you are right; and,*

10) *Can be something you believe you can escape, bury, or run from, and never have to deal with it.*

## Tim Tebow's Confession

Tim Tebow has transitioned his success with the Florida Gators as one of the greatest quarterbacks in college football history to become a serious NFL quarterback. His resume includes two BCS national championships, becoming the first sophomore in NCAA history to win the Heisman trophy, and being drafted in the first round of the NFL draft by the Denver Broncos, all under relentless media coverage. Huge expectations have dominated his life and young career, and he's honored Jesus consistently through them. His newly released book, *Through My Eyes*, is Tim's unfiltered take on the challenges and purpose of his life. He's an unapologetic Christ-follower, who coincidentally had the #1 selling jersey in the NFL for 2010. But he doesn't make decisions based on what the media is saying or fans might do. After a 136-day NFL lockout, the August 12, 2011 Denver Broncos season opener against the Dallas Cowboys gave Tim an opportunity to excel—and he did. But after a wild 3rd down play in which Tebow scrambled around and crossed the line of scrimmage before stepping back and unloading a pass, which drew flags and even chuckles from the officials, it was typical Tebow to confess, "...in the QB room I got fined for it because of three penalties on one play."[4] Success hasn't changed Tim's heart.

That's a high profile confession, even if it's funny. When you confess, particularly to an individual, you have to be careful what you say. No explicit boundaries are given in James 5:16— *"Confess your sins"*, but the goal there is clearly what follows— *"so that you may be healed"* (KJV). Whatever is necessary for healing—i.e., getting it right for everybody involved—must be on the table. Even if the confession is summarily rejected, you have to create an opportunity for physical and relational healing. Here's the disclaimer: you should only confess to another person the sins of which the other person is aware and involve that person alone (see Matthew 18:15; 5:23-24). Any more than that is TMI (Too Much Information) and can create confusion and hurt. For example, telling your boss that you have had bad thoughts about him, or a guy confessing to his buddy that he's had lustful thoughts about his buddy's wife, is unnecessary—not to mention just plain stupid—and can destroy credibility in relationships. All our speech is to be limited to what is encouraging (see Ephesians 4:29).

## Home Depot and D-I-Y (Do-It-Yourself)

Home Depot, the large chain home improvement stores, advertise "More saving. More doing." Their stores offer free DIY (Do-It-Yourself) workshops for inexperienced people like me to learn the "how to" steps of a weekend home project. Why? Probably because Home Depot doesn't want people to fail due to not knowing how to use the tools and supplies they just bought on a maxed-out credit card. A frustrated weekend-project husband might evolve into a customer casualty. Makes sense.

So it also makes sense that people should get informed about the steps, the proper way to do a "confession project." The next in the process is getting the biblical principle that *the size of the confession should equal the size or impact of the sin* (see Matthew 18:15-20). If the sin is public, the confession must be as big and visible. When the sin is against a friend, it is excessive and punitive to believe that confession has to be done before a large audience. Basically, confess only to the people you have sinned against. If your sin is known to the church, confess in front of the church. Simple. President Clinton needed to confess to a world-wide audience because his sin was known. If you have lied to someone, just go to the person directly involved, period.

And you need to know timing to get it right. When is the right time to confess? Immediately if not sooner. *The speed of your response controls the success of your recovery.* Real confession is always prompted by the Holy Spirit making you aware of what you have done wrong or how you have failed to do right, the very moment you get off track. His primary target is your internal moral compass, the conscience, which either accuses you or excuses you (see Romans 2:15). According to John 16:8, the Holy Spirit's role is to immediately make you totally *aware*—i.e., *convict* you—of the sin. It's ridiculous to think you could evade, deceive, or by-pass the Spirit (who knows all truth—see John 16:13), who will repeatedly surface that sin to you or expose it to others—the incident, the conversation, the people involved, the date, location, etc. Why? So you can get it right with God and not be killed by Satan or guilt. You know you've got to deal with it, so pushing a planned confession into the future makes you powerless against Satan, plus...to delay confession is to deny responsibility and initiate God's discipline or judgment track. Lame excuses, shifting blame, or laughing it off only postpones the inevitable and makes things worse. Stand up and take your chewing out like a man, a Marine, or a mid-level executive. Get it over with. Let God do what He needs to do, people say what they need to say, and move on! Don't let it become a "cold case." Wrap it up now! Nothing gets better with time. You either go deeper into bondage, justifying the sin over and over again, or conquer it by calling it out. God is going to surface the sin. He won't forget it until you confess AND He will never remember it once you confess!

If you don't confess sin(s), according to scripture you risk triggering some of the following consequences:

1) *God's direct discipline (Genesis 3:23 / Numbers 12:1-11 / Jonah 1:17). Why wait for God to chase you down and make you look like a coward, a jerk, a failure, or an idiot in public, when you can get it over quickly with God in private?*
2) *Deeper sin and shame (Luke 15:16-18 / 2 Corinthians 2:5-10). Either you will beat yourself up repeatedly or Satan will make you feel worthless.*

3)  ***Extreme regret, depression, or suicide (Jonah 4:9 / 1 Kings 19:4
    / Matthew 27:3-5).*** *Running from confession makes you its slave,
    eventually deceiving you into believing you CAN'T make things right
    and have no reason to live.*

4)  ***Grieving or quenching God's Spirit and losing His power (Eph-
    esians 4:30 / 1 Thessalonians 5:19).*** *Deliberate sin is like a NFL-
    style "personal foul" against the Spirit. When you attempt to do damage
    to Him, you are only isolating yourself from your exclusive source of
    strength.*

5)  ***Death (Acts 5:3-5).*** *This was the ultimate penalty brought on by a
    conspiracy to cover-up a financial scheme that would destroy many
    lives,*

6)  ***Loss of God's favor on your ministry/career (1 Samuel 15:9-26).***
    *How can God do amazing things through you if you are hiding stuff
    from Him, making excuses, or minimizing what you've done?*

7)  ***Broken relationships and bitterness (2 Samuel 13:22-38 /
    Hebrews 12:15).*** *Unconfessed resentment poisons your relationships
    and evolves into a deep-seated anger that seeks out victims.*

8)  ***Spreading defeat (Joshua 7:10-12).*** *Like the financial mismanage-
    ment of Enron executives that brought down an entire company and
    ruined the lives and retirement accounts of thousands, Joshua sending
    troops into battle unprepared proved that protecting your sin can hurt
    others.*

9)  ***Fear (Genesis 50:15).*** *Covering up sin puts you in bondage to a fear
    that you will one day be discovered and pay a huge price.*

10) ***Being dominated by your enemies (Nehemiah 1:4-9; 9:36).*** *If
    you don't deal with your sin, God has been known to give people over
    to their enemies to wear you out and the confession is squeezed out!*

## Do It Again, Dad!

A father gave a true, first-hand account of one of a parent's worst fears.
After he and his wife had put their preschoolers to bed, they heard a horrifying scream coming from the room of their 3-year-old son, Ryan. When dad
burst into the room, Ryan was sitting up in bed, crying uncontrollably. He
appeared to be okay, but through the sobs and tears, dad heard him say repeatedly, "I swallowed a penny. I'm going to die!" Nothing dad said calmed his
fears. In desperation, the quick-thinking dad pulled a penny out of his pocket,
hid it in the palm of his hand, and explained to his son that he could pull the
penny out of him. Dad brushed his son's ear with the hand hiding the penny,
and then opened his hand to reveal the rescued coin. His son stopped crying,
but then his eyes got big, and a smile broke out as he snatched the penny from
his dad's hand before dad could react, popped it in his mouth, and said, "Do
it again, Dad!"

Wow! Parenting is brutal…and never guilt-free! My totally unprofessional theory, now that I'm in parental-recovery, is that about 90% of parenting is endurance—just outlasting your kids by staying up longer, refusing to pick up their clothes, making them eat something green every day, and getting them through algebra…and for me, through driving lessons in Atlanta, Georgia traffic! But some days I feel like 90% of parenting is dealing with parental guilt over everything from missed ballgames to not knowing how to motivate kids to do homework…or how to get them past losing friends, being bullied, managing Facebook, settling for non-designer label stuff, and swallowing pennies.

So, the obvious black-hole of confession is what happens if we die with guilt…basically, the carryover regret from unconfessed sin? Salvation is not a business deal with God where believers are trying to confess and repent of every sin they commit before they die. Security with God is not based on whether you have confessed and repented of every sin. Yes, we should confess our sins to God as soon as we are aware that we have sinned. Jesus died to pay the penalty for all of our sins—past, present, and future—so that issue was resolved when you originally surrendered (or eventually choose to surrender) to become His follower (see Colossians 1:14). Done. Can't be reversed. You can't be "unforgiven" any more than you can be "unborn" again. Daily or situational confession by believers serves primarily to maintain intimacy in your relationship with God, not to protect your salvation (see 1 John 1:5-10). So, confession is relational. Salvation is positional—we already have right standing with God secured through the forgiveness that is given by accepting Jesus as your Lord and Savior.

Still, people routinely feel guilty, even after confessing sins to God. Why? Maybe because you are…

1)  *Relying on feelings rather than believing what God says in scripture as the truth. Obeying God's Word is the key. Confession is not based on feelings, and neither are God's promises. In 1 John 1:9 we are told that confession will bring forgiveness and cleansing from God. God promises to remove the guilt and record of your failure through forgiveness. Stand on the verses that promise forgiveness. Repeat them out loud. Confess those things regularly! (Romans 8:1). You don't have to "feel" forgiven to be forgiven—just go back and act like you are!*

2)  *Allowing Satan to accuse you falsely (i.e., say that you are not worthy or the change won't last). Our invisible enemy (Ephesians 6:12) manipulates people easily through undeserved and unresolved guilt, trying to destroy your confidence in God or yourself. Reject those dark thoughts because they are not from God.*

3)  *Basing your relationship to God on performance. Believing that God only loves you when you do good puts you in bondage to perfec-*

tionism. *Some call it "works", because you live under the impossible standard that God loves you only for what you do, not accepting you as you are. Trying to perform, or live right after the sin, hoping that it will make God approve or accept you, is a "failed policy". God allows "restart", not "do-overs".*

4) **Lying to God.** *Another possibility is that you really didn't either have a heart-confession in the first place. That seems to be the most frequent cause of lingering guilt.*

5) **Unwilling to make things right.** *Maybe you didn't follow-through with your confession to the next step of repentance and complete the restoration or reconciliation. In other words, if God expects you to apologize to someone, and you stopped at just asking His forgiveness, the confession is incomplete and will always trigger guilt (Psalm 32:5—"Finally, I confessed all my sins to you and stopped trying to hide my guilt. I said to myself, "I will confess my rebellion to the Lord." And you forgave me! All my guilt is gone", NLT).*

6) **Thinking that you are superior to others, including non-believers and are therefore exempt from confessing.** *Confession is a God-requirement and has nothing to do with whether the status of the victim—i.e., whether you like them or not, whether they will deserve your patience or not, whether they will ever change, or whether they believe in your God or not. Let's say you are married to a non-believer and sin against them. It is absolutely right to confess (1 Corinthians 7:12-14). Confession is all about your sin, not their relationship to God. You may have to confess to somebody that is totally offensive to you and God if you have hurt them. In another situation, the person may already even be dead. Confession is a step for believers regardless of the ability to confront them or not, your mental stability, your emotional vulnerability, or outcome.*

## SPAM and King Kamehameha

Since American soldiers imported it to the islands during WWII, Hawaiians have had a love affair with SPAM! More than 6 million cans of SPAM are eaten every year in Hawaii alone, making it America's highest per capita consumption of Hormel's canned pork.[5] In December, 2010, a vacationing President Obama was back in Hawaii, enjoying *musubi*, a sushi-like serving of teriyaki-fried Spam on rice, wrapped in nori seaweed. They also serve Spam with eggs, top it with pineapple, combine it with mac and cheese, stir-fry it, or toss it in salad. It's even on the menus of McDonald's and Burger King, creating "Spam Wars". Spam is mainstream in the island state.

But unusual trends have ruled Hawaii before. In the late 1700's, Hawaii's tribal ruler, King Kamehameha II, was well-known for serial adultery, possessing at least 5 wives. In an anecdotal story, when missionaries first arrived in Hawaii they warned the King that if he did not repent of this sin, God would punish him in hell. Supposedly, King Kamehameha responded defiantly: "What do you mean God will be angry and punish me? I am God!"[6]

Failure to confess means you think you are God! Confession will never be totally hip or trendy. Most people will put it in the same category as Spam—something that's all about personal tastes and preferences, or unique to the religious crowd or some underground spiritual culture. People don't have to hear or know the law and commandments to understand they have sinned or done wrong in defiance of God (see Romans 1:20; 2:14-15, 18, 27). That's why God gave us the pre-installed spiritual memory software called "conscience", created in the human heart long before King Kamehameha worshipped idols or Hawaiians took the first bite of Spam. The sidebar is that both sin and Satan can blind people to their offense (see 1 John 1:8, 10 / 2 Corinthians 4:4).

So, you can't argue that you don't need to confess sin because God already knows what you've done or He's already forgiven it. It's because God knows our sin that we must confess. Because we have offended God, we are accountable and must get it fixed. Confession of sin is for you, not God. God doesn't need to get free from guilt or the power of sin—you do! You would never confess anyway unless God pursued and convicted you. He already knows what's in your heart and everything you've done (Hebrews 4:13—*"Nothing in all creation is hidden from God. Everything is naked and exposed before his eyes, and He is the one to whom we are accountable"*, NLT). Again, the function of forgiveness at the point of confession is not about salvation or whether you will go to heaven, but about intimacy with God—worship, trust, growth, strength, peace, and effectiveness in living right.

And you can't argue that confession is impossible because there might be times when you're not even aware that you've sinned. The Greek word for that is "baloney!" There is no evidence I've found in scripture that says any person, especially a believer, can sin and not know it. Regardless of whether you label it "sin", describe it in Bible language, defend it or deny it—even if you got away with it and have faced zero consequences—*you own it.* Romans 1:18-19 indicates that even non-believers have full knowledge of truth…and have to seriously work to suppress it to keep it from constantly surfacing in thoughts. Both pre-believers and seasoned believers have a conscience. And there's more. If we justify or rationalize sin, we can ultimately *"deceive"* ourselves (1 John 1:6-8, KJV) into believing we have no sin.

But there has to be some rules or real confession ceases to exist. Without rules, angry parents could get away with attacking referees at their kids' games, and politicians could accept bribes. Look at the following excerpt from an online discussion to see why rules or a final authority is important.

> **Q:** *How do you know something is sin or not?*
> **A:** *First, pray for guidance. Second, ask Christian friends whom you completely trust. Third, judge how you feel when you are*

*contemplating an action; and if you go ahead, how you feel afterwards. If you feel bad about it, don't do it again. God knows we are imperfect, and takes our intentions into account when judging our actions.*[7]

That answer sounds good but is really weak. Feelings rule. What if you go ahead with something that is really wrong but you feel good about it before *and* after you do it? The Bible is full of stories about people who lived by their feelings instead of truth (see Luke 23:23). The reply is classic relativism. No final authority. No absolutes. Right and wrong are defined by feelings and opinion polls with friends. Sin and confession must be ultimately defined by and based on what the Word of God says—not prayer, feelings, or friends. If any doubt exists—if there is any question mark over what you're thinking or doing—all you have to do is search the Word of God to know if something is a sin or not!

Sin is not limited to breaking God's rules with some ugly, out-of-control behavior like first degree murder or stealing. It can include holding back on God—passing on doing something that is legitimately good or desperately needed (James 4:17— *"it is sin to know what you ought to do and then not do it"*, NLT). Withholding that generous donation to Sudanese refugees, refusing to forgive the person who ruined your reputation, or failure to confess sin itself can be a sin!

Reality check? Just because you confess your sins does not guarantee that you will get the guy you want, suddenly ace your geography tests, become wealthy and hang out with Warren Buffett, be able to argue constitutional law in front of the Supreme Court, win at Wimbledon, have 1 million followers on Twitter, relationships will be restored, or you will be promoted. But if you honor God, He will honor you: *"...God opposes the proud but favors the humble. So humble yourselves under the mighty power of God, and at the right time he will lift you up in honor"* (1 Peter 5:5a-6, NLT). Confession opens the pipeline of blessing that God had already funded through the sacrifice of His Son. And that includes some physical blessings. If you have a physical illness, and that sickness is connected to your sins, you can be healed, according to James 5:16. Sin can cause physical illness (see Deuteronomy 28:58-61 / Psalm 32:3-4; 38:3 / Mark 2:5-12 / 1 Corinthians 11:30 / Ephesians 6:2 / 1 Thessalonians 5:23-24). Confession just might remove it.

Withholding confession burns bridges with God and others.

That's **BIG**.

Confession of sins can build a bridge for physical or relational healing from God to occur.

That's even **BIGGER**.

*Chapter 8*

# I'd Like That RARE, Please!

Matt Slot and his wife brought their newborn son, Adam, to the pediatrician for his first checkup. As he finished, the doctor told them, "You have a cute baby." Smiling, Matt said, "I bet you say that to all new parents." "No," he replied, "just to those whose babies really are good-looking." "So what do you say to the others?" Matt asked. "He looks just like you."[1]

Honesty can be a precise art. You shouldn't have to calculate what to say or fake anything. And nobody should have to lie about you. There shouldn't be apologizing, exaggerating, making excuses, or hedging from your friends when they are asked if you and God are doing well. According to a 2010 survey, men tell 3 lies every day on average, and women only tell 2 lies per day. The top lie for men was "I didn't have that much to drink", and for women it was, "Nothing's wrong. I'm fine."[2] Been there, haven't you? In the same survey, 75% of men and women believe lying is acceptable if done to protect someone's feelings.[3] Try having any kind of a life while simultaneously covering up something risky or embarrassing. And try coming up with fresh, creative ways daily to stay mobile with that indulgence. It's not going to happen.

**PLUS Size?**

So, moving forward, knowing God is omnipresent and omniscient (i.e., possessing infinite and preeminent knowledge—bigger and smarter than we'll ever be), the next step in the process of discarding the excess weight and the "sin" is to confess it and separate from it. Confession must first be directed toward God in order to be valid, because all sin is ultimately a rejection of Him and His authority over your life. God's commands—His rules, laws, and principles detailed in the Bible—are an expression of His holy, perfect character, and totally unconditional love toward us (Romans 5:8; 13:8-10 / 1 John 4:7-10). He has revealed the truth about the whole *life/sin/happiness-balance issue* and set boundaries, not to make us miserable but to **protect us from**

**repeating really bad choice**s and ultimately signing off on an eternal separation and judgment in hell. God has ensured that His laws, or rules to save life, have been widely publicized and distributed so that when we naturally test the boundaries and get burned, we'll realize that sin really owns us deep in our nature and be redirected to God for help.

> 7 But I can hear you say, "If the law code was as bad as all that, it's no better than sin itself." That's certainly not true. The law code had a perfectly legitimate function. Without its clear guidelines for right and wrong, moral behavior would be mostly guesswork. Apart from the succinct, surgical command, "You shall not covet," I could have dressed covetousness up to look like a virtue and ruined my life with it.
> 8-12 Don't you remember how it was? I do, perfectly well. The law code started out as an excellent piece of work. What happened, though, was that sin found a way to pervert the command into a temptation, making a piece of "forbidden fruit" out of it. The law code, instead of being used to guide me, was used to seduce me. Without all the paraphernalia of the law code, sin looked pretty dull and lifeless, and I went along without paying much attention to it. But once sin got its hands on the law code and decked itself out in all that finery, I was fooled, and fell for it. The very command that was supposed to guide me into life was cleverly used to trip me up, throwing me headlong. So sin was plenty alive, and I was stone dead. But the law code itself is God's good and common sense, each command sane and holy counsel.
> (Romans 7:7-12, The Message)

The one word that captures confession's logical outcome—separation and permanent change—is *repentance*. Repentance then becomes the final proof of your authenticity—the evidence that you want to honor God and make good choices that benefit you and others.

Repentance is the admission that you have sinned PLUS an attitude change PLUS a new direction. Repentance will show regret for past conduct PLUS a change of mind about practicing the things that hurt you and shamed the life and blood sacrifice of Jesus PLUS a radical new lifestyle. And, just like an infomercial pitch, *"There's more!"*

Stated another way, at the core, repentance is **submission toward God** (Acts 20:21) PLUS real **sorrow over sin** (2 Corinthians 7:10) PLUS **separation from the past** (Matthew 3:8). Under that framework, repentance will always be visible (as public as your sin), radical (cost you something), and verifiable (all the people involved will know you've taken responsibility and changed).

Shock. Numbness. Anger. I felt all that and more when one of my close friends in ministry, a model husband and father, a leader in a former church, sat down in my office and said, "I've found my soul-mate. I'm in love with somebody else besides my wife. I plan to marry her and I know it's God's will." When the blood returned to my brain and I recalled the state penalty for murder, I asked, "And how do you know it's God's will?" Without blinking, and showing total confidence, he explained, "We [he and his new girlfriend] both prayed about and agree that God is telling us to do this. We feel so happy." How blind. How insane. How selfish. Classic mistake. I felt like showing him some different kind of "feelings". His wife was awesome and his kids great. He was throwing it all away.    Totally unrepentant.    It was all about him…his needs…his feelings…NOT about grown-up morals, accountability, truth or reality. So I tried an intervention. I held up my Bible, leaned over the desk to get in his face, and gave him a reality-check: "The Bible gives us God's will. There is nothing in it you can use to justify breaking up your marriage. What you are planning to do is wrong. It is not God's will." But regardless of my arguments, pleas, and warnings, he smiled all the way through, confident nobody else understood that "God had given him these feelings". Watching him selfishly insist on the affair and a divorce, listening for hours and months to the crushing hurt from his wife and kids, slogging through their tears, disillusionment, parenting battles, and financial hardships that resulted when he abandoned them to start a new life, I witnessed first-hand the personal disaster from a refusal to repent.

At one time or another, you will be faced with both having to repent or expecting somebody else to repent. That's why repentance creates difficulty and controversy. It implies accountability to somebody for your actions. That's an *authority* issue. And it requires a person to decide their moral limits. That's a *truthfulness* issue.

## Abraham, Martin, & John

Ancient Jewish patriarch, Abram, made the "Faith Hall of Fame" in Hebrews 11, but had some huge strike-outs and losses recorded in his biography that surfaced the repentance/accountability issue. The embarrassing story that stuck to old "Teflon-Abe" was a moment of weakness with an employee. Desperate for children and weary of waiting on God to fulfill a decade-old promise for a family, Abram's wife Sarai convinced him to have a sexual relationship with her servant, Hagar, in hopes of a baby by adoption. Creative way to keep God from being embarrassed, right? No surprise here that Abram didn't hesitate to help the cause! Realizing the actual impact of sin and adultery only after her servant Hagar conceived, a quickly embittered Sarai ejected her new rival from the camp (see Genesis 16:1-6), while Abram apparently had duct tape over his mouth. You could hear the crickets chirping. No repentance there from the 86-year-old Chaldean immigrant, who told his wife the pregnant servant was her problem, not his. More creative leadership, huh?

Sort of a B.C. (comic strip) flip, like the "unevolved" ancestor of Lanny Donoho's concept in his book, *Think Orange*. Lanny argued that the two combined influences of church and family can make a greater impact on the next generation of children or create a better solution by partnering, than if they functioned as two separate influences. Abe never evolved into a "Donoho" in his thinking. He capped out with his "tent theology"—what happens in the tent, stays in the tent! The son, named Ishmael, born from that craziness in wife-swapping, is the progenitor of the Arabic tribes with a prophetic wall of hostility between his descendants and the Jewish race that still exists today.[4]

Civil rights activist and Nobel Peace Prize recipient, Dr. Martin Luther King, sacrificed his life in a non-violent peace campaign challenging America to *repent* of the sins of racial prejudice and injustice. I remember standing silently near the spot where he was assassinated on April 4, 1968, on the balcony of his room in the Lorraine Motel in Memphis, Tennessee. My mind was flooded with questions about the mysterious convergence of circumstances that would allow a bullet from the 30-06 rifle of a criminal like James Earl Ray to be forever linked to the life of a world-changer. Thoughts drifted back to sad and ominous tones of his now historic speech the night before his tragic assassination: "I've been to the mountaintop and I've seen the Promised Land. And I might not get there with you". I personally believe Dr. King knew his resolve never to compromise his message or his convictions would cost him his life. Repentance remains divisive.

Similarly, John the Baptist ultimately lost his life at the hands of insane and evil King Herod, because he refused to back away from one word— REPENT! (see Matthew 3:1; 14:1-11). His political mistake was demanding that the Roman ruler, Herod the tetrarch, repent of his adultery with his brother's wife! John was committed to his ministry before Jesus came as back-up! If you are waiting on better conditions, more people to agree with you because you are afraid to stand alone, or someone else to help, you have just become the proud owner of an excuse! John's purpose was to define repentance for the crowds of spiritual seekers, and it broke down this way: recognize guilt, respond with sorrow, and reverse direction away from sin while simultaneously moving toward God and forgiveness.

## LIPSTICK and MIRRORS

A number of 12-year-old middle school girls were beginning to use lipstick and would put it on while in the school bathroom. That was fine, but after they put on their lipstick they would press their lips to the mirror leaving dozens of little lip prints. Every night, the janitor would have to clean the mirror and the next day the girls would put them back. Finally the principal decided that something had to be done. She called all the suspect girls to the bathroom and met them there with the janitor. She explained that all the lip prints were causing a major problem for the janitor who had to clean the mirrors every night. To demonstrate how difficult it had been to clean the mirrors, she asked the janitor to show the girls how much effort was required. He took out a long-handled squeegee, dipped it in the toilet, and cleaned the mirror with it. Following that, no lip prints appeared on the mirrors!

**Repentance is rare. It's hard. It's controversial.** That 3-syllable word engenders hostility. Nothing has changed. It was just as shocking when John and Jesus introduced it as the first step for genuine commitment. Jesus even used the "R" word to comment on 2 major news stories of His day in 1st century Palestine—the tragedy of 18 people killed in a building collapse and the genocidal act of the Roman Governor Pilate, murdering people during a religious service (see Luke 13:1-5). Do you realize that repentance is an issue in every marriage, in every career, in every relationship, and in every business? You will not be able to escape either the controversy or the consequences.

Why is it valuable to understand repentance? Because it forces you to deal with the tough questions that give you the option to get right spiritually and get healthy emotionally. Is it sufficient just to say you are sorry? Do certain words confirm repentance? Does repentance apply only to certain sins? What does a person have to do or say to meet your definition of repentance? What standards do you use to trust someone again? How do you know if someone has really changed? Can you explain what you are looking for in your son or daughter's attitude after they have sinned? Repentance is a live issue because when you have to evaluate an employee, build trust in a mate, help children understand salvation, discipline teenagers, be sure of an honest business deal, escape guilt, be effective as a coach, decide how to discipline a student, or apply the law in a courtroom, you can't go forward without it!

## PEELING M & M's?

There are actually 5 pieces (stages or steps are equally good analogies) to the repentance puzzle. Even if only one is missing, the picture of genuine turnaround is incomplete.

The first step is to **own the selfishness** of what you have done. Drop the defense. Give up the self-pity. There are many convincing emotional substitutes for repentance: guilt, regret, depression, fear, complaining, embarrassment, promises, and even worship! Frequently offered substitutes for repentance include making demands like, *"Why did this happen to me? Things should have gone differently! You've got to change, too!"* Or a convincing substitute is giving in to despair: *"Look what's happened to me. I'm the victim.* Sometimes falling into the ditch of doubt feels like the pain of genuine repentance: *"Things always happen to me. I'll never get any better. Nothing will ever change."* Believing those arguments work is as much a waste of time as peeling M & M's to make chocolate chip cookies.

Repentance is only triggered when you come to the end of your selfishness. It's owning the reality that your sinful choices created distance in your relationships. Denial damages your plans, desires, and desperation. When you don't do the repentance thing, you evolve into something you were not before, like the old Snickers candy bar TV ad campaign that tells us that we become divas when we get hungry! You think you are protecting self interests, but holding back on getting things right ultimately destroys peace and deprives you of what you really need from God and other people.

Sometimes when you struggle to come up with a clear definition of something, it helps to state "what it's NOT". For example, repentance is NOT:

✓ *regret over a choice*
✓ *promising to improve when there is less stress*
✓ *saying you understand what is wrong*
✓ *stopping at confessing a failure or sin*
✓ *hoping for acceptance*
✓ *expecting other people to change*
✓ *planning to change*
✓ *blaming a person, the past, or a circumstance*
✓ *explaining your motives for what you did*
✓ *making excuses or trying to justify your choices*
✓ *defending your rights*
✓ *providing reasons for your choices*

Repentance is sorrow over sin—*REGRET over hurting God*—not just to admit something because you got caught or are tired of covering up, or apologize because you are tired of lying and see your chances for a happy life slipping away. Acts 20:21 defines the real direction: *"repentance toward God"*. How weird would it be if you blew past a red light in your car, totaled another person's car, and then randomly apologized to a clueless friend that knew nothing about the accident? You should repent to the person you have actually hurt or offended. In our case, God is the first and ultimate conversation.

In 2 Corinthians 7:10, the Bible actually talks about "fake" or "false" repentance like it's the TERMINATOR: *"For godly sorrow produces repentance leading to salvation, not to be regretted; but the sorrow of the world produces death"* (NKJV). Godly sorrow is simply realizing that your really bad decision—your *sin*—was an offense to the love, patience, and character of the Holy God. The godly sorrow of repentance results in realizing you have been wrong and it hurt God. It is NOT just realizing you have created problems, wished you had not done something really stupid, or are miserable because you are suffering humiliation and lost opportunity.

The second step of valid repentance is to make a decision to **separate from the sin.** Why make multiple mistakes with the same issue? Again, the big picture view is that we are running a race and need to get rid of the sins and hindrances that hold us back from God's best, so that we don't repeat the bad choices. You have to assume personal responsibility for a change. Nobody should have to beg or bargain with you to do it. Step up. You can't transfer blame. If your issue forced you to appear in front of a Congressional Committee hearing, you would automatically know it was over. No more excuses. Same here. If you want to survive, you'll have to break all connections with the sinful attitude, situation, habit, or relationship. This is a real move, not a temporary relocation. Change your schedule. Get a new attitude or you'll get sucked into the destructive stuff again. Submit to God in the sense of opening your mind and decisions to God's standards for the next decision. It's about replacement. You have to be willing to replace the failed method with what God says works. Then release control. Simply surrender to what Jesus' purpose was for you in the first place. For example, if you were in the wrong relationship, repentance means starting over by asking Jesus what kind of relationship He wants you to have and "why". Confess that you have a new direction.

Third, to qualify for legitimate repentance, be willing to **name the sin.** Use the right label. CAUTION: You need to enter a no-spin zone! Our American culture is flooded with empty apologies. In 2009, with 3 words, "I've screwed up," President Obama abandoned his nomination fight for Tom Daschle to become Secretary of Health and Human Services when it was revealed that Daschle had failed to pay taxes. When baseball's mega-star Alex Rodriguez confessed to using banned steroids he used 5 words plus a trailer: "I screwed up, big time....I knew we weren't taking Tic Tacs." After winning a record 8 gold medals in the 2008 Olympic swimming events, 23-year-old Michael Phelps gave his mea culpa for getting caught using drugs: "I acted in a youthful and inappropriate way." You will qualify for your own "mea culpa" moment (i.e., "my fault, my bad"). **Name the sin immediately, specifically, and repeatedly if necessary.** 1 John 1:8-10 says:

> *If we claim that we're free of sin, we're only fooling ourselves. A*
> *claim like that is errant nonsense. On the other hand, if we*
> *admit our sin . . . He won't let us down; He'll be true to him-*
> *self. He'll forgive our sins and purge us of all wrongdoing. If we*
> *claim that we've never sinned, we out-and-out contradict*
> *God—make a liar out of him. A claim like that only shows off*
> *our ignorance of God.* (The Message)

The word translated "sin" in that verse means agreeing with God on specific things. Just a generic, random, wild, "hope-it's-enough-to-get-me-by-with-God-and-avoid-getting-killed" statement like "God forgive me", fails the test of scripture. You see, that's how you distinguish God's voice speaking to you from our enemy's voice. Yes, the enemy is real. He is a person and has a name. No, it's not your ex or your former boss! It's Satan. The Bible calls him "*the accuser*" (Revelation 12:10). Satan's role is to keep you distant from God. Or if you buy-in and become a devoted lifetime follower of Jesus, his goal shifts to deceiving you into denying God. Either way, he wants to make sure Jesus is never real to you and keep you from doing anything to make Jesus real to others, because if you do…they *will believe* in Him.

When the missionary entrepreneur and mentor, Paul, profiled his friends in the Greek city of Thessalonica, the phrase he thought best captured their spiritual transformation was that they had *"turned to God from idols"* (1 Thessalonians 1:9, NKJV). These original pagan idol worshippers identified false and worthless beliefs, and threw those beliefs under the bus. When you have built your beliefs and lifestyle around priorities that are in competition with pursuing Jesus, those must be seen as worthless, wasted, and wrong! If a person is offended and insulted at such an extreme or radical standard, it is because repentance is a direct challenge to reject dead-end beliefs and lifestyles. Repentance is controversial in large part because it forces you to compare yourself not against some other unhappy or unsuccessful person, but God. All of our choices must be directly overlaid on God's standards. It's easy to look good when you line yourself up against the dumbest criminal, repeated loser, or the most evil person you can find. Clearly, when that happens, our defense disappears. To confirm how ridiculous we sound, in Lee Strobel's book, *God's Outrageous Claims*, one man argued, "I may be a drug dealer, but I'm not a bad person."[5]

The fourth step in the process of credible repentance requires that you **demonstrate an attitude of humility**. A frustrated mom felt she was losing the argument to convince her two elementary-age boys that they had to go to school the next day. "Boys, if you don't go to school, they will put me in jail." After a brief pause, she heard, "Mom, how long would you have to stay?" Real repentance is packaged with humility before God. A humble attitude contains no bargaining, no rights, no demands, no excuses, and no lies. Someone said that a recent survey revealed 9 out of 10 people like chocolate and the 10th person lies! Don't even think about lying. Lying kills trust. In her article, "7 Lies Men Tell Women", Dr. Joyce Brothers explains what's at stake:

> In his book *The Varnished Truth*, David Nyberg, professor of education at State University of New York at Buffalo, states, "Occasionally there is a lot to lose by telling the truth, and something to be gained by not telling the truth." Still, it's important to remember that lies are at heart deceptions, and repeated deceptions destroy intimacy. Real intimacy is only possible to the degree that we can be honest about what we

are doing and feeling. When lying comes to predominate in
a marriage, the relationship begins to deteriorate. A husband
and wife can sense the trust erode, and feel their hearts growing colder. The healing oxygen is truth.[6]

Tragically, on April 21, 2010, a Deepwater Horizon oil rig located 50
miles off the coast of Louisiana went down in a titanic explosion that killed 11
of the 126 workers and created a massive oil spill that migrated toward the
coast. A mega-column of flames and oil spill were directly traceable to that
incident. In the same way, an oil spill points to an accident, complications and
confusion point to a sin that requires repentance. Until you "cap the source
and put out the flames" it doesn't stop.

To complete the fifth step of authentic repentance, you must **make things
right**. Whatever it takes to get right, do it! Many people want things to be
restored and forgiven immediately, bypassing the hard work of rebuilding spiritual and emotional bridges. You cannot act as though nothing ever happened
or announce that your past is suddenly off limits. People got hurt. Damage
was done. Bridges were burned.

Look at the proactive strategy of the first century believers in Corinth,
Greece: *"For observe this very thing, that you sorrowed in a godly manner: What
diligence it produced in you, what clearing of yourselves, what indignation, what
fear, what vehement desire, what zeal, what vindication! In all things you proved
yourselves to be clear in this matter"* (2 Corinthians 7:11, NKJV). These Jesus-
believers had crossed-over from lifestyles like idol worship, alcoholism, theft,
extortion, homosexuality, and prostitution. In their struggle to embrace being
a new creation in Christ (see 2 Corinthians 5:17), they had both fallen back
into some of their former destructive tendencies and had bragged about their
tolerance of a young guy in the church who was having sex with his father's
wife (see 1 Corinthians 5:1-2). When their spiritual mentor, Paul, called them
out on it and busted them for it, they got it and chased repentance with the
same enthusiasm as they chased their former reckless sinful behavior. So
someone has commented that 2 Corinthians 7:11 sets the standards with 7
signs of bona fide repentance:

- ✓ **Diligence:** *you try to do what is right without somebody
  having to be in your face motivating you.*
- ✓ **Clearing:** *you want to make restoration known.*
- ✓ **Indignation:** *you are angry over what you have done.*
- ✓ **Fear:** *you have a new reverence for God.*
- ✓ **Desire:** *you want complete restoration.*
- ✓ **Zeal:** *you have a new energy and love for both God and peo-
  ple.*

*✓ **Vindication:** you make things right regardless of the cost, and have no desire to protect yourself or withhold anything.*

In an anecdotal story, evangelist Junior Hill focused on the "whatever-it-takes" app of repentance with a 20-yr-old waitress working in a small town downtown café. Wrestling with huge guilt over a really bad decision, she confessed to her boss that she had stolen $20 from the cash register. She risked the job she needed just to make it right with God and her employer. Her boss was so impressed by the genuine turnaround that he accepted her confession without penalty and committed his life to follow Jesus as a result.

## You Can't Give What You Don't Have

Actor Kirk Cameron played the role of Caleb Holt, a small town fireman, in the 2008 movie FIREPROOF. The plot centered on the collapsing marriage between Caleb Holt and his wife Catherine, a hospital public relations director. Caleb raged with anger over what he felt was rejection by Catherine. Depressed, Catherine leaned toward an extramarital affair because of what she interpreted as neglect from Caleb. After a breakthrough moment of total humbling for Caleb, when he believed he had wasted 20+ days of serving his wife to rescue the marriage, Caleb repented of his sins to Jesus and received a new life start. After 40 consecutive days of what Caleb called "The Love Dare", small acts of respect and kindness, Catherine was overwhelmed by his expressions of love. Drained by her confusion and skepticism over Caleb's new attitude toward her, Catherine stayed home from work one day, faking illness. It gave Caleb the opportunity he was seeking to break the silence between them and officially "repent" to her. Kneeling beside the bed, with tears, Caleb tenderly confesses: "I am sorry. I have been so selfish. For the past seven years, I have trampled on you with my words and with my actions. I have loved other things, when I should have loved you. In the last few weeks, God has given me a love for you that I have never had before. And I have asked Him to forgive me. And I am hoping, I am praying, that somehow you would be able to forgive me too. Catherine, I do not want to live the rest of my life without you."

True repentance is actually produced by God's work of grace in a heart (see Acts 11:18). Nobody can fake that. It cannot be permanently imitated or duplicated. Earlier in the movie, the real source of Caleb's conflict is revealed during a conversation with his father, John, which becomes confrontational.

> **John Holt:** *Caleb, if I had to ask you why you're so frustrated with Catherine, what would you say?*
> **Caleb Holt:** *She's stubborn. She makes everything difficult for me. She's ungrateful. She's constantly griping about something.*

**John Holt:** *Has she thanked you for anything you've done in the last 20 days?*

**Caleb Holt:** *No! And you'd think after I washed the car, changed the oil, do the dishes, washed the house, that she would try to show me a little bit of gratitude, but she doesn't. In fact, when I come home, she makes me feel like I'm an enemy! I'm not even welcome in my own home, dad! That is what really ticks me off! Dad, for the last three weeks I have bent over backwards for her! I have tried to demonstrate that I still care about this rela-tionship. I bought her flowers, which she threw away. I have taken her insults and her sarcasm, but last night was it. I made dinner for her. I did everything I could to demonstrate that I care about her, to show value for her, and she spat in my face! She does not deserve this, dad! I am not doing it anymore! How am I supposed to show love to somebody over and over and over, who constantly rejects me?*

**John Holt:** *[John Holt strokes a wooden cross, and turns to Caleb] That's a good question.*

**Caleb Holt:** *Dad, that is not what I'm doing.*

**John Holt:** *Is it?*

**Caleb Holt:** *No. Dad, that is not what this is about.*

**John Holt:** *Son, you just asked me: how can someone show love over and over again when they're constantly rejected? Caleb, the answer is: you can't love her, because **you can't give her what you don't have** [emphasis mine]. I couldn't truly love your mother until I understood what love truly was. It's not because I get some reward out of it. I've now made a decision to love your mother whether she deserves it or not. Son, God loves you, even though you don't deserve it. Even though you've rejected Him. Spat in His face. God sent Jesus to die on the cross for your sin, because He loves you. The cross was offensive to me, until I came to it. But when I did, Jesus Christ changed my life. That's when I truly began to love your mom. Son, I can't settle this for you. This is between you and the Lord. But I love you too much not to tell you the truth. Can't you see that you need Him? Can't you see that you need His forgiveness?*

**Caleb Holt:** *Yes.*

**John Holt:** *Will you trust Him with your life?* [Caleb nods yes][7]

***"You can't give what you don't have."*** Wow. That's so true it's crushing. If you've never really repented to God, then you don't know the love and for-giveness of God, and thus don't have any love and forgiveness to transfer to anyone else. You can't forgive big until you've been forgiven big! You can't love big until you've been loved big! You can't live big until you've repented big!

Jesus defended an extravagant act of worship from a prostitute whom He forgiven (see Luke 7:36-50). When she emptied an alabaster flask of uber-expensive fragrant oil on Jesus, it offended a self-righteous religious leader at the dinner party. Jesus uncovered that religious phony's failure to repent by connecting the dots for him: *"She was forgiven many, many sins, and so she is very, very grateful. If the forgiveness is minimal, the gratitude is minimal"* (Luke 7:47, The Message). Are you running on empty?

Because God doesn't want you to be confused, multiple unfiltered examples of both artificial repentance and pure repentance are displayed on the pages of the Bible. Repentance was the one thing Jesus required for a church to come back into His favor (see Revelation 2:5). Judas, the disciple who sold-out Jesus to the Jewish religious authorities, was remorseful and tried to return the 30 pieces of silver he was paid for the betrayal before committing suicide (see Matthew 27:3-5). That was counterfeit, only an image of repentance and surface-level regret that couldn't remove the guilt that made him self-destruct. King Saul apologized for only partially obeying God's command in a military battle (see 1 Samuel 15:17-30), but it was insincere and too late, falling totally short of bona fide repentance. That faux pas, plus his impatience in offering an unlawful sacrifice (see 1 Samuel 13:11-14), cost him his career and protection from God. The diminutive Jewish tax collector, Zacchaeus, proved his heart was pure on the issue of repentance when he promised Jesus that he would give 50% of his wealth to the poor and provide damages of four times the amount he had swindled from people (see Luke 19:8-9). Finally, in Revelation 9:20-21, the 6th Trumpet Judgment of Plagues will be unleashed on the planet during the 7 years of the Great Tribulation judgments, destroying a full one-third of the population because people who know the truth refuse to repent.

### AWKWARD!

One woman said that when she and her husband moved to a new city, they joined a fitness center in search of friends. So one day she struck up a conversation with the only other woman in the gym. Pointing to two men playing racquetball in a nearby court, she said to the other woman, "There's my husband." Then she added, "The thin one—not the fat one." After a slightly uncomfortable silence the other woman replied, "And that's my husband—the fat one."

AWKWARD! Sometimes there's nowhere to go, nowhere to hide. The only thing you *can do* in some situations is what you *should do*—make it right.

Someone has suggested the following 10 things you can say (in order to avoid repentance), when you get caught sleeping at work:

10) "They told me at the blood bank this might happen."
9) "This is just a 15 minute power-nap like they raved
about in that time management course you sent me to."
8) "Whew! Guess I left the top off the White-Out.
You probably got here just in time!"
7) "I wasn't sleeping! I was meditating on the mission statement
and envisioning a new paradigm."
6) "I was testing my keyboard for drool resistance."
5) "I was doing a highly specific Yoga exercise to relieve work-related stress.
Do you discriminate toward people who practice Yoga?"
4) "Man! Why did you interrupt me?
I had almost figured out a solution to our biggest problem."
3) "The coffee machine is broken..."
2) "Someone must have put decaf in the wrong pot..."
1) ".....in Jesus' name, Amen."

Put the right ending on the wrong start.
Fix your original mess-up by repenting "in Jesus name"!

*Chapter 9*

# Two Bare Feet On The Dashboard?

A wife, desperate for encouragement, cried out to her husband, "This is the worst meal I've ever cooked!" The unthinking husband replied, "No it's not!"

Men need warning labels...or is it women? Thankfully our life-race instructions come with a warning label. Whenever God attaches a descriptive phrase to sin, pay attention! It's like a side effects list on a drug prescription warning label. In this scenario, we're taking on sin that *"so easily entangles"* (Hebrews 12:1, NIV). Normally, the axiom goes like this: *the easier some sin is to import, the harder it is to export.* In plain language, the most addicting stuff is the most pleasurable to start and the hardest to get rid of. The phrase points to unhealthy, destructive, or hurtful stuff that is readily accessible, creating a distracting competition for the runner that is close by. It pictures something that is constantly *appealing* (e.g., maybe stuff you used to do before Jesus changed your life, thinking, and desires—because once you choose the bad stuff, you remain weaker or more vulnerable in that area long term). Another action image conveyed by the phrase is constantly *attacking*, or getting in your way (i.e., the sin doesn't go away by itself and CHASES US!)—constantly surrounding from all sides, and tempting you.

So, as runners in our customized life-race, we're not faced with just some random course obstacles or unpredictable weather conditions, but really cool, compelling, convincing, and yes, *"like a preschooler that keeps saying mommy"*-type, irritating, interrupting options to disobey God. And that stuff doesn't go away—it's unrelenting, pursuing you for the entire life race! 1 John 2:15-17 captures the tension well:

> *15 Do not love this world nor the things it offers you, for when*
> *you love the world, you do not have the love of the Father in*

> *you. 16 For the world offers only a craving for physical*
> *pleasure, a craving for everything we see, and pride in our*
> *achievements and possessions. These are not from the Father,*
> *but are from this world. 17 And this world is fading away,*
> *along with everything that people crave.*
> *But anyone who does what pleases*
> *God will live forever.* (NLT)

## A Redneck's last words?

What is identified in other translations as *"the lust of the flesh, the lust of the eyes"* (NKJV), *"the desire to have everything we see"* (CEV), and *"wanting your own way, wanting everything for yourself, wanting to appear important"* (The Message), is comparable to unending terrorist threats. Or compare the pressure and assault to frustrating internet pop-up ads that you have to "click" to close out, or TV commercial ads that interrupt your favorite movie and force you click "previous channel" on your remote. In the animal kingdom extreme, it's like being chased by lots of pit bulls every day, surrounded by great white sharks while you are bleeding in the water, attacked by a bear on Kodiak Island, Alaska, or getting run down like a Thompson gazelle by cheetahs on the Serengeti plains in Tanzania, Africa.

Just like we need a reality check on the persistence of temptation, we need to be educated about the latent, hidden, embedded energy of sin. Its power to deceive, lure, capture, torture, and enslave is legendary, but largely marginalized and underestimated. Debunk the myth quickly. **I'm personally convinced that most people, including seasoned, veteran believers, are functional or practical agnostics on the issue of entanglement.** Merriam-Webster lists one slice of the definition as "to wrap or twist together".[1]

*Entanglement* practically means you get involved in something and it starts to control you. Point of order! It's not just the stuff that you think is off limits according to the Ten Commandments. It can be good stuff that is misused, transformed into your personal idol, or run past moderation on the scale—pushed to excess. The late Pastor Adrian Rogers once commented, "First the man shapes the idol and then the idol shapes the man."

So…bad choice options that can wrap you up in knots and trip up your biggest dreams, are not limited to sex, drugs, rock-'n-roll, work, investments, or alcohol. You can become anything from a political junkie, band groupie, lottery addict, shopping-maniac, party animal, or a foodie (chasing food trends with a food-obsessed personality), to a sports-obsessed student, career-driven chef, compulsive volunteer, or a snow-boarding, deer-hunting, sky-diving, country-music-singing, 4-wheeling, mega-texting, fast-driving, bar-hopping freak. Almost any desire carries the potential for locking you in and sucking the life out of you with amazing ease *(or more accurately, stealing your God-given potential),* or being substituted for what's best for you and your family. No guy thinks he would do something stupid just by innocently listening to, say, Kenny Chesney's 2005 song, *Summertime*, with lyrics like:

> *Bikini bottoms underneath*
> *But the boys' hearts still skip a beat*
> *When them girls shimmy off*
> *Them old cutoffs*
>
> *And it's two bare feet on the dashboard*
> *Young love and an old Ford*
> *Cheap shades and a tattoo*
> *And a Yoo-Hoo bottle on the floorboard.*

Why? Because **guys really don't think!** Rarely does a person engage in risky behavior—whether it's Wall Street greed, Las Vegas Boulevard gambling, or Bourbon Street sex—believing they'll become a slave to it. When you first plunge into the deep end, you always think you can swim or at least tread water. "I'll never be an addict!" you boast like a politician trying to convince the voters when down in the polls. Sort of like comedian Jeff Foxworthy's familiar line that a redneck's last words are, "Hey, watch this!" "My company and clients will never interfere with my marriage," you brag. Right. No teenager taking their first drink ever believes they will be the victim of date-rape or the idiot with the BAC (blood alcohol content) level to t-bone another car and kill someone as a result. Some husbands wouldn't admit porn controls them even under questioning from a Congressional Committee.

Enough images. You get it. Now make the choice. Oops. Correction. Make the right *choices* in the right way. A choice is a moral and spiritual weapon, and you'd better be trained to handle it or somebody's going to get hurt! Problem is that when we make unguarded choices we go down! And sometimes we take other people with us! Bad choices mean we get more entangled, more wrapped up, in deeper than before. A friend of mine, whose life crashed because of adultery, once insightfully warned:

**An Undetected Weakness + An Unexpected Opportunity = A Casualty**

## Here's Your Sign!

There are highway signs, business signs, political campaign signs, restroom signs, and even miraculous signs. Signs of addiction are also out there. How do you know when a really bad, stupid, deceptive, or destructive choice has you entangled? What are some easy-to-read, *i.e., you've-got-a-problem-even-if-you-can't-see-it-or-don't-believe-it,* signs?

✓ *you can't shake an undercurrent of guilt*

✓ *you don't ever seem to feel truly forgiven*

✓ *you haven't been able to quit or change*

✓ *you start building your attitudes, relationships, schedule, or separate life around it*

✓ *you have to explain it, apologize for it, hide it, cover it up, or lie about it*

✓ *you ignore jokes, attacks, criticism, or comments about it from friends, family, or co-workers who are obviously aware of your choices*

✓ *you dismiss any bad consequences as irrelevant or unconnected*

✓ *you have anger or anxiety you can't explain*

✓ *your thoughts keep going back to it*

✓ *you develop other bad habits because of it*

✓ *you really enjoy the thought, desire, experience, or choice to the point you let other priorities slide*

✓ *you lose interest in God and wonder if you've stopped believing*

✓ *you feel like you are not worthy*

✓ *you begin to feel other people are against you*

## TEMPTATION 101 and Reality Shows

Your assignment?  Make the right choices.  No, this is not Mission Impossible 5.  If it were, you'd get an exemption from judgment and an apology from God for allowing you to be stressed.  That's a partial explanation for the phrase in Hebrews 12:3, *"Let us look only to Jesus, the One who began our faith and who makes it perfect"* (NCV).  Jesus modeled successful choices under the worst possible conditions.  His worst moment?  A whole lot worse than yours.

No, I'm not minimizing the pressure you might feel to lie to close a deal, the surging desire for sex, the panic of not being able to make the payment, or even the pain of surgery or chemotherapy on your child that tempts you to shout curses back to God.  For Jesus, there was the unprecedented double darkness of being tortured by Roman execution pros and absorbing the torture of hell itself—and every filthy sin ever committed—in His ravaged body on a cross.  Philippians 2:8 is a select summary of the principle that dominated His life: *"And being found in appearance as a man, He humbled himself and became obedient to death—even death on a cross!"* (NIV).

The issue with temptation is not about its appeal or pressure.  Wrong focus.  Quit talking about the stuff that can pull you down and wear you out, the huge desire you feel, the history of your past mistakes, indescribable pain from your darkest moments of hurt...or the pressure you feel from friends…or career. Start talking about what you are going to do to please God and make His fame and name known. Obedience is the issue. It was the same scenario for Jesus also, totally obvious when He tasted the same sense of abandonment in suffering you feel: *"My God, My God, why have you forsaken Me?"* (Matthew 27:46, NKJV). But the death of Jesus meant nothing, was wasted and meaningless, and certainly wouldn't rise above the death of any other martyr for a cause, if…**IF**…He had not lived a perfectly obedient life. It was His consistent choice to reject every temptation that could *disqualify* Him, that ultimately *qualified* His sacrifice for our sins as acceptable to God.

For example, after the spiritual high of hearing the Father in heaven speak approval at His baptism, and following 40 days of fasting in a desert, Satan shows up to negotiate with Jesus in person! For all three recorded temptations from Satan to get Jesus to quit, give up, walk away from His assigned life-race and chase other things, Jesus responded with specific scriptures to demolish Satan's twisted appeals (see Matthew 4:1-11). Part of Jesus' purpose in coming to the planet, beyond dying for our sins, was living an obedient life to prove that it could be done: *"So then, since we have a great High Priest who has entered heaven, Jesus the Son of God, let us hold firmly to what we believe. This High Priest of ours understands our weaknesses, for He faced all of the same testings we do, yet He did not sin"* (Hebrews 4:14-15, NLT).

Because of *that* undefeated record and having the truth about choices and pressure, there's no excuse for our failure. Yes, of course, there's forgiveness…but no excuse. Have you ever said that it's easier to get forgiveness than permission? Another really bad idea! Don't go there. If believers have these promises, it's all good. Look at this verse: *"The temptations in your life are no different from what others experience. And God is faithful. He will not allow the temptation to be more than you can stand. When you are tempted, he will show you a way out so that you can endure"* (1 Corinthians 10:13, NLT).

So, educated by that verse and enrolled in TEMPTATION 101, you can't say your temptation is unique—that nobody has ever been hurt, abused, pressured, or felt a desire like what hit you. Neither can you say there was no way out. And you cannot blame God for not showing up with answers. All of who He is and what He can do is on the table if you will access it. Besides, according to your "believer's bill of rights" in that verse, there's always an expiration date on the temptation. Even if it feels like eternity, temptation doesn't last forever. By the way, somebody said the definition of eternity is four blondes at a four-way stop. Just kidding. Pleeeaaasssee…no blogging or emails.

Temptation is seasonal, even if it is **personal** (fits your unique personality and circumstances), **powerful** (appeals to your deepest desires), **perplexing** (the real issue is rarely obvious), and **persistent** (repeats and returns). God controls the temptation and will intervene if you are actually getting anywhere close to reaching your breaking point. Why? He doesn't want you to go down, any more than He was casually standing by when Jesus faced the ultimate temptation on the cross to give up. God isn't some sadistic, profit-and-ratings-driven reality show producer that keeps setting up obstacles to discourage you into acting out something that entertains viewers.

There is an amazing story of how all this works and how it's done right in Genesis 39. Check it out.

# PART FOUR:

# The Choices

*Chapter 10*

# What Happens In Cairo...

## The Office

If there had been an American Eagle store nearby, he would have been wearing "Athletic Fit". He was maybe early 20's, "hot", bronzed, athletically-trimmed, well-dressed, articulate, ambitious...*and* the personal manager for the head of secret service for the world's most powerful leader. Enter the "cougar". The chase was on. His boss' wife checked him out and wanted him. Maybe she was lonely. Maybe the cougar was trying to prove she still had "the look". Maybe she was sexually addicted. Maybe it was about revenge for something her husband had done or failed to do. Maybe it was a bet, proving to her lunch crowd or BFF that she could conquer him. Usually the person who initiates the adultery is not doing it for the first time anyway. Her boldness was probably proof that she was not the rookie virgin. We can't access the details or guess at motives because the primary witness chose not to release them. He focused on excellence at the office—she focused on him.

So at the right moment...right there in **"the office"**...at his workplace...she offers sex—no fears, no limits, no consequences. That, audience, is *real* temptation. He never saw that coming, but still got past it. How? Or better yet, maybe you are asking why would he want to pass on this one?

## Bungee Jumping on the Zambezi

Script this one, and it's one of the most engaging and realistic—and RELEVANT—scenes recorded in the Bible. Men and women are in that mix daily in the workplace, bar, ballpark, or on the school campus. Attracted by the adrenaline rush of doing something crazy and spontaneous, people still take that bait so often that with some crowds it's considered routine...normal...expected.

In his hit song, *I'm Yours,* Jason Mraz makes the point with his line, "And nothing's going to stop me but divine intervention." Actually, that's true.

God can interrupt your life. Back to the point. Tucker Max, the self-promoted pick-up artist and author of New York Times bestseller, *I Hope They Serve Beer In Hell*, said, "Why should I feel guilty for doing something everybody else is doing?" At least he's honest about how he's chosen to run his life-race. His website says, "I get excessively drunk at inappropriate times, disregard social norms, indulge every whim, ignore the consequences of my actions, mock idiots and posers, sleep with more women than is safe or reasonable....But, I do contribute to humanity in one very important way. I share my adventures with the world."[1]

Sin makes you stupid. More sin removes fear. Even more sin makes you a celebrity...because, after all, we worship the *successful*...AND the *survivors* (check out the autograph lines if you don't believe it). An unchecked life of sin also means you die...over and over again...forever. Hopefully, because Jason and Tucker tell the truth about being reckless, it will result in more people asking for a more sane approach to life, or where God is at the morning after.

On New Year's Eve, December 31, 2011, Australian Erin Langworthy, 22, survived a terrifying moment when her 111-meter bungee jump over Victoria Falls went horribly wrong. The bungee rope snapped, and with her feet still tied she plunged headfirst into the crocodile-infested rapids of the Zambezi River, which runs the borders of the African nations of Zambia and Zimbabwe. Amazingly, she reached shore with only a broken collarbone and bruises. "It went black straight away and I felt like I had been slapped all over", Erin recalled.[2]

Playing with sin is like doing that 111-meter Victoria Falls bungee jump toward the Zambezi River with a faulty rope. At some point reality hits. What you were doing and believing comes to an abrupt end. It doesn't work anymore. Sin will always have an "Oooohhhh, NO!" moment, made up of equal parts of fear, regret, and panic, when you finally realize the truth...about God, about yourself, and about the situation—that you don't qualify for a do-over!

The guy in this drama knew it. He triggered another kind of adventure...no, more like a competition...when he refused the cougar the first time. That brush-off apparently just created more passion and determination. Result? She obviously loved the challenge...or was ticked off with his rejection. You didn't say "No" to the boss' wife. So the game was on. It became a daily thing. Every day a revealing look. A seductive smile. A suggestive remark. A passionate touch. A revealing outfit. The sexual tension was mega-powerful. Yet she didn't win.

**Why?** Let's work through the crime scene.

## "GO TO JAIL. DO NOT PASS GO. DO NOT COLLECT $200!"

You've rolled the dice. You've played the board game, MONOPOLY, hoping to hit it big. And then you got the *GO TO JAIL* card. Maaannnn! It ruins everything! You are in jail while others are buying property, making money and bad jokes, and waving their success in your face. Your life is put on hold. It's not fair! Or is it?

His name was Joseph. He was a slave. But she didn't own him. Nobody did. That is, except God. Because God was real to him and that made running his life-race "priority one". Joseph was the consummate professional. She was the wife of Potiphar, captain of Pharaoh's elite palace guard. The setting was ancient Egypt, but the story is as familiar as the next Hollywood celebrity meltdown on *Entertainment Tonight.* We're talking pyramids, gold chariots, the sun god Ra, moonlit sails on the Nile, probably pomegranate cocktails…and zero future if you were a slave. A vacation destination where "what happened in Cairo *didn't stay* in Cairo!" A 2012 comparison? It was like a random college student being offered a White House job for sexual favors. Where did this come from? It doesn't make sense except that *Joseph-the-slave* believed he was not destined to be a slave forever—that his life-race was bigger and more valuable than a secret sex romp.

How smart was that? Really smart. Because when you put a price tag on your dream…actually, your soul…you realize it shouldn't be for sale. Jesus framed it this way: *"What will you gain, if you own the whole world but destroy yourself? What would you give to get back your soul?"* (Matthew 16:26, CEV). Even Jim Kramer (CNBC's *Mad Money* host who entertains with his take on stocks, investing, and market analysis) will tell you, "don't buy high and sell low!"

Here's the background. Genesis chapters 37 and 39 in the Bible explain that after being abused by his brothers, a 17-year-old Joseph was sold from a desert pit in Canaan into slavery in Egypt, and purchased from the auction block to serve in the household of Potiphar, captain of Pharaoh's elite and highly-screened palace guard…*Enter the cougar.*

Just when you are tempted to whine about how tough things are in your life, God presses the play button on Joseph's biography (Genesis chapters 37, 39-50), and all your excuses for giving in to temptation are destroyed. Remember his backstory. He's been abused by his brothers, sold into slavery in Egypt, fought his way into a trusted position, and then gets propositioned by his boss' wife. When he refused her advances, it's "GO TO JAIL. DO NOT PASS GO. DO NOT COLLECT $200!"

Yet he wins. How? He has no family support network in Egypt. He doesn't know the language or culture. He is now the new ethnic minority with zero freedom as a slave. Somebody else controls his life and makes the decisions. All he has to fall back on is God…PLUS a dream from God that came to him as a 17-year-old that he had a big destiny—that his life was worth something to God. Yet that's miraculously enough. And he does more than survive. His life had impact. What he did challenged the belief system of everybody who knew him and forced them to deal with the reality of God. Of secondary importance is that his peak career achievement was becoming the equivalent of the Vice-President of Egypt, the most dominating empire-country in that segment of history.

Joseph was successful on all levels. WHAT? How can a teenage slave ultimately flip the culture that threatens to eat him first? Because he didn't become what anybody else wanted him to be. He stayed true to who he was...and what God expected him to become. Conspiring brothers couldn't kill his spirit. The sex-crazed wife of a government official couldn't conquer him. Two years in prison didn't embitter him. Betrayal by friends couldn't depress him. He didn't become like them. How did he do it? Joseph made 7 consecutive right choices without a mistake. 7 wins, 0 losses in that streak. A record like that is no accident. Joseph didn't just get lucky. No pun intended. Repeated success is not an aberration. He was doing something right. And doing it well.

## 1st Right Choice: Build integrity.

Genesis 39:2-6 reveals Joseph's simple secret of integrity—giving your best in every circumstance:

> *2 The Lord was with Joseph, so he succeeded in everything*
> *he did as he served in the home of his Egyptian master.*
> *3 Potiphar noticed this and realized that the Lord was*
> *with Joseph, giving him success in everything he did. 4*
> *This pleased Potiphar, so he soon made Joseph his personal*
> *attendant. He put him in charge of his entire household and*
> *everything he owned. 5 From the day Joseph was put in charge*
> *of his master's household and property, the Lord began to*
> *bless Potiphar's household for Joseph's sake.*
> *All his household affairs ran smoothly, and his crops*
> *and livestock flourished.*
> *6 So Potiphar gave Joseph complete administrative*
> *responsibility over everything he owned.*
> *With Joseph there, he didn't worry about a thing—*
> *except what kind of food to eat!* (NLT)

Joseph gave his best effort—consistently and reliably doing what was right—in his new role as the personal manager for Potiphar. How? With humility and excellence in his performance. It was classic servant leadership—investing in someone's need to make God known. That kind of a record is more valuable than any position, title, achievement, or portfolio. You don't trade it or sell it. If you ever do sell your integrity, you'll find it almost impossible to buy back! In fact, the integrity that earned the trust of his boss (master) was the first defense Joseph used to deflect the come-on from Potiphar's wife:

*8 But Joseph refused. "Look," he told her, "my master trusts me*
*with everything in his entire household.*
*9 No one here has more authority than I do. He has held*
*back nothing from me except you, because you are his wife."*
(Genesis 39:8-9, NLT)

Leadership coach and best-selling author John Maxwell believes trust is critical to relationships and success: "'Do my people trust me?' is the central question of leadership, and leaders must continually monitor the level of trust that exists on their team."[3]

Comply with *biblical* work standards, and whether you work at a restaurant or play in the NFL, you'll be radical in today's corporate culture. When you respect and submit to authority (see 1 Peter 5:5, NLT), play by the rules (see Romans 13:1-5, NIV), give more than the minimum and do it passionately (see Colossians 3:22-25, The Message), and pray for those in authority over you (see 1 Timothy 2:1-3, The Message), you'll be isolated, labeled weird, or maybe pressured. But there is *power* in serving. It's simultaneously intimidating and compelling, mostly because unselfishness is so radical—it's so anti culture—to be concerned about what's best for other person first (i.e., the strategy and mindset of Jesus when He gave up heaven to come die for us, see Philippians 2:5-8). And it's controversial because the choice to serve with respect can only be explained as God-driven, because everybody—including a CEO—knows that we're not good enough or big enough to create that kind of an attitude and sustain it on our own.

## Honeymoons, Hangover 2, Facebook, Dating Sites, Mercy Ships, a 4-lb. Tumor, and $16 Margaritas

Success can hide a lot of problems. Good times can cover up a lot of stupidity, sloppiness, or sin. For example, weddings and honeymoons aren't real life. Whether you did a honeymoon in Aruba or Pigeon Forge, real life starts when you get back to face $100,000 of wedding indulgence or school debt on your Visa card. Nobody at the wedding was questioning your financial discipline—they just danced and went back for seconds at the buffet. Nobody in your sorority or in your row at the stadium asked how you were going to pay for college—they were too busy tailgating. When things are going good, you look good. When people party, they normally don't have a plan for tomorrow. Case in point? Check out the movies *Hangover* and *Hangover 2*. When people celebrate, they aren't thinking about cleaning up. Riding a wave of corporate growth, celebrating a winning streak, or cashing in on an investment can provide convenient cover for someone to temporarily ignore character flaws, questionable decisions, and undisciplined behavior. Another example? Israel's first king, Saul, owned a string of military victories and the trust of the nation until Samuel the prophet confronted him about intentionally lying to appear successful by propping up a battle story (see 1 Samuel 15:13-23). Competency can only take you so far. It takes character to sustain success. Your giftedness can actually outgrow your godliness. Winning gets you recognized—it doesn't make you a better person or change who you are baseline. Nobody seems to worry about integrity until a 2001 Enron collapse results "in the loss of $60 billion in market value on Wall Street, almost $2.1 billion in pension plans and 5,600 jobs."[4] Whether it's hundreds of thousands lost in 401(k)'s, former Toronto Blue Jays strength coach Brian McNamee testifying in court he injected pitcher Roger Clemens with steroids and HGH, or John Edward's vice-presidential campaign contributions are allegedly diverted to hide his mistress, success without standards eventually crashes. Whether it's your virginity or identity stolen, hardball questions sadly come later in most cases.

Take the Facebook flip...or is it "flap"? Under the ticker symbol "FB", social-media transformer Facebook's IPO (Initial Public Offering) opened at $38 per share after weird delays and glitches, had 82 million shares trade in 30 seconds, increased the net worth of twenty-eight-year-old CEO Mark Zuckerberg by $19 billion,[5] then plummeted to $29 per share within a week and became the target of a class action lawsuit accusing Morgan Stanley of sharing negative information with institutional investors. What looks cool and successful on the surface can sometimes be deceiving. Ask anybody who's ever done the match-thing with an internet dating site! Skinny success for Scott Harrison eventually triggered a big question as well.

"What would the opposite of my life look like?"[6] After 10 years of throwing parties for MTV, VH1, ABC TV, Cosmopolitan, ELLE Magazine, Universal Records, Bacardi and Anheuser-Busch,[7] chasing models, socializing with NYC elite, and sampling drugs like cocaine and ecstasy,[8] a then 28-year-old New York City nightclub and fashion event promoter, Scott Harrison, asked that life-changing question. He had a "crisis of conscience" during a Uruguay vacation,[9] questioning his life and career: "I was selling selfishness and decadence[10]....[feeling like] the most selfish, sycophantic and miserable human being....[and]....the worst person I knew."[11]   Scott's vacation epiphany, a spiritual re-awakening, brought him back to the Christian faith he had abandoned in college. The answer to his question motivated the desperately unhappy NYU communications grad to head for Liberia, West Africa in 2004 as a volunteer photojournalist for Mercy Ships. It was a Christian charity he'd never heard of (paying them $500/month to serve!), which operates a fleet of hospital/surgical ships offering free healthcare to the poorest nations.[12] The change? Scott shifted from living in a 1,500sf loft with grand piano to a 150sf ship's cabin, complete with cockroaches and strange roommates; from going to work at 11pm doing parties and coming home drunk at 5am, to this:

*I fell in love with Liberia, a country with no public electricity,*
*running water or sewage. Spending time in a leper colony and*
*many remote villages, I put a face to the world's 1.2 billion liv-*
*ing in poverty. Those living on less than $365 a year—money I*
*used to blow on a bottle of Grey Goose vodka at a fancy club.*
*Before tip. Our medical staff would hold patient intake "screen-*
*ings" and thousands would wait in line to be seen, many*
*afflicted with deformities even Clive Barker hadn't thought of.*
*Enormous, suffocating tumors—cleft lips, faces eaten by bacteria*
*from water-borne diseases*[13]....[Referring to an incident in
Benin] *The first person I photographed was a 14-year-old boy*
*named Alfred, choking on a four-pound benign tumor in his*
*mouth, filling up his whole mouth. He was suffocating on his*
*own face. I just went into the corner and sobbed."*[14]

Photographing Alfred and breaking down was Scott's "a-ha" moment.
Nobody could have been prepared for what the team encountered on that day,
Day 3 in Africa. Cotonou, Benin. 5:30a.m. On the first day of patient
screening, volunteer doctors and surgeons were confronted with over 5,000
people from all over West Africa, standing outside a stadium, desperate for
treatment. It was overwhelming: 1,500 surgery slots available...3,500 suffering and dying people would be turned away.[15]

After a successful surgery, Scott took Alfred *[mentioned above]* back to his village in Benin, West Africa. But it was Scott that was changed! "I saw everybody
celebrating, because a few doctors had given up their vacation time," he said.[16]
Scott returned to New York two years and 13,000 photos later, broke and sleeping on a friend's couch, but he had a plan. That vision resulted in launching
**charity: water**, with a mission to provide clean water to the planet. Called a
"marketing machine," by Jacqueline Novogratz of the Acumen Fund, Scott is
"lifting one of the most critical issues of our time in a way that is sexy and incred-
ibly compelling—that's his gift."[17] With more than half a million followers on
Twitter (the United Nations has 3,000), his group has raised $10 million, pro-
viding clean water to nearly 1 million people in Africa and Asia, and making sure
every penny from new donors goes to specific projects in the field. [18]

Scott came back to New York from Africa with a different perspective and
a fresh motivation:

*It's $32 for two margaritas when $16 buys a bag of rice for a*
*family for a month. I've bought that $16 bag of rice and deliv-*
*ered it. It's a different concept of wealth. Instead of getting*
*angry, I've just tried to talk to people about ways they can help*
*either financially or volunteering. I've tried to make it positive*
*and not guilt anyone.*

*You know, I'm personally motivated by my Christian faith. I read something in the book of James a long time ago, and it really stuck. James 1:27 says that true religion is two things. Looking after widows and orphans, and keeping yourself from being polluted by the world. That's what motivates me. Service to the poor, a relationship with God and trying to live with integrity.*[19]

Service. Scott Harrison is not just doing it. He's living it...with integrity.

## HORRIBLE BOSSES!

Apparently, issues with employers are so common that the 2011 movie, **Horrible Bosses**, starring Jason Bateman, Charlie Day, Jason Sudeikis, Jennifer Aniston, Colin Farrell, Kevin Spacey, and Jamie Foxx, asks the big question: "What can you do when your boss is a psycho, a man-eater, or a total tool?" Everybody is trying to cope with the personality and quirks of the people at the top of the corporate food chain. But it's not all about the boss. So let's rip the Band-Aid off!

One boss was fed up with a certain worker who had developed the habit of arriving late for work on a regular basis. "Do you know what time we start work here?" he yelled when he saw the employee arrive late that day. "No sir!" the man answered. "Every time I get here everybody is already busy at work. How should I know?"

There are higher standards for believers vs. non-believers, but anybody who chooses to play by God's rules will be blessed. Joseph chose to honor those in authority over him, even if he disagreed with the system or felt his boss didn't deserve it. Respect for authority is not based in the person who currently occupies that role of authority, but linked to a higher spiritual principle: *submission honors God.*

There are plenty of bosses who could give a flip about you or God. Stanley Bing identifies five types of difficult bosses—The Bully, The Paranoid, The Wimp, The Narcissist, and The Disaster Hunter—and some strategies for coping, in his book, *Crazy Bosses* (Harper Collins). For example, he says The Bully boss requires enemies in order to function properly, and if none are handy is not averse to creating them.[20] Normally, employees don't have any trouble categorizing their boss. One guy's criteria was the knot in his stomach when the boss showed up.

Despite Kevin, Jennifer, and Colin's characters in the movie, there are some good bosses. An Ajilon Finance (an accounting and financial staffing company) survey discovered 79% of workers have great respect for their boss, and identified as key traits: leading by example, strong ethics or morals, knowledge of the business, fairness, overall intelligence and competence, and recognition of employees.  Randall Hansen argues that bad bosses pop up in all organizations:

> *Maybe you have a boss who is sexist or racist. Or perhaps a boss who takes all the credit for himself. Maybe your boss thinks you have no life outside work and makes you stay late every day. Or perhaps a boss who gives out too many tasks with impossible to meet deadlines (or constantly changing deadlines). Maybe your boss is a pathological liar. Or perhaps the boss plays favorites. Bad bosses — whether ogres, control freaks, jerks, microman-agers, or bumbling fools — can be found in all organizations. Pop culture loves to make fun of bad bosses, from the pointy-haired boss in the Dilbert comic strip, to the completely insipid boss from "The Office," to the…compulsive and mean boss of the movie Office Space… but bad bosses are no laughing matter when you have to face him or her every working day. And, unfortunately, with the rightsizing of the last several years, there are probably more overworked and undertrained bosses than ever. It's also possible, though, that bad bossing is just part of the organization's corporate culture. One study found that almost 80 percent of the employees surveyed identified their boss as a lousy manager. And almost 70 percent in that study conducted by Delta Road stated that their immediate superior had "no clue" what to do to become a good manager. Author Harvey Horn-stein, Ph.D., estimates that 90 percent of the U.S. work force has been subjected to abusive behavior at some time. He bases his conclusions on a survey of nearly 1,000 workers over eight years.*[21]

So, even if you *know* your boss is wacko and unpredictable, your co-work-ers unethical and undependable, and company policies unfair and unbending, God says…"So?"  The reason He can require respectful behavior with authority is because He controls the outcome.  He decides when to call a time out, change coaches, or hit the buzzer to end the game.  The laws of His kingdom are unchangeable.  Stay humble and honor Him, and He will promote you:  *"God opposes the proud but favors the humble.…So humble yourselves under the mighty power of God, and at the right time he will lift you up in honor"* (1 Peter 5:5-6, NLT).  Translation?  Do it God's way, and God will promote you and jerk the boss around at the right time.  God is CEO of justice, not vengeance.  Even if nobody—including your boss, priest, wife, kids, buddy, tail-gating friends, client, highway patrolman, personal trainer, babysitter, doctor, patients, teacher, princi-pal, bank teller, or pizza delivery guy—sees, understands, recognizes, rewards, or applauds your integrity—God does! *No sin escapes God's scrutiny. But neither does service!*

**SIDEBAR: Here's my simple biblical definition of service:** Investing in a need to move someone forward in their awareness of God. Whether you are serving your boss, husband or wife, the community food bank, a boys and girls club, a local school, your kids' sports teams, a church, mosque, temple or synagogue, a physically-disabled person, or a homeless shelter, there are three distinctives that make service for God unique:

1. **PURPOSE:** Biblical service is making people aware that God is real, that God cares, that God owns the truth about life, and that God has a purpose for every life to give hope. Brad Pitt and Angelina Jolie gave millions for an Ethiopian health clinic and housing in New Orleans. That's awesome and commendable. Applaud them. Appreciate them. Thank God for them. It was definitely a good work. But without a clear message attached—that *stuff* eventually perishes and doesn't qualify as biblical service. Only God can give real life. In every contribution, you have a choice to promote yourself or God! To meet the test, do it in His name (actually bring it up in the conversations), for His glory (brag on God), and love ALL the people recklessly...like Him.

2. **PASSION:** *"And whatever you do, do it heartily, as to the Lord and not to men, knowing that from the Lord you will receive the reward of the inheritance; for you serve the Lord Christ"* (Colossians 3:23-24, NKJV). Ultimately, you serve Jesus, not your boss, mate, the poor or a friend. TRANSLATION? If you get that right—that a believer's goal is exclusively to please Jesus—then you are less likely to quit, get mad, or withhold service when the other person behaves badly, never changes, lacks proper appreciation for what you've done, or takes advantage. And...it shifts the responsibility for outcome back to Jesus—i.e., you are not responsible for results, recognition, or being appreciated. You serve. God rewards. Period. Joseph got promoted in prison! And if you are really serving Jesus—passion actually *increases* because you can't forget what He did to forgive *you* and launch a new life for you FIRST! A believer serving up good works without excitement means they are dissatisfied with their role, disgusted with the person they serve, or disappointed because they haven't become a celebrity! POINT? Take the passion test. The best servants are having a blast!

3. **POSITION:** With this universal definition, service can be anything on the scale from mowing someone's lawn to moving legislation forward as a governor or flipping a low-performing school as a principal, as long as people are more impressed by the love of Jesus coming

through what you do, and know you are in it for Him.  Any position, role, or job can become a lifeline with God's power and compassion flowing through you.  Nobody is insignificant.  God is not limited, no matter how *risky* it is to represent Him or how your position is *rated*, from minimum-wage earner to a Mark Zuckerberg planet-changing role.  Your position has worth because God is in it!  Value is not determined by the size of your paycheck but by the size of your passion.  Not by the visibility of your act of service, but by the visibility of God working through you.

The result is that respecting authority not only honors God, but it validates a believer's claims in the eyes of non-believers, and also preserves relationships and institutions.  In the home, biblically, both husband and wife are required to submit to each other in marriage, even  though the husband is the designated authority (see Ephesians 5:21-25).

Truthfully, that's usually why some people try to get by with the minimum, only doing what is required of them and no more.  They don't want to play by God's rules or don't believe He really has ultimate control.  And typically, people don't look at job performance as a category of accountability to God.  We ignorantly tend to segment our lives, as though God just sees what we do at worship in the church, synagogue, temple, or mosque, or that our career is somehow exempt from evaluation by God.  Some people actually believe God left their workplace long ago!  Once the job is done, the 40 hours up, or the checklist is complete, they check-out!  It's because down deep inside they want to retain the right to decide if God or their boss deserves their best effort.  Doing the minimum required is more than lazy, undisciplined, or unmotivated—it's a sign of unconquered resentment.  **Got a horrible boss?**  Do what you have to and go home!  That's the reasoning.  Nobody normally gives their best to something they don't like.  Big donors invest in the Republican, Democrat, or TEA parties because their beliefs and passions align with that particular group.

### Good to GREAT!

In the multi-million selling book, *Good to Great: Why Some Companies Make the Leap...And Others Don't,* author and former faculty member at Stanford Graduate School of Business, Jim Collins, revolutionized corporate thinking about the factors that determine ultimate success.   Research and comparison focused on the 15-year histories of 28 elite companies (e.g., Coca-Cola, Intel, General Electric, Merck) to surface reasons why some companies made the leap from good to great and others failed.  His team discovered the most successful leaders, "Level 5" leaders, built enduring greatness with a mysterious blend of personal humility and professional will.  With surprising results about what elevates some companies to sustain performance at higher levels, Collins reflected on another connection between excellence at work and meaning for life:

> When [what you are deeply passionate about, what you can be best in the world at and what drives your economic engine] comes together, not only does your work move toward greatness, but so does your life. For, in the end, it is impossible to have a great life unless it is a meaningful life....Indeed, you might even gain that deepest of all satisfactions: knowing that your short time here on this earth has been well spent, and that it mattered....Faith in the endgame helps you live through the months or years of buildup.[22]

Joseph may have been the original Level 5 leader! He went from good to great as the proto-typical blend of humility and strong will. It was ultimately faith that propelled him past the opportunities disguised as setbacks to success—*faith* in the sense that Joseph gave his best for God, not just for his boss or to advance his own dream. That was smart from five perspectives.

*First, that attitude was the best defense against living in bitterness from the past.* You can't excel with a divided heart. If you are always thinking about what somebody else did to hurt you or your family or your career, there's no way you are focusing on what's in front of you.

*Second, excellence is always rewarded by God and frequently recognized by superiors.* That's why he had God's favor that gave him wisdom and a promotion. Excellence is always discovered! Sometimes it's even uncovered!

*Third, it is an expression of a worshipful heart, and a worshipping heart creates a winning attitude.* You WILL be focused on worshipping and pleasing someone—either yourself, others, or God. Worship of God always evolves into a desire to serve the needs of others. People are naturally attracted to those who invest in and encourage others.

*Fourth, even the smallest compromises in telling the truth, giving your best effort, or honoring those in authority create an opening for temptation.* For example, if you think you can withhold your best effort because of the way your boss, mate, coach, or friend has treated you, then you will begin to believe that you deserve some other special treatment or indulgence. You begin to think that it's okay to cut yourself some slack, or give yourself a break when it comes to complete obedience and follow-through.

*Fifth, giving your best kills the kind of stress at work that increases your desire to quit.* In their book, *The Service Prescription*, T. Scott Gross, Karyn Buxman, and my friend, Dr. Greg Ayers, promote what they label as "Positively Outrageous Service" as the new gold standard for the healthcare industry, but it's a universal principle because it's biblical. In one example, they cite the shocking stat that "One in every five nurses plans to leave the profession within the next

5 years due to unsatisfactory working conditions. One in three nurses under 30 plans on leaving her job within the next year! The cost to replace a nurse is approximately four times higher than the nurse's salary."[23] The desire to quit, or just to escape stress is epidemic. They humorously argue that the sign of nursing burnout is that every time a nurse makes a patient's bed they have the overwhelming desire to lie down in it![24] Choose to excel. It builds your confidence...and God's confidence in you! When you give your best effort, you'll never have to apologize or back up. As long as you know you've done your best and God knows it, everything is good! You produce the excellence. God will provide the encouragement.

But be careful not to slide into the ditch on either side. This trap comes standard with two extremes. The first ditch is *perfectionism*. Pride blinds. Arrogance makes you weak. Perfectionism is false assurance. The danger is in thinking that because you have done so well you can handle anything or deserve anything. In Joseph's case, that would have translated to believing that he deserved some sexual fun because of his achievements—which basically would have meant he forgot it was God's favor that made him successful.

A second ditch is *processing*—specifically, processing failure wrong. Listening to Satan or critics that say—*"You are a failure...You didn't have the abilities...You are unimportant...You don't have influence...You are unworthy of God's love and forgiveness...You'll never achieve anything...Things will never change"*—makes you think that obeying God is not worth it. If you have already failed, Satan argues, "then who cares?" I once heard a young single woman say, "If I've already had sex with so many guys, it's no use *[to change or want a better life]*. Nobody would want me." You've just moved into a really classic older home on Failure Street if you start thinking like that. Don't let stress, customers, patients, bosses, co-workers, or critics steal your potential by tempting you to slow down or give less than your best.

### Timing *IS* Everything!

No surprise that Joseph faced some upper level temptation. The more you succeed, the more you will be tempted. Not the reverse. It's when you give your best that you will be attacked or tempted. And timing is everything for the believer's spiritual adversary, Satan. When you get the promotion, hit the home run, close the deal, give your life over to Jesus, get baptized, promise to stay pure, commit to giving thousands to charity, or come home from the honeymoon, *get ready*...because you will be slammed with Satan's most difficult and deceptive tactics! He schedules temptation to immediately follow a life-changing experience or big-direction commitment in order to shut down your potential—basically to get you to quit before you've had the chance to succeed. Of course, his short-term goal is to create an inconsistency in your life, to make you look like an idiot, feel like a jerk, think like a failure, and back up on your commitments to God!

So, Satan's pattern—the timing and trajectory of his attacks—is normally on the front-end of your commitment. I mean, if you were the enemy, wouldn't you want to take out the opposition early, before they could produce a significant impact? Think about it. When did Satan prompt King Herod to kill all baby boys, 2-years-old and under, that lived near Bethlehem? It was when that insane Roman dictator learned of the birth of Jesus, the Messiah. In other words, as Jesus' earthly life began, Satan was trying to eliminate or reduce Jesus' effectiveness for God. Question: When did Satan appear to personally tempt Jesus in the desert? Answer: Immediately following Jesus' baptism and public commitment to the ministry God had given Him. If Satan can disable your confidence with a big mistake initially, he will have succeeded in discrediting, denying, delaying, or destroying the success God has planned for your future. So brace yourself for a certain assault right after any success or serious commitment. Here's a huge truth: we usually don't fall or mess up when suffering comes. We're more likely to just shut down. It's when we get serious or enjoy success that it's easiest to lose focus and chase a convincing substitute.

So, how do Main Street or Wall Street believers survive? Same way. By integrity in choices. Whether you drive a BMW or ride a bicycle, live in Boston or Bangladesh, play a didgeridoo or drum, or eat biscuits in Australia or bolinhos de arroz (fried rice balls) in Brazil, every one of the nearly 7 billion people on the planet lives or dies within the integrity maze. Remember, Joseph had no back-up or friends, and yet his integrity stood the most extreme test. God and character may be all you have, but that's enough!

Joseph's striking physical attributes made him a convenient target. Those good looks were a weakness in the sense that it made him vulnerable to wrong desires. Know your weaknesses. A weakness can be defined as things like an unfulfilled desire for something good or bad, an unguarded decision that overrides counsel and conviction, an unimproved character flaw that fractures your honesty, unresolved guilt that leads you to give up goals and avoid starting over right, an undetected sin that opens the door for worse sins, an undisciplined thought that stirs curiosity, an uncontrolled emotion that seeks release—or the classic, like Joseph's good looks in this case—an under-valued strength.

But regardless of circumstances—your past, the pressure of threats or lusts, love or hate for your position, preparation or lack of it, or level of pain or passion you feel—YOU are responsible for your decisions! The core of a Jesus-follower's life is OBEDIENCE! You must continue to obey God when nobody agrees, nothing changes, and no answers surface. Joseph made his decision to honor God in total isolation, when there was no crowd to applaud and no immediate reward. Integrity means you focus on God's love and provision for that moment as sufficient…simply because, at the end of the day, God is worthy! Especially if you have already tasted His forgiveness and life in Jesus, you owe Him your best— *"You were bought at a price. Therefore honor God with your bodies"* (1 Corinthians 6:2, NIV).

## In The RAW

Here's a key truth to absorb in preserving your integrity: *a loving God withholds NOTHING that you really need* (see Psalm 84:11). Ultimately, your view of God's character determines your effectiveness in sustaining the right choices. It's what you know of God that's real and accurate that drives the right decisions. Big dream means you have a BIG GOD! And a standing strong for your convictions means you know you have a BIG GOD! The size of your dream and your determination reflects the size of your God!

One of my favorite indulgences is *Sugar In The Raw*, natural cane sugar from the tropics. Those golden crystals are full of natural molasses and are advertised to add a deep, rich flavor to any food or drink. I dump it in huge amounts in my ice tea. It's a flavor adventure like none other. I like "raw" except in the same sentence as steaks, sushi, and sores.

Natural is best…except when it's a wrong desire or a good impulse headed in the wrong direction. Sex is good. God designed it to be incredible…but it only works long term by God's rules in marriage. But that's not the issue. Never is. Strip a temptation of its packaging and all that's left exposed is a substitute for worshipping God. Take our example. Joseph's "temptation in the raw" was not sex with his boss' wife. The *real* temptation was to substitute that woman *and* a few seconds of heavy breathing—at that moment in his career— for the wife, timing, career, and passion of committed love that God intended to give him later. Temptation is always sweetened with the *you-can-enjoy-it-now-rather-than-later* offer. The big lie is that honoring God means you get nothing and miss out on the good stuff. BIG lie! God has never failed in His "rewards program". Reward comes AFTER. The University of Alabama football team didn't get the 2012 NCAA Championship crystal football trophy BEFORE they played the game. Reward is LATER…even if you want it sooner. And the reward is *not* for holding back your desires so you can have a no-restraints Mardi Gras celebration moment or like getting drunk on your 21st birthday! Reward is for WINNERS…those who do it right…again and again. Don't forget that.

So, define integrity then! All right. Integrity is doing what is right. Period. In every situation, under every condition, in every decision, and in every relationship…including with God. There's more though, because it means you have to be consistent or it's not really integrity. Doing right 75% of the time does not qualify as integrity. Your mate would kill you if you bragged that you only committed adultery 25% of the time! Let me toss this to you: **INTEGRITY is doing the right thing, at the right time, in the right way, with the right motive (to please God), which almost always means postponing a desire that compromises character in order to honor God and get something even better later!** Translation? Sex is better with the mate God will give you for waiting!

Pressure is never from God. Conviction? Yes. *"Take-your-breath-away-moments-to-make-you-think-about-God"*? God designs those too. He allows guilt, but not condemnation. Tension, but not temptation. Stress comes from God? Sure it can. Sometimes suffering. Pain possibly, but not pressure in the classic sense of manipulation or force that could override your will or capacity to choose (see 2 Corinthians 12:7-10 and James 1:12-17). Those verses tell us God pours His power through us in times when we are weak or hurting, and *He never tempts us to trip us!* Simply stated, God doesn't set you up, man! God is committed to your success. Period. Interest rates change. God doesn't.

## HONEY, I'M PREGNANT!

Satan is into pressure. He's all about creating the stress—or maybe even urgency driven by the fear or panic of missed opportunity for fun or success—that says you have to *"go-for-it-now-or-you-may-never-have-another-chance-to-enjoy-it-again"* or *"you-don't-have-to-put-up-with-that-stuff"* kind of sales tactic. Satan pushes. God leads. Why? Because God's strategy is to make you an independent, crazy healthy, solidly mature, totally balanced, raging confident, multi-functioning disciple that actually gets results in people's lives. Jesus cast the vision in John 15:16— *"You did not choose me. I chose you and sent you out to produce fruit, the kind of fruit that will last. Then my Father will give you whatever you ask for in my name"*, (NLT). Resistance to temptation is a method God uses to teach the value of waiting. Waiting can preempt big mistakes from impulsive and reactionary decisions. Don't you think God deserves a moment to weigh in on what could alter your life race?

Of course it requires trust. That's the overlooked secret in the profile of a different Joseph (earthly father of Jesus, husband of Mary). After learning that his fiancé, Mary, was pregnant, he's reviewing all options on the scale from a quiet, secret divorce to enforcing the penalty of stoning in Jewish law. Imagine the hurt when the woman that you thought was totally pure now has an explanation that goes like this: "I was like, uh, picking grapes in the vineyard, then like…uh, this guy shows up, and…oh, by the way, HONEY, I'M PREGNANT!" Actually, there was more that probably came out like, "…then this guy in white appears, says he was from God, and I was chosen to have this baby." Not the most believable story, even if it's followed by, "This baby is the Messiah". Yet, Joseph put the brakes on his emotions long enough for God to speak to him in a dream, explaining that God expected Joseph to go forward with the marriage because the baby was created supernaturally inside Mary by the Holy Spirit, and Joseph was supposed to name him JESUS. Even with the dream and explanation, the second miracle after Mary's Immaculate Conception is Joseph's "Immediate Commitment". He went through with the wedding plans and kept the name! The bigger the decision, the more critical the need to wait until you know God is leading.

## Rookies and Temptation

Again, we've closed the loop and come back to the point: *Temptation is anything that pressures you to accept false substitutes for worshipping God.* The street language for violating God's standards (i.e., sin), showing out *disrespect* for God, is *dissing* God. So when you actually show God respect by obeying Him you are, in effect, worshipping Him. How? Because the heart of worship is trusting that God is simultaneously wise, loving, and good; that He knows best what you need; and, withholds nothing that you really need.

Now, back to Egypt. Joseph's refusal to have sex with his boss' wife equaled worship—like saying, "God, I am passing on this offer because it will honor You to do life YOUR WAY and wait for what You say is THE best." Satan's basic DNA desire is to destroy WORSHIP—to remove any trust and praise that might go to God, even for one brief moment! Remember the rookie believers Paul wrote in Corinth? Here *again* is the closing argument he used to make the appeal for resisting temptation:

> *12 Just because something is technically legal doesn't mean that it's spiritually appropriate. If I went around doing whatever I thought I could get by with, I'd be a slave to my whims. 13 You know the old saying, 'First you eat to live, and then you live to eat'? Well, it may be true that the body is only a temporary thing, but that's no excuse for stuffing your body with food, or indulging it with sex. Since the Master honors you with a body, honor him with your body!* (1 Corinthians 6:12-13, The Message)

Survival under the uber-intense appeal of temptation is driven by integrity in choices. But you don't walk away from the deception unless the motivation is really deep and ingrained, and the reason is worth it. Honoring God is worth it. Remember, if you do, He'll not only have your back…He'll pay you back! ("*…God opposes the proud but favors the humble.…So humble yourselves under the mighty power of God, and at the right time he will lift you up in honor*", 1 Peter 5:5-7, NLT).

## STARBUCKS IS CLOSED!

In 2010, Starbucks annual revenue soared over $10 million from serving nearly 60 million store visitors a week in 16,000 stores in 54 countries. More than 200,000 employees, or "partners", represent the Starbucks values every day. But it almost didn't happen. After three decades of success, on February 26, 2008, in an unprecedented move, customers at 7,100 U.S. Starbucks stores were asked to leave. For the next 3 hours, every barista was re-trained in the art of making the perfect cup of coffee. That radical action was prompted by 8 years of crazy-fast expansion at the expense of quality. It was a $6 million dollar gamble by Howard Schulz to re-ignite their original passion for coffee! Starbucks founder, Howard Schulz, who had stepped down as CEO in 2000, came out of semi-retirement to save not just the stock price, but the company itself, as told in his business memoir, *Onward*. Schulz felt Starbucks problems were not because competitors like McDonald's created *McCafe's* with cheaper coffee or Dunkin' Donuts stepped it up. Nor did he conveniently blame the slide on a crumbling economy, an emerging ethic-conscious consumer, or negativism from the largely uncontrollable blogosphere. He was doing his own review, in his words, with never any "intent to attack or assign blame."[25] In a private memo to Starbucks CEO, Jim Donald, and the leadership team, he argued that there was a "dilution of the experience."[26] Schulz's life or death memo that even referenced things like "loss of aroma" in the stores was ultimately leaked and created a huge public relations nightmare. Yet, Schulz didn't back down, fighting back in the media for his company's survival with statements that were from the heart: "We believe that success is not an entitlement and that it has to be earned every day."[27] Refusing to focus on the mistakes of the past, he operated from the conviction that Starbucks was "better than that" and refused to be a bystander as Starbucks slipped toward mediocrity.[28] Expressing total confidence that it could be turned around, Schulz challenged his team: "I am going to ask more of you than has ever been asked before,"[29] and added, "I'm in this 100 percent. My passion. My commitment. This is the most important thing in life other than my family. This is 25 years of my life, and I don't like what has happened."[30] His goal was nothing less than to "help get this company back, find our voice, find our soul, and make our customers and partners proud to be associated with Starbucks."[31] Howard Schulz made it happen because he went back to core values that made Starbucks successful.

Want to find your voice?

Want to find your soul?

Want to make God proud that you are wearing His name?

Want to prosper?

Want to get promoted?

Decide that *integrity* is worth everything. Promote God's standards!

Yes, God expects YOU to go first!

*Chapter 11*

# Butterbeer and Broomsticks

An aggressive guy and a fearful girl landed back on the front porch of her home following their first date. As they stood in front of the door, he propped himself up with his hand on the door frame, boldly leaned toward her, and asked for a kiss. She refused, "I can't." "Don't you like me?" he argued. "Yeah, but I just can't," she replied. "Why not?" "Well, what if somebody saw us, I mean like my parents?" He pressured, "Who's gonna see in the dark here?" "Well, I don't know, but I just can't." "C'mon!" he insisted. "No. I'd be embarrassed." "Pleeeease???" he came back "NO!" she said sharply. He didn't give up: "Just one kiss?" "No!" Then suddenly the porch lights came on and the door swung open. The girl's young sister stood there in her pajamas: "I've got a message from Dad. He says you can kiss the guy. If you don't want to, I can do it. If I don't want to, he can come down here and kiss him. But just tell him to take his hand off the intercom button!!!" Busted! The whole family knew what he wanted.

What's your dream? What are you willing to do? Better yet, what does God want for you? How do make sure you don't give in prematurely, accept a substitute, or compromise the dream? It's discipline. Jesus said we *can* figure out God's will if we really want to (see John 7:17).

**2nd Right Choice: Discipline thoughts.**
Life is about outcomes. There are built-in trade-offs. If you want the best outcome, you have to pay the price of discipline. It's about focusing exclusively on God and a goal. Devoted lifetime followers of Jesus use the term *obedience*. Obeying God creates a destiny just as much as disobeying God shapes a future. The process is: thoughts control decisions, which create habits, which shape character, which determine a destiny. Want to know someone's destiny? Easy. Look at what they are doing right now. Want to drill deeper? The outcome for a life is actually based on what you are THINKING right

now! Believers have a radical responsibility for screening and securing thoughts:

> *It is true that we live in the world, but we do not fight from*
> *worldly motives. The weapons we use in our fight are not the*
> *world's weapons but God's powerful weapons, which we use to*
> *destroy strongholds. We destroy false arguments; we pull down*
> *every proud obstacle that is raised against the knowledge of*
> *God; we take every thought captive and make it obey Christ.*
> (2 Corinthians 10:3-5, GNT).

Joseph wasn't making a similar typical mistake of information-obsessed American Christians in 2012. For years, people have worn me out with one question, "How can I know God's will for my life?" Frequently, that is a cover for, "I need answers from God NOW!" It is their real scantily-clad demand, as though that were the ultimate objective for a devoted follower of Jesus. Instead, Joseph lived the basics he knew God expected and the will of God became obvious.

The discipline in his thought life was as stunning as Kate Middleton's bridal gown at her April 30, 2011 Westminster Abbey wedding to Prince William. Mrs. Potiphar made a brazen offer (minus the price tag): *"Sleep with me."* (39:7, Amplified Bible). Having negotiated and settled the difference between right and wrong, the confident teenage slave fired back a stinging, prosecutorial-style question/accusation: *"How then can I do this great evil?"* (Genesis 39:9b, Amplified Bible). He called it evil. In microseconds. That's impressive. His thinking survived without damage as a result. "Props" to the guy whose thinking didn't have to be "propped up".

**SIDEBAR:** Do you know what happens every time you stand for what is right, speak your convictions, refuse to do what is wrong, or make statements that bring clarity and biblical reality into a situation? God comes with it and creates conviction! That's right. Conviction. ***Conviction is the immediate awareness of right and wrong PLUS the instant sense God is there, knows everything, and you are accountable.*** Every time. No exceptions. Increased tension? Yes. Controversy? Yes. But it's all generated from somebody feeling the internal pain of God's holy truth about what's right, intersecting with pre-meditated rebellion. Conviction is the invisible, holy God busting down the door hiding a person's wrong desires. It's impossible to keep God out of your mind and those moments!

Why? Because God speaks, like Joseph's comeback in Genesis 39:9, through words in real-time moments like that—directly to the heart and con-science of people who are urging, considering, or agreeing with, bad behavior. It doesn't make any difference if the person suggesting sin admits it or not. Mrs. Potiphar felt conviction. That's ultimately why she became angry and tried to destroy Joseph. Not because she was sex-deprived, or full of hatred because she was let down after over-valuing men, or a control-freak with men. She did payback later because her attempt to bring down God's man was a camouflaged attempt to invalidate the truth from Joseph's lips that she had sinned and was fighting God! Truth [from God's Word], like Joseph spoke it—razor-sharp clear and concise—cuts through the mental maze of pre-planned arguments and exposes to that person their real intent and guilt that normally only God knows (cf., Hebrews 4:12-13— *"For the word of God is alive and powerful. It is sharper than the sharpest two-edged sword, cutting between soul and spirit, between joint and marrow. It exposes our innermost thoughts and desires. Nothing in all creation is hidden from God. Everything is naked and exposed before his eyes, and He is the one to whom we are accountable"*, NLT and *"God means what He says. What He says goes. His powerful Word is sharp as a surgeon's scalpel, cutting through everything, whether doubt or defense, laying us open to listen and obey. Nothing and no one is impervious to God's Word. We can't get away from it—no matter what"*, The Message).

Enticement is real. Seduction is about what you don't see. Movie producers make hundreds of millions setting up your imagination. Without showing any actual contact, and sometimes zero skin, they create sexual tension between characters, and meticulously craft images of touching and clothing on the floor, or anything that suggests uncontrolled passion. You don't have to see any naked bodies. Why? Because they know a biblical fact: the mind rules! The scene is already being played out in your mind. In chapters 5 to 7 of Proverbs, the same type of scene was originally scripted to warn you of how it goes down—so you can bail out early! There I found 12 signs of enticement from a woman wanting sex, planning for the escape, and willing to throw away the rules to get it:

1.   *Gives compliments & convincing conversation*
2.   *Makes herself irresistibly attractive*
3.   *Gives signals with direct eye contact*
4.   *Willingly arranges meeting times & places*
5.   *Dresses seductively*
6.   *Presents a fun & edgy image*
7.   *Adventurous: loves to experience new things*
8.   *Uses lots of physical touching*
9.   *Boldly talks about intimate things*
10.  *States you are the one she's been looking for*
11.  *Willing to do anything sexually*
12.  *Makes plans to deceive her family*

If any of those signs are visible right now in your relationship with someone, don't explain—***escape!*** Long before any physical act, casual sex is a mind thing. That's just one reason why there are repeated statements in the New Testament books about **guarding, controlling, disciplining, redirecting, or replacing your thoughts**. Like overkill with an ad campaign that hits you everywhere you go, God wears you out with multiple warning signs like Romans 12:1-2:

> *I plead with you to give your bodies to God because of all he has done for you. Let them be a living and holy sacrifice—the kind He will find acceptable. This is truly the way to worship Him. Don't copy the behavior and customs of this world, but let God transform you into a new person by **changing the way you think**. [emphasis mine] Then you will learn to know God's will for you, which is good and pleasing and perfect.*
> (NLT, see also 2 Corinthians 10:3-5 / Ephesians 4:21-24 / Philippians 2:5; 4:8)

## Butterbeer and Broomsticks

We have a cultural DNA bias that categorizes people and their choices as smart or dumb, winner or loser, profitable or costly, protected or risky, safe or unsafe, guilty or not guilty, successful or failure, but almost never in terms of right or wrong, good or evil. It takes somebody like Osama bin Laden for the American media to even come close to using the word "evil" to describe any-body. Apparently only a few people like Bin Laden, Hitler, Stalin, Idi Amin, suicide bombers, and child murderers can do things that reach that status or level. Maybe it's because if we admit somebody's evil or doing evil, then we also have to admit that evil is in all of us? Maybe Harry Potter has helped us more than we think—to see evil is real? Maybe the Butterbeer and Broom-sticks at *The Wizarding World of Harry Potter* in Universal Studios Orlando aren't just for kids after all?

Flashback to 1960. South America. In a bold raid, Israeli secret agents kidnapped Adolf Eichmann, one of the men responsible for Nazi Germany's Holocaust of the Jews during WWII, and returned him to Israel to face war crimes trials. Yehiel Dinur, a former concentration camp prisoner who sur-vived the infamous Auschwitz death camp, was summoned as a witness to tes-tify against Eichmann. In his classic book defining what it means for Christians to engage the culture, *Being The Body*, Chuck Colson described Dinur's unexpected reaction when entered the courtroom:

> ...Dinur entered the courtroom and stared at the man in the bulletproof-glass booth—the man who had murdered Dinur's friends, personally executed a number of Jews, and presided over the slaughter of millions more. As the eyes of the two men met—victim and murderous tyrant—the courtroom fell silent,

filled with the tension of the confrontation. But no one was prepared for what happened next. Yehiel Dinur began to shout and sob, collapsing on the floor. Was he overcome by hatred…by the horrifying memories…by the evil incarnate in Eichmann's face? No. As he later explained in a riveting *60 Minutes* interview….Dinur came to the stunning realization that sin and evil are the human condition. "I was afraid about myself….I saw that I am capable to do this…exactly like he….Eichmann is in all of us."[1]

Evil does exist. In us. Yeah, totally embodied in Satan and some select personalities, but in all of us. One frustrated husband said, "I know Satan is real because I married his sister." Evil is also in the *best* of us. Romans 3:10-12 is cold: *nobody's good.* Proof? Do what Romans 3:19-23 says, compare yourself to the gold standard—God Himself—not some jerk down the street or a terrorist, and what happens? Nobody makes the cut. We're all guilty of big stuff or small, secret stuff that violates the standards of a perfect, holy God who knows your every secret.

Make no mistake. The offer for sex from Joseph's boss' wife was *evil.* More than skin was exposed by the cougar. It was an indictment not merely on her marriage, but on the condition of her heart. And you don't defeat evil with Butterbeer and Broomsticks, a cappuccino-flavored laugh, legislation, campaign promises, love, tolerance, vacations, money, the peace sign, or a tear-jerking story. Your thought-life had better be in sync with God. He will warn you. He will protect you. Take the very powerful real-life moment when evil touched the life of the founder of Focus on the Family ministry, James Dobson, and his wife Shirley:

> *I'll never forget the time when our daughter had just learned to drive. Danae had been enrolled in Kamakazi Driving School, and the moment finally arrived for her to take her first solo flight in the family car. Believe me, my anxiety level was climbing off the chart that day. Someday you will know how terrifying it is to hand the car keys to a 16-year-old kid who doesn't know what she doesn't know about driving. Shirley and I stood quaking in the front yard as Danae drove out of sight. Fortunately, Danae made it home safely in a few minutes and brought the car to a careful and controlled stop. That is the sweetest sound in the world to an anxious parent!*
>
> *It was during this era, when we lived in Southern California, that Shirley and I covenanted between us to pray for our son and daughter at the close of every day. Not only were we concerned*

*about the risk of an automobile accident, but we were also aware of so many other dangers that lurk out there in a city like Los Angeles. That part of the world is known for weirdos, kooks, nuts, ding-a-lings and fruitcakes. That's one reason we found ourselves on our knees each evening, asking for divine protection for the teenagers we love so much.*

*One night we were particularly tired and collapsed into bed without our benedictory prayer. We were almost asleep before Shirley's voice pierced the night. "Jim," she said. "We haven't prayed for our kids yet today. Don't you think we should talk to the Lord?" I admit it was difficult for me to pull my 6'2 frame out of the warm bed that night. Nevertheless, we got on our knees and offered a prayer for our children's safety, placing them in the hands of the Father once more.*

*Later we learned that Danae and a girlfriend had gone to a fast-food establishment and bought hamburgers and Cokes. They drove up the road a few miles to eat the meal when a city policeman drove by, shining his spotlight in all directions. He was obviously looking for someone, but gradually went past. In a few minutes, Danae and her friend heard a "clunk" from under the car. They looked at one another nervously and felt another sharp bump. Before they could leave, a man crawled out from under the car and emerged on the passenger side. He was very hairy and looked as if he had been on the street for weeks. He also wore strange-looking "John Lennon" glasses down on his nose. The man immediately came over to the door and attempted to open it. Thank God, it was locked. Danae quickly started the car and drove of...no doubt at record speed.*

*Later, when we checked the timing of this incident, we realized that Shirley and I had been on our knees at the precise moment of danger. Our prayers were answered. Our daughter and her friend were safe! It is impossible for me to overstate the need for prayer in the fabric of family life. Not simply as a shield against danger, of course. A personal relationship with Jesus Christ is the cornerstone of marriage, giving meaning and purpose to every dimension of living. Being able to bow in prayer as the day begins or ends gives expression to the frustrations and concerns that might not otherwise be ventilated.*

*On the other end of that prayer line is a loving heavenly Father who has promised to hear and answer our petitions. In this day of disintegrating families on every side, we dare not try to make it on our own.*[2]

Because James and Shirley's thoughts were focused on listening to God, they were able to follow His prompting to intercede with prayer for their daughter Danae, who never realized how desperately she needed God's protection at that critical moment. At any moment, your thoughts are either disciplined or drifting.

**For believers, the mind is the battleground.** Our best defense is the "remodeled" thinking that I referenced earlier. ***Consuming the truth of scripture is what changes your perspective.*** There is no substitute for studying the Bible. God's Word is truth (see John 17:16), and getting the truth from the ultimate "No Spin Zone" is critical for making right choices. Since the Holy Spirit speaks to you through the scripture (see 1 Corinthians 2:10-16; John 16:12-14), wrong thoughts get exposed and you absorb the right balanced perspective on desires and decisions, ambitions and adultery, sin and guilt, commitment and escape, selfishness and generosity, or love and emotions.

Competing thoughts fight 24/7 for supremacy in your mind. You WILL give in to one of them—truth or lie. Unless you are packing the truth, you'll get killed by some "random bullet" argument that sounds good at the time. Believers are at war with internal impulses and cultural philosophies that divert thoughts from God's best plan. Those thoughts have to be managed:

*The world is unprincipled. It's dog-eat-dog out there! The world doesn't fight fair. But we don't live or fight our battles that way—never have and never will. The tools of our trade aren't for marketing or manipulation, but they are for demolishing that entire massively corrupt culture. We use our powerful God-tools for smashing warped philosophies, tearing down barriers erected against the truth of God, fitting every loose thought and emotion and impulse into the structure of life shaped by Christ.*
(2 Corinthians 10:3-5, The Message)

## What Men Want

Every act of casual sex (adultery, or any other sin, for that matter), begins with a single, unguarded thought. It can be thoughts like: *"I deserve it...it feels right...I need this...this sex is good...this is normal...I can have this relationship **AND** still have my career, marriage, girlfriend, boyfriend, etc., and be a good student, parent, friend, and employee...nobody will ever know...there's nothing wrong with it...everybody has done something like this before...God will forgive me...my* *mate doesn't need to know...I am actually helping this person work through their problems...I'm the only person in the fraternity/sorority who hasn't done it...I missed God's will when I married this other person...this person can make me happy...it makes me a better person or mate...it's okay as long as I don't do it too much...OR...I can stop this anytime."*

The wrapping paper for every temptation is deception. Either you are deceived and not thinking right, or somebody else is wrapping it to get your attention and create maximum appeal. When Satan does the gift-wrapping, he is effective in deceiving you into *overestimating your strength* and *underestimating the cost.* If married, keep your thoughts focused on your mate with every strategy available. Brag on your mate constantly in front of friends and kids for random reasons. Call or text them often during the day. Put photos of them in high-traffic places. Discuss your problems exclusively with your mate. Do community, school, and ministry projects together. Never be alone with the opposite sex for any reason, even business. Travel together. Give gifts regularly for no reason. Keep a weekly date. Copy them on emails where there is risk with the opposite sex. Give up your passwords, including Facebook! Confess your thoughts and temptations to them. Pray out loud over each other. Single? Find that trusted friend of the same sex and create similar accountability links. Link...or sink!

Guarding your thoughts primarily means guarding your eyes, according to Jesus: *"Your eye is a lamp that provides light for your body. When your eye is good, your whole body is filled with light."* (Matthew 6:22, NLT). It's especially true for guys because **sight** comes right before sex in the male dictionary. What men see usually determines what they want. But it's not all sex. Whether it's sex, an NFL game, a beer, a truck, an autograph, a championship, a closed deal, a boat, a position, a dirt bike, a tattoo, or a large pizza, it's like all based on sight (i.e., the impulse of the moment and the thrill of competing, conquering, and controlling). Proverbs 4:25 says, *"Let your eyes look straight ahead"* (NKJV). Easy to understand why God inserted *that* vision restriction. Without a focus, you'll be tempted by magazine racks, internet sites, videos, ads, programs, movies, images, people, or places that create lustful thoughts.

One salesman said that on extended trips away from home, he asks motel managers to remove the TV from his room to avoid any temptation. That's radical and weird and extreme for some, but it's consistent with Jesus' words in Matthew 5:29—*"So if your eye—even your good eye—causes you to lust, gouge it out and throw it away. It is better for you to lose one part of your body than for your whole body to be thrown into hell"* (NLT). Tell your skeptic friend *that* is hyperbole, and the Master Communicator used it effectively to grab attention on the subject of temptation. Jesus never suggested self-mutilation—although I've seen some really bad tattoos on athletes that look like the leftovers from a suicide attempt. He simply insisted only that we take every step necessary— even if it looks insane to people who don't believe hell, heroin, or hormones are real issues—to prevent engaging the sins that could destroy our lives or prevent us from making it to heaven.

But it's bigger than adultery, even if studies reveal that about 50% of all married people engage in extramarital sex at some time or another during their relationship.[3]   Sexual passion is so powerful and explosive, but it still lags behind anger—and its fully-*devolved* version, called "bitterness"—on the temptation charts.   Anger is like the *Australopithecus afarensis*[4] of bitterness. Anger is "off the charts" the most universal temptation.

Don't worry.  Keep reading.  We're *going* to deal with this.

*Chapter 12*

# Is Stupidity Contagious?

Stealing is always wrong and seldom executed well. Stealing from a Wal-Mart store covered with 5 billion security cameras is never brilliant, but 22-year-old Timothy Clark's decision to do some "unauthorized" early Christmas shopping in December, 2011, elevated him to the status of the criminally stupid. The first mistake was thinking he could get out of the store and parking lot with $635 worth of PlayStation 3 and Xbox 360 games and accessories stuffed into his pants and sweatshirt. No way those bulges show! Right. The second, and biggest mistake, was planning it on "Shop With A Cop" day. No less than 50 uniformed officers were roaming through the store as a part of the national event where law enforcement officials spend time shopping with needy or neglected children. Mr. Clark was arrested before he got to the exit.[1]

But while the laughter dies down, and just before you click SEND to email that story to your buddies, think about another outcome. If Mr. Clark had pulled that off, we'd be furious with the cops and fearful that security was a joke. Cops are supposed to be resisting lawbreakers. With all the resources, the cops still had to go after the guy trying to steal and stop him.

Bridge? Think about the people around you every day in your routine, crowd, and culture, who are acting with brazen stupidity—surrounded by believers who have massive spiritual resources—to steal your convictions and embarrass your God. If you don't do something...if you don't speak out...they win and you lose.

### 3rd Right Choice: Speak convictions.

Up front. Early. Decisively. That's how Joseph "spoke" his convictions. Joseph got out in front of the temptations PLUS he went VERBAL! Not a bad idea if you're actually going to drive your choices instead of being run over by them like a victim. Joseph's response was textbook perfect! When you speak your convictions, besides complying with God's rules in order for you to survive, they have to be precise and unambiguous.

## Wall Street Is Laughing!

Wall Street had a laugh over the January 23, 2012 cover letter from a New York University student making his case for employment with the J.P. Morgan firm and hoping for an interview during Superdays, when aspiring investors are grilled by entire teams of analysts. Here's an excerpt: "I am unequivocally the most unflaggingly hard worker I know, and I love self-improvement. I have always felt that my time should be spent wisely, so I continuously challenge myself...I decided to redouble my effort by placing out of two classes, taking two honors classes, and holding two part-time jobs. That semester I achieved a 3.93, and in the same time I managed to bench double my bodyweight and do 35 pull-ups....Egos can be a huge liability, and I try not to have one."[2] After a Bank of America Merrill Lynch director forwarded the cover letter to his entire team, offering drinks "to the first analyst to concisely summarize everything that is wrong with" the letter, it passed through investment banking and accounting teams at Goldman Sachs, Morgan Stanley, Nomura, Citi, Deutsche Bank, PricewaterhouseCoopers, KPMG, Wells Fargo, Keefe, Bruyette & Woods, Perella Weinberg Partners, and Barclays Capital.[3] That guy spoke his convictions! Nothing held back. He made it clear. Like him or laugh at him, at least you know where he stood. That's Bold with a capital "B"...or Stupid with a capital "S", depending on how it hit you. As you might expect, the letter received mixed reaction. Investment bankers normally prefer a pretense of humility, but his letter is the only one from tens of thousands of undergrad Wall Street wannabes that made the news! Sometimes boldness pays. But God obviously prefers boldness with truth! His truth!

## Angels and Heroes

After his 2001 debut in major league baseball, Albert Pujols became the first player in baseball history to hit 30 or more home runs in each of his first five seasons. There's been no power outage yet, with the 3-time National League MVP hitting 3 home runs for the St. Louis Cardinals in Game 3 of the 2011 World Series against the Texas Rangers. Neither his success, nor his 2011 trade to the California Angels in a $254 million, 10-year contract deal, has changed his core. Like Joseph, his professional success as one of baseball's biggest talents is balanced by an ultra-clear conviction: "It doesn't matter if I hit a home run. It doesn't matter if we win a game. It doesn't matter if I go four for four. Whatever happens at the end of the day, as long as I glorify His name, that's what it's all about. I always say God doesn't need me, but I need Him in my life to survive in this world and over temptation. That's Who keeps me humble every time....The kids look at me, 'Ah, you're my hero.' I want to teach those kids. 'Hey listen, God is my hero. He died on the cross for my sins, and He's the one."[4] His wife Deidre was equally bold about the responsibility and risk that goes with the moment when success arrives: "We can retire…when we get to heaven. I mean now is the time God has put us in a position…of great power. I believe in speaking out on His behalf and really speaking out on what is right."[5]

Do it like Albert and Deidre…and our buddy, Joseph. Rather than viewing yourself as a potential victim, look at the moment of testing as a platform of awesome power that gives you an opportunity to speak out for God!

## Tim Tebow and Convictions

Inexplicably famous for the image of being on one knee with head bowed in prayer (dubbed "Tebowing"), Tim Tebow is controversial for all the right reasons. As a playoff game-winning quarterback for the NFL's Denver Broncos, and author of *Through My Eyes*, Tebow had the ultimate response to the 2011 scandal that erupted over alleged violations of NCAA rules by jailed Ponzi scheme artist Nevin Shapiro involving University of Miami football players. Shapiro confessed to Yahoo Sports that he even put a bounty on Tebow when Florida played Miami, and provided Miami players with perks including cash, prostitutes, cars, and other gifts over the past 10 years. Tim said, "…high school and college athletes need to be prepared in case they're approached by unscrupulous individuals offering illicit or illegal benefits….Hey, no matter what comes at me, I'm going to say no to it, not 'What is it? How nice is it? How nice is the perk? If they're thinking anything like that, then temptation can overcome you and you give into it and then regret it later on down the road."[6] Tim's simple protection against that unfolding scandal that could ruin lives, families, and careers? "Just say no!" It does work. How? It has to be spoken up front. It has to be a conviction.

What is the difference between a conviction and a preference? A **conviction** is a non-negotiable core belief that ultimately shapes your character and decisions. Convictions energize you. Convictions drive priorities. Convictions make you practice your guitar or give money to a charity, candidate, or cause. It's the reason you stay up with sick kids or postpone having kids until after med school. It's more than something you would rather not change or give-up. *Better yet, it's something that changes you when acted upon.* It's who you are when nobody's looking or when everybody's looking and you have to pay a price. When it costs you something to follow-through on, defend, or keep that belief, idea, or value, then you've identified your conviction. Believers normally agree that convictions should be sourced in scripture.

In contrast, a **preference** is an idea or choice that can change or flex based on desire, motivation, circumstances, or pressures. Preferences are not generally life and death stuff. Refusing to get an abortion because you believe life begins at conception is a conviction. Choosing to eat Mexican food tonight or go barefoot on the beach are preferences.

Long before Mrs. Potiphar offered sex to Joseph, he had apparently decided adultery was not only risky and stupid—*it was a sin against God.* Although Joseph's passive daddy, Jacob, didn't personally play by God's rules when it came to the *one-man-for-one-woman-for-life* concept,[7] in a sort of schizophrenic-hypocritical way, Jacob did communicate his version of God's standards for marriage and purity to his son. Well, *teach* is more accurate because kids tend to believe lifestyle more than words. Maybe seeing the train wreck in his own home with his daddy's decisions about multiple wives made Joseph more averse to testing the boundaries. Some kids of alcoholics survive the abuse and neglect swearing they will never have the stuff in their refrigerator or even pass a beer down the row at a ballgame.

Everybody has convictions, including the late Osama Bin Laden. Where you get your convictions matters. Joseph's were definitely linked to God's standards. If you are interested in peace and happiness in this life, then get your convictions from scripture. The alternative is to borrow them from current culture—convenient sources like the entertainment universe, the political zoo, or religious traditions. You can choose Bill Clinton or Billy Graham as the source, but your convictions will bend to the situation if not tied to eternal truth. Basically, check out the results, or check out the fruit, as Jesus said, and you will know if the convictions will pay off eternally.

## Where's Oprah?

Where will your beliefs take you? As Charles Lowery asked, "If you get where you are going, where will you be?"[8] Andy Stanley observed, "Your direction determines your destination." So, what will be the outcome of following hormones or holiness? Something's not true merely because it's effective, but what is true will be effective. Is there really a talk-show host, politician, or religious ceremony that is going to prop you up, back you up, or make you pause, when you are thinking about what to do while you stare at a naked woman, lie on your tax return, reach for the 4th drink, or scream at your son? Oprah can't be everywhere you know, even if she's not doing a daytime show anymore!

The original standards weren't inspired or developed in a sanctuary but on the streets. Think about what Paul, the 13th apostle, wrote to the new believers in the hip, 1st century metroplex culture of Corinth, Greece. Many of them had come from backgrounds of reckless sex, over-the-edge drinking and partying, and homosexual lifestyles, so they needed an "Intimacy 101" course to update their sex lives to match God's standards:

> *There's more to sex than mere skin on skin. Sex is as much spiritual mystery as physical fact. As written in Scripture, "The two become one." Since we want to become spiritually one with the Master, we must not pursue the kind of sex that*

> *avoids commitment and intimacy, leaving us more lonely than*
> *ever—the kind of sex that can never "become one." There is a*
> *sense in which sexual sins are different from all others. In sex-*
> *ual sin we violate the sacredness of our own bodies, these bodies*
> *that were made for God-given and God-modeled love, for*
> *"becoming one" with another. Or didn't you realize that your*
> *body is a sacred place, the place of the Holy Spirit? Don't you*
> *see that you can't live however you please, squandering what*
> *God paid such a high price for? The physical part of you is not*
> *some piece of property belonging to the spiritual part of you.*
> *God owns the whole works. So let people see God in and*
> *through your body.*
> (1 Corinthians 6:16-20, The Message)

Either you believe you are a spiritual person, designed to honor God with body, passions, and your potential, or your body will become a cheap piece of real estate, traded multiple times and headed for foreclosure.

### Symptom vs. Source: "Are Those Potato Chips?"

Sue Ater said that shortly before her 25th wedding anniversary her husband sent 25 long-stemmed yellow roses to her at her office. A few days later, she plucked all the petals and dried them. On the night of their anniversary, she spread the petals over the bed and lay on top of them, with only minimal clothing. As she had hoped, she did get a reaction from her husband...but *not* what she expected. When he saw her, he shouted, "Are those potato chips?"[9] Some guys may always be clueless. Joseph wasn't! And yet...people still focus on the "chips". That is, the symptom—the visible appeal—versus the source. How did Joseph get his focus? Why did it work?

The proof that Joseph's belief system was organized and sealed early in life is in his response: *"How then can I do this great wickedness, and sin against God?"* (Genesis 39:9, NKJV). That's *not* the first thing you say when a woman offers you sex...unless you have wrestled with the issue, decided what you would say if it went down that way, and repeatedly rehearsed your answer— or had lots of practice turning down women. And if he didn't label it as **sin** and speak God's name in microseconds, he had to have known he would have given in! Why? He's a man and all men have limits...or they are liars! Yes, ALL men!

So who gets to define sin? Actually God does...*if* you believe the Bible's contention that He is the ultimate Creator, Judge, and Authority. Want to know the kind of bible statements that made me mad as a pre-Christian skeptic? Lines like Psalm 12:4— *"those who say, 'By our tongues we will prevail; our own lips will defend us—who is lord over us?'"* (NIV). Meaning what? Simply this. If God is not your ultimate authority, the only alternative is that you assume that position, and become both the dictionary and the decision-maker. I was angry that Christians would attack my belief that I was actually in control of my life. But since the Bible defines reality, just because you announce you are in control of your life doesn't cancel God's authority. I've heard men announce that they are the boss in their marriage, too! If you stick with the illusion that "nobody is lord over you", then the question becomes: "Does it work?" not, "Are you happy with it?" The answer is that it doesn't *and* you're not, because *that* universe can't resolve ultimate questions (like forgiveness, love, and eternal life), and will always compete with the next guy's universe. Translation? Sex ≠ love. Money ≠ happiness. Success ≠ peace.

The implication is that unlike the American Constitution, God's definitions can't be amended or re-interpreted by any court or culture. Iconic definition? *Sin is any thought, decision, choice, or action that breaks one of God's rules* (see 1 John 3:4). At the core, it's just substituting our desire for His plan, and our pleasure for His praise. Every sin is an act of defiance against a Holy God, whether it's a secret random selfish thought, well-publicized raw greed in an investment scam, life-stealing reckless drunk driving, or socially-acceptable criticism of your boss. **Universal truth: everybody is driven to sin by the desire to cover-up a bigger issue: rejection of God's authority over their life.** Any substitute for total worship of a totally holy God qualifies as sin. Pushing back or rebelling against God, and His truth, is the *source* of all sin. It's what's happening underground—in your mind, emotions, and spirit. Above ground, breaking biblical commands is the fruit—the *symptom*—of that basic rejection of God's authority. Any and all sin creates spiritual death (*"the wages of sin is death"*, Romans 6:23, KJV). And people can miss God and heaven by just trying to be "good"—dealing only with the *symptom*. Going to rehab is a good choice, but it was never designed to fix the ultimate *source* issue. A husband can apologize for adultery and give his wife flowers, but there is a deeper heart issue that must be resolved. You can drill wells and fund clean water all over Africa (which you should do!), but still never deal with your real soul-thirsts.

Joseph bundled his answer to his boss' wife with God's definition of sin— *"wickedness against God"*. When you can do that, it avoids another costly mistake—believing that you have to apologize for your beliefs, explain your motives, or defend your position! Don't take the bait! Satan capitalizes on your fear of offending the other person(s) involved, wanting you to feel obligated to hang around and explain, argue for the right to express your beliefs, defend your right to have a place in the group, moderate your position, or justify your weirdness to them. Normally, you don't even have the bonus time to make adjustments. When the issue on the floor is resisting temptation— *standing strong*—do it. But get it done and walk out! The longer you camp out on that yellow line in the middle of the highway, the greater the chances of you getting run over.

## Skinny Jeans

Satan would love for you to slow down and tone down the rhetoric because it signals you are keeping the door open for discussion and re-negotiation. There are times when it's not only okay to put up a **CLOSED** sign on a conversation, but it's the only right thing to do (Ephesians 4:26— *"don't give the devil a chance"*, CEV). Our spiritual enemy prefers you wearing "skinny" confidence, not just skinny jeans. Satan is always trying to locate an opening—a vulnerability in your thinking or desires or the skinniest uncertainty in your confidence—scanning your conversation and daily routine for gaps in your personal moral firewall. Satan knows that marginal confidence in either beliefs or method of response sets you up for major confusion. A *small* definition of sin leads to *big* mistakes. Weak answers are a gift to Satan!

Upside to convictions? Once convictions are defined they are hard to "undefine". And in the same universe, once you compromise convictions, it's really hard to rewind what you've said, done, or changed. Basically, people don't change much—or often—especially when those convictions are imbedded in a real life experience with God, the war in Iraq or Afghanistan, mom and dad in church, a civil rights movement, gay pride, cancer treatment, rape, Super Bowls, coaching soccer, or investing with Bernie Madoff. In order to win under pressure, your stand has to be ***believable, brief, bold***...*and yes*, ***biblical***. Why biblical? Obviously because it's the only truth and it works. But also because if you know deep in your soul that what you believe is a lie, or wrong, or totally destructive, at some point you will cave. You will walk away when the price tag of holding on to those beliefs exceeds the value you've placed on them. Simply stated, everybody has limits. Every conviction has a threshold. You've got a tipping point. People don't take abuse or die for stuff they think is worthless or they know is a lie.

Joseph's conviction was not based on what mama and daddy believed, how cool Jewish religion was, corporate ethical standards for slaves, or some romantic view of marriage. You don't play the "sin" card unless you actually believe God took a position on the issue and it matters...AND there are consequences...AND you will face God one day and have to explain before you get judged. An eternal destination is at stake in God's commands, rules, and laws. In fact, use the "S" word ("Sin") today in a conversation, an interview on talk shows or cable news, research article, political decision, or party, and you'll get laughs, be called narrow-minded and bigoted, be labeled as outdated, and generally be caricatured as a religious freak. However, if your convictions are based on the truth of God's Word and not culture or convenience, you will NOT make a mistake. Point? Olympic-style training with scripture wins. You gotta really *study* the Bible *consistently* or you're going to bite on whatever is in the next pretty package.

## Under-Performing?

By the way, when God labels something as "sin" in His Word, the Bible, His purpose is always protection. Sin is normally interpreted to mean that God is calling your fun off limits—that God is all about postponing or ruining what makes life enjoyable. The average person views biblical precepts as restrictive, and the God who wrote and manages them as repressive. *Freedom is the result of having the power NOT to be enslaved to, owned by, addicted to, or captured by, any desire, person, experience, or idol.* It is NOT the right to chase whatever your body, mind, or emotions tell you.

Just to be *laser*-honest, the Bible says that a non-believer's life without God makes them "dead" spiritually in their sins (unresponsive to God), ignorantly performing for Satan (who temporarily rules the planet), and slaves to whatever spontaneous thoughts or desires surge through their minds and bodies (see Ephesians 2:1-3). Application? A big reason that extra-marital or pre-marital or casual sex is a category 1 sin with God is because He intends to protect the institutions of marriage and family—the very foundation of a society. Life does not equal sex…or any other desire. There's a bigger purpose.

## Sin and Domino's Pizza

Besides, casual sex (or ANY other unchecked desire for that matter) only creates a desire for more that can never ultimately be satisfied. That's just a basic reality. You can't change it. A recent *desire-based* trend (March, 2011) was a website started at the University of Chicago (not affiliated with UNC), exclusively for college students who simply wanted to hook-up for casual sex, called *.eduHOOKUPS*. A random UNC student said that the school's reputation was "Where fun goes to die," and obviously somebody wanted to change that image. The trailer was that as the site expands nationally, there was no expectation of any long-term relationship. Opinions were split between outrage and "so what?" attitudes. One skeptical, not necessarily moral, post to the site quickly challenged: "$20 says this site is all dudes." They claimed that "chastity is curable if detected early." What you would get apparently, is organic sex—ordered, packaged, and shipped separately from friendship…or love…or marriage…or trust…or future plans. But in reality…not consequence-free. It never is. The deception—the ridiculously obvious scam—is that all that stuff is what we really chase on the "soul level" but think it can be experienced somewhere during or after the hook-up.

There's more really scary news about choices that break God's rules. It's in the fine print. You'd think an attorney wrote it, because nobody really wants to think about it until "after". Here goes: **any sin is an artificial, quick fix for the real stuff your soul craves, and will always leave you wanting more.** It never fills you up…never satisfies completely. Commit it once and there will be a stronger desire to do it again next time. And the next time, it takes more rush or more risk to keep the physical or emotional high at the same level. Unlike Domino's Pizza, sin *doesn't* deliver! Lasting fulfillment, that is. By definition then, sin is not only attractive and fun, it's uncontrollably addictive. That's why there are tons of biblical warning labels: *"I beg you to avoid the evil things your bodies want to do that fight against your soul"* (1 Peter 2:11, NCV). Hosea 4:11-12 says even people who believe in God lose their understanding—specifically, have their **heart enslaved**—when they participate in casual sex and drinking.

Outcome? SIN CAN MAKE YOU STUPID! You want to go back and do it again! Sin has the power to capture and control you because it is universally (i.e., in **all** cases and places) *"deceitful"* (e.g., Matthew 13:22— *"deceitfulness of riches"* and Ephesians 4:22— *"deceitful lusts"*, NKJV). Yes, it's possible for someone to be totally oblivious to making the wrong choice and messing up their life because they are fooled by the packaging. Even devoted followers of Jesus are capable of being deceived. The Bible pronounces you a *liar* and *self-deceived* if you, as a believer in Jesus, argue that you don't sin (1 John 1:8).

At first, sin is SWEET! But eventually, sin causes you to lose the ability to hear God's voice and think right about God, yourself, choices, consequences. At some point you will throw away everything you've worked for to enjoy a temporary indulgence (i.e., *"the fleeting pleasures of sin"*, Hebrews 11:25, NIV). The biblical terminology for that is "hardening" your heart (see Exodus 9:34 / Mark 6:52 / Acts 19:9). Capitalizing on the analogy of that language, the heart becomes like concrete, thoughts and emotions almost impenetrable, where neither God nor friends seem to be able to get through to you. It's like you put up a big wall to keep friends who care, God, and truth out of your space and mind. Keep chasing and surrendering to the wrong stuff and you get locked-in to sin to the degree you not only don't want to deal with it— you CAN'T change, repent, or get out of it by yourself! What you once owned, will own you! And you will be powerless. Once you import sin, it's really hard to contain it, regain control, and replace it with the right thoughts and choices. Getting back to normal can get ridiculously hard when you can't control it, contain it, or cap it. Like a stray cat desperate for a meal that races inside when you open a door, because you are not the boss, you have to chase it down and set it back outside. And just saying, "It's the new normal" is not an answer and doesn't solve anything.

FACT: Fulfillment is sourced in the soul, in exclusive worship of the One who created you. Sex or success can be idols substituted for worship of God just like anything else.

## Confusion Isn't 1 of America's 57 States…is it?

Just saying that he wasn't interested, or that somebody might find out, would not have been an adequate defense for Joseph. Totally incomplete. That kind of a reply means you've already hedged what you believe. And, on the other end of the response scale, knowing or believing the right stuff about

God does not guarantee you have God's power or protection. The implication here, though, is that Joseph was already a devoted God-worshipper, driven by a desire to honor God in the toughest moments and biggest decisions. It takes surrendering to God's Spirit inside of you, giving you clarity of thought and the courage to speak what's right. Just knowing biblical stuff doesn't automatically make you mature, strong, smart…or translate into successful life management.

When you know God intimately, you will love what He loves, and hate what He hates—namely sin—and your first thought will always be, "What can I do to honor Him and make Him known?" The closer you are to Jesus the easier it is to see what's right. The longer you wait to walk away from temptation, the more likely you are to give in to it. Resistance drops at warp speed if the temptation is intense and possible. It's an inverse relationship. Waiting makes you weaker. The longer you **stare** at a questionable opportunity without **standing**, *the more* you get confused and *the more* the temptation seems reasonable and non-threatening.

## No Dumpster Diving!

A new believer called, and in a panicked, desperate voice said he wanted me to come to his home. Something was wrong and he needed guidance; some real answers. No explanation. This was long before I got my concealed weapons permit, but I was prepared for the ultimate shock of some spontaneous confession. I knew he was already a miracle story, coming to know Jesus out of an unbelievably difficult background of dysfunctional family and jail time. After sitting down in his media room, he revealed what to him were the two worst possible scenarios. In a guilty tone, he dumped the first: "I've got to quit smoking. It's killing me. But I just can't seem to do it." Not what I expected. So with some relief, I looked around the room and discovered a carton of cigarettes on top of his TV. He continued, "I read my Bible. I pray. But I just keep doing it." Totally sincere but totally wrong. I asked him to explain to me how the cigarettes got into his living room. They didn't just magically appear! With some embarrassment, he confessed he bought them at a nearby convenience store. "There's your problem," I stated firmly. "Listen, you walked to the store, picked out your brand, paid for them, put them in a sack, carried them home, placed them on top of your TV, and started praying, 'God, help me not to give in.' And you pray constantly while you are staring at the cigarettes. You had plenty of opportunities at every step to prevent that from happening but you didn't." He got it.

Then he quickly shifted focus to his 15-year-old son, who had also just gone public with his belief in Jesus. Getting serious, he asked me to talk to his son because he had caught his son with some porn magazines. Since his son was open to dealing with it right then, we went to his bedroom for privacy and I asked him to explain. He told me that a friend had given him the magazines, and even though he felt in his heart that it was wrong, he couldn't seem to resist staring at the photos for hours. Then, basically because he had no biblical instruction and minimal parental guidance, but because the Holy Spirit that now lived in him was convicting him to take action, he had come up with his best strategy to avoid the porn and prevent the addiction: *hide the magazines under his bed and pray God would help him not to pull them out!* Both father and son committed the same mistake. Again, same principle: the longer you stare or hang out close to the wrong stuff, the weaker you become, and the more likely you are to rationalize participating. I recommended they put the cigarettes and the magazines in a dumpster they couldn't access later. SEPARATION, man! Get radical with sin! Throw the stuff into a dumpster…and no dumpster diving! You *have* to get that strategy down!

Here's a practical definition of confusion: *the result of negotiating with temptation and delaying a response.* Randy Raysbrook is more definitive:

> *"Life is a series of choices. Whether we are aware of it or not, we choose before the fact whether we will be victorious or suffer defeat. When we do not decide how we will respond to temptation before it occurs, we are choosing defeat by default.…Think through the various situations in which you might be called upon to compromise and decide an appropriate response before you face them: How will you respond to unwelcome advances on a date? Will you ask to be taken home? Will you explain your convictions? If your boss pressures you to be unethical in reporting certain business expenses, what will you do? Will you refuse and quit? Will you appeal to your supervisor and try to reason with him? If someone pours you a drink at a party and you feel that it is wrong for you to drink, how will you react? What will you say? Decide your position on these issues before the heat of the moment. Otherwise you might begin to bend a little to avoid offending someone."*[10]

### You ain't no Peyton Manning!

The scripture offers multiple effective and proven strategies to deal with temptation. Many are issue-specific, depending upon the category, frequency, and intensity of the temptation. With some temptations, like adultery, you don't investigate, debate, or think—you RUN! (1 Corinthians 6:18— *"Run from sexual sin!"*, NLT). Mostly because when it comes to sex, your hormones or emotions do your thinking for you.

Survival depends upon the principle of preparation—just ask Bear Grilles.[11] He didn't reach the peak of Mt. Everest at age 23 without intense training, mapping the slopes, packing the right gear, and studying the history of previous expeditions in order not to repeat fatal mistakes.

Be ready for the lack of oxygen at the summit. It's hard to think clearly in the pressure of the moment. Things get blurry when your boss tells you to exaggerate or cover up in the sales pitch, a friend offers you answers to the test, a co-worker attacks a friend in your presence, a girl at school offers sex, or a drunk driver totals your car. Will you yell, cuss, confront, argue, refuse, lecture, leave, forgive, give in, expose, sue, or remain silent? It's your choice. A lot is at stake. God's watching. Just thinking *"No worries. I'll think of something,"* usually becomes the 6 words put on your headstone when they bury you.

You must choose ahead of time what you will say and do. Rehearse your lines. Know the scripture that fits. Have an escape plan. Be more prepared than Jason Bourne in an assassination attempt. Unless you are Peyton Manning, quarterback of the NFL's Indianapolis Colts—who can use an audible at the line of scrimmage like a heart surgeon uses a surgical instrument—you can't wait until you are in the moment to figure out where you stand or what's right to do.

Here's why. You aren't as strong as you think and Satan is the best salesperson who ever lived. His pitch is so good—in a bad way, of course. Satan wants you to believe that the *next* experience is the one that will make you happy. So create real boundaries. Blurry lines and fuzzy beliefs are like IED's[12]—they make casualties—really fast. Speak out against your temptation. Name it. Put some light on it. Bring it out into the open. Make it sound and feel shameful. Make somebody in the room feel guilty about even considering an alternative that dishonors God. The very moment you are confronted with temptation, choose to do the right thing. STAY ON THE OFFENSE! Here's a bonus strategy: Go positive. Expose the stupidity of sin. David Letterman is a pro at it. Letterman does it nightly on his show—and does it well—usually with his Top Ten lists…and people laugh and applaud. You want to look smart and strong, not stupid and vulnerable, when you hit the intersection of temptation and truth. God seems more real to you *and* skeptics when you get serious, loud if necessary, bold, and clear. Pick your position and stick with it…for God's sake! Really.

In reality, there is less pressure later because you don't have to keep explaining your position. There's no federal law that says you have to apologize for *NOT* participating in the sinful stuff that weights you down and wears you out. It's not a felony if you refuse to answer everybody's questions or objections to your beliefs. You don't owe anything to anybody except God. Mess up though, and it *is* law that you have to explain to God why you turned on Him! In most cases, you will actually get weaker and sloppier if you stick around and argue or defend what you are doing that's right. The quicker you speak and the more often you speak up, the bolder and stronger you become.

## The "IN-Convenience" Store

People are fascinated by boldness in any form. Whether it is the evil to rob banks, fearlessness to skydive, the risk-loving enterprise to start a business, the heroism to rescue someone in a burning building, or the courage to vote against the majority in Congress, we have an inexplicable, sometimes even almost sick curiosity with those who act on their convictions. Like a morbid preoccupation with Lee Harvey Oswald's role in the November 22, 1963 assassination of President John F. Kennedy.

Or curiosity with boldness like in the dramatic struggle to save a baby on November 24, 2010. A couple had stopped at a Kansas City, Missouri gas station to fuel up during their move from Colorado to Missouri. With the car running after the fill-up and their 6-month-old inside, Aaron and Melanie Richman, both 22, stepped away from the car to talk with their friends. Surveillance video showed a man who appeared to be entering the convenience store but suddenly jumped into their car, backed it out, and tried to speed away. Without even thinking, Aaron jumped into the car, while Melanie was being dragged through the parking lot, clinging to the passenger door. Inside the vehicle, police said, Aaron hit and kicked the driver as he tried to save his child. The beating caused the carjacker to crash the car. Their baby was saved but the evil man remains at large. What would you have done? Their conviction, that their child was more important than their own lives, kicked-in immediately and their baby was saved.

A conviction is natural. It spills out in a crisis. Nobody can force a conviction on you. It's what you know is true to the degree that you don't even think about checking polls, coming up with talking points, thinking about who you'll have to explain to, or dancing around the issue. Boldness comes from convictions.[13] And just like Joseph in our biblical example, you and I have to speak and act on those convictions up front—decisively and early—to survive.

Regardless of whether the boldness is instinctive or insidious, illegal or legal, ethical or unethical—boldness tends to create more boldness. Want to be bold? Act bold! In fact, pray for it and you'll get it, like the early disciples of Jesus in the first church in Jerusalem (see Acts 4:29-31). Rather than pray for relief from persecution and beatings, they asked God for boldness to keep speaking the message of Jesus. Want to be wise? Start acting smart! Here's a universal reality: the more you practice doing something, the more entrenched and natural a response it becomes. If it's recklessness with temptation, over time your decision-making process and conscience will gradually adjust to the new reality. Giving in to temptation will seem less radical and more reasonable. What is morally uncomfortable or questionable in the beginning will become spiritually tolerable if repeated. The second lie is always easier than the first. There's a bizarre and deadly side effect of compromise. Within minutes, you start feeling really comfortable with it. *In fact, if you keep putting the sinful, negative stuff in your backpack, not only will you quickly and almost imperceptibly begin to enjoy it, you'll start defending it or bragging about how tolerant and trendy you are!*

Yes, there's more. And NO, it's not a happy ending. At the end of the day, you will be miserable, empty, and feeling worthless, like the young, wealthy heir that partied his way through his entire fortune (see Luke 15:17-19).

How embarrassing and humiliating that any temptation could own a believer in Jesus! Totally wrong optic. Three things should never happen. Presidents should never do anything that could result in impeachment. Coca-Cola should never change their classic recipe again. And believers should never be caught doing something stupid!

*Chapter 13*

# Bully-Proof!

Most bullying occurs from the fourth through the eighth grades, which makes school a really scary place, according to Steve Henson, Senior Writer and Editor for *Yahoo!* Sports. "Experts say that more than 150,000 children miss school every day because they are afraid of being bullied. More than half of all schoolchildren have witnessed a bullying incident and three of every four students say bullying is a problem at their school."[1] Gracie Academy in Torrance, California even offers an intense 5-day self-defense training program to give kids a blueprint for handling bullies and building self-confidence.[2] In another category, anybody can be "bullied" by simple, ordinary, everyday temptations. There's a free self-defense training program available to become *temptation bully-proof!*

### 4th Right Choice: Be consistent.

A successfully proven way to get past temptation is simply to avoid it if possible. No drug addict ever took the first hit believing and hoping to achieve a lifetime addiction and destroy as many lives as possible. Every druggie started with just the thought of escape for that moment. If you don't go to the party, it's 100% certain you won't drink or shoot up.

But...and this is where most of us are at...when you can't change your job, commute, office location, schedule, friends, itinerary, home, team, class, locker, school, family, co-workers, boss, clients, or contracts, Plan B is activated—you have to **be consistent** in your resistance. Even if the argument changes daily or the offer improves, sticking with your original position will make the difference. It doesn't make any difference if you are a minority of one—the only one committed to what is right. Your only chance of survival is to resist even the smallest, most insignificant concession to what you know is risky behavior when you are surrounded or closed in by serious pressure to compromise.

Open the door and you may not be able to shut it later, even if you want to. The late Pastor Adrian Rogers once said, "What you are in the small things is what you are. What you are in the secret things is what you are." Joseph revealed his character in those secret encounters set up by an Egyptian star of a "Sex and The City"-style production. Genesis 39:10 illustrates that under steady, sustained, relentless pressure that never took a day off, Joseph held his ground and refused sex with Mrs. Potiphar: *"She kept putting pressure on Joseph day after day, but he refused to sleep with her"* (NLT). Not just once. Every day. EVERY day. Joseph could count on his boss' wife giving her offer a different spin every time he showed up for work. He knew he would have to face it. She obsessed with marketing her stuff. Whatever he decided to do in response had to *meet and exceed* the skill, deception, desire, frequency, and force of her appeal—*or he loses.* It's not like he could feel good about himself and his integrity if he slept with her only 3 days out of 7. And the ironic thing about this kind of conflict? It's never locked in to one level of exchange. The words get sharper, the responses more tricky, and the sensitivity more acute. Tension didn't decrease by Friday of each week—it increased!

By definition, achieving consistency means somebody else could care less about your mistakes or mess. The crowd is party-driven and you are stuck with trying to be pure, right? For consistency to resonate from your example, you have to process doubts about losing your own mind when they surface. When everybody else seems to disagree or oppose you, it makes you feel like you could be wrong, or at least should re-think your convictions. Maybe you are too extreme in your views? That's a frequent criticism in American culture. Be more tolerant. Loosen up. Have a bipartisan approach. By the way, in American politics that usually can be translated, "Give up your position and agree with me." After all, you don't have a monopoly on the truth, right?

## The Mistake That Killed Lincoln

It was Saturday, March 4, 1865. Exhausted by the demands of leading a country through a Civil War but hopeful that the South's great leader, General Robert E. Lee, pinned down for 250 days at Petersburg, Virginia, would soon surrender, President Abraham Lincoln walked through rain toward the inaugural platform. In their New York Times No. 1 best-selling book, *Killing Lincoln*, co-authors Bill O'Reilly and Martin Dugard describe the scene: "Fifty thousand men and women stand in pouring rain and ankle-deep mud to watch Abraham Lincoln take the oath of office to begin his second term. His new vice president, Andrew Johnson, has just delivered a red-faced, drunken, twenty-minute ramble vilifying the South that has left the crowd squirming, embarrassed by Johnson's inebriation. So when Lincoln steps up to the podium and delivers an eloquent appeal for reunification, the spiritual message of his second inaugural address is all the more uplifting. 'With malice toward none, with charity for all, with firmness in the right as God gives us to see the right, let us strive on to finish the work we are in, to bind up the nation's wounds...'".[3] But nobody was aware of the seething, pathological bitterness toward the President and the North that was about to explode from the heart of a man near the front of the crowd. A dashing, charismatic, 26-year-old successful Broadway stage actor, John Wilkes Booth, was about to trigger a long-planned conspiracy—a well-timed assassination plot. Even though a determined Lincoln suspected he might not have long to live, he could not have known Booth's hatred would be delivered with a bullet in Ford's Theater just 6 weeks later. The amazing trivia fact is that it might have been prevented! O'Reilly and Dugard note, "Just before Lincoln's speech, as the president stepped out onto the East Portico, Booth's carefully crafted conspiracy was instantly forgotten. Though he had no gun or knife, Booth lunged at Lincoln. An officer from Washington's Metropolitan Police, a force known to be heavily infiltrated by Confederate sympathizers, grabbed him hard by the arm and pulled him back. Booth struggles, which only made Officer John William Westfall grasp him tighter. Like everyone else in the city, Westfall is well aware that there are plots against Lincoln's life. Some say it's not a matter of if but when the president will die. Yet rather than arrest Booth, or even pull him aside for questioning, Westfall accepted Booth's excuse that he merely stumbled."[4] A big mistake. The evil was not confronted, so it was never exposed. The assassination may never have happened if Westfall had been *consistent*— just followed through on the right thing to do.

### Will you go to the Prom with me?

Consistency is a big deal. As I write this chapter, the consistency issue is making national news again everywhere. ABC World News reported a bus driver caught on video with a cell phone in each hand...while driving! A government official just released a story that U.S. Navy Seals discovered a huge stash of pornography in the bedroom of Osama bin Laden during the raid on his compound in which he was killed. So much for the terrorist leader's rants against American morals. Then, Shelton, Connecticut High School senior James Tate was suspended from school (and by default, the prom) for hanging a prom invitation in 12-inch cardboard letters on the school entrance. According to the school's Headmaster, Ms. Rodriguez, this was a violation of historic school rules. The consequences, including exclusion from prom, had been explained multiple times to the seniors prior to this incident. However, after 10,000 tweets, 175,000 hits on a newly created Facebook page to rally support for him, and a state legislator writing an appeal, the Principal reversed the decision, promising to review the violations on a case-by-case basis. Apparently, rules are okay until somebody popular violates them or you can exert enough pressure to make those in authority back down. Inconsistency in any venue sends a message that you really can't believe what somebody says, and that you don't always have to play by the rules. It not only creates confusion. It creates anger.

*Consistency in choices is the discipline and courage to maintain your position on an issue even when it doesn't seem worth it.* After all, consistency is important in everything from respecting courtroom procedure, to umpire calls, judging on American Idol, making Subway sandwiches, completing IRS forms, printing $20 bills, or following the recipe for Twinkies. Subway is known to have asked applicants during employment interviews to name the most important part of one of their sandwiches. Answer? The smile. Apparently it works, because they are all about consistency. But I always thought it was the fresh bread.

There was nothing Joseph could change about his role or his residence, so…he didn't change his resistance! No negotiation. No weakening. No sell-out. No adjusting his beliefs downward. No thought of "doing it" once and moving on. But why should he have accommodated her, even if she had authority and influence? He was in the right! Somewhere in the mix of daily suggestive remarks, provocative poses, and strategic touching from the cougar, the tense drama between them morphed into a battle of wills. She was leveraging her power to pull him down. Joseph knew it wasn't about sex. It was a threat. She owned him…or on paper, at least 50% of him if ancient Egypt had marital property laws like California.

It was literally a "power grab"…no pun intended. The cougar wanted him, plain and simple. Maybe she always got what she wanted. Maybe she was abused as a young girl or as a wife. Maybe it was just what socialites or Egyptian "desperate housewives" did in those days. Maybe it was all the above, but at a minimum, it was a sense of entitlement. No love. Even if he caved, there would be no relationship. And that's the dirty little secret that your obnoxious friend(s) have withheld on you. Once you agree to do what they are enticing you to do, it's over. They have no need for you. Why? The game is over. They won. You went down their way. You became like them.

### Virgin is not JUST an Airline!

One high-school girl who went public with a purity vow, promising to abstain from sex until marriage and remain a virgin, was routinely taunted and brutally harassed by other girls who were sexually active. After a sustained resistance, she took her final stand: "I can become like you anytime I want, but you can never be like me again." Wow! That could be voted No. 1 comeback of the year. But her point is valid. Compromise with sin leaves scars. You can survive some accidents but still have the scars.

On the flip side, truth is, when Jesus forgives you, your purity is restored in God's eyes. Because Jesus paid once and for all the punishment for your sin, when you surrender your life to Him, He changes your status before God, giving you right standing, accepting you as though you had never sinned! (see

Psalm 103:12 / Ephesians 1:7 / 2 Corinthians 5:21). Romans 8:1 explains that there's no condemnation—*that means no guilt, no accusation, no attack, no bringing up your past, no punishment*—from God toward anybody who has turned from rebellion and become a lifetime follower of Jesus.

## Hotel California and iTunes

"You can check-out any time you like, but you can never leave!'" Those are the final words of *Hotel California*, the iconic 1976 song from the biggest selling American band in history, *The Eagles*. Drummer and lead vocalist, Don Henley, one of the founding members, said the song was "really about the excesses of American culture and certain girls we knew."[5] The lyrics at the beginning tell the story of a guy checking out a girl in a doorway, saying, "And I was thinking to myself, 'This could be Heaven or this could be Hell'". Okay. He gets it.

So…back to our little "resistance movement" point. Once you give in to the pressure, it's not the outcome you think. It could be Hell, like Henley said. You give up and *they* win. Why? No more challenge. It never is about being a part of their life or their group or their network. It's about whether or not you'll keep playing their games and repeating the party talking points. You will be "de-friended" quicker than a 4G iTunes download—like so 27 seconds ago! You are entertainment, an experiment, a barrier, an escape, a challenge, a laugh—something they want to experience, conquer, use, brag about, and discard like a used napkin when they are done with you. Giving in is way overrated. In fact, it's a lie.

That's why you have to stay in control. Be consistent in holding the line. Like Ephesians 6:13-14 says, once you've done everything you can do, just stand, man!

> *Be prepared. You're up against far more than you can handle*
> *on your own. Take all the help you can get, every weapon*
> *God has issued, so that when it's all over but the shouting you'll*
> *still be on your feet.*
> (The Message)
> *Therefore put on the full armor of God, so that when the day*
> *of evil comes, you may be able to stand your ground, and after*
> *you have done everything, to stand.*
> (NIV)

## CHRISTMAS Memories with Senator John McCain

Too many quit right before the breakthrough. Former Presidential candidate, long-time Arizona Senator, and true American patriot, John McCain, endured unbelievable torture for 7 years as a POW in Vietnamese prison camps, and emerged a confirmed hero. In McCain's memoir, *Faith of My*

*Fathers,* he talked about one unexpected private moment with a Vietnamese gun guard that brought him encouragement in his resistance:

> *On Christmas Day, we were always treated to a better-than-usual dinner. We were also allowed to stand outside our cells for five minutes to exercise or to just look at the trees in the sky. One Christmas, a few months after the gun guard had inexplicably come to my assistance during my long night in the interrogation room, I was standing in the dirt courtyard when I saw him approach me. He walked up and stood silently next to me. Again he didn't smile or look at me. He just stared at the ground in front of us. After a few moments had passed he rather nonchalantly used his sandaled foot to draw a cross in the dirt. We both stood wordlessly looking at the cross until, after a minute or two, he rubbed it out and walked away. I saw my good Samaritan often after the Christmas when we venerated the cross together.*[6]

When you keep on standing up for what God wants, you get God's strength, and you WILL make it! It's not impossible—no matter how hot the other person looks, how good the stuff makes you feel, or how easy you can do it.

## Consistency in Iran

As I write this, 34-year-old Iranian Christian Pastor, Youcef Nadarkhani, a follower of Christ since his teenage years and a pastor for over 10 years, remains in prison in Lakan, but may have received his final execution order. Youcef was arrested in 2009 by the secret police because he protested a government policy requiring the school attended by his two sons, Daniel and Yoel, to teach all children Islam, including those from Christian families. At his initial hearings the court pronounced him a Muslim because his parents were Muslim, and demanded he recant (see Acts 4:13-21). He refused. His faith endured. He was running his life-race with excellence, looking to the author and finisher of his faith, Jesus. Because he did not compromise, his wife Fatemah was arrested, charged with apostasy, and spent four months in prison in a failed attempt to increase the pressure on him. Authorities doubled-down, threatening to take their children away and give them to a Muslim family. In 2011, Youcef's death sentence—to be hanged for the crime of apostasy—was upheld by the Supreme Court. Islam is the official religion in Iran, and according to the CIA, 98 percent of the country's population is Muslim.[7] Even the White House has weighed in on this basic human rights issue with an unambiguous statement: "This action is yet another shocking breach of Iran's international obligations, its own constitution, and stated religious values....The United States stands in solidarity with Pastor Nadarkhani, his

family, and all those who seek to practice their religion without fear of persecution—a fundamental and universal human right."[8]

PresentTruth Ministries, a global advocacy group for persecuted Christians reported:

> During one hearing he was told to recant and he responded,
> "You ask me to recant. Recant means to return. What do you
> wish me to return to? The blasphemy that I was in before
> Christ?" The judges responded, "To the religion of your
> ancestors, Islam." Youcef replied, "I cannot." The Muslim
> attorney that is working to help him had this to say about his
> client, "Physically he looks weak but emotionally his belief in
> Christ is keeping his spirits high."[9]

That is God's definition of consistency!  Under Islamic Sharia Law, an
apostate has three days to recant.  Youcef missed their deadline...but honored
God's deadline for sticking with his message!  Only God's grace could sustain
a person to that level under all those threats: *"But He said to me, 'My grace is
enough for you. When you are weak, my power is made perfect in you.' So I am
very happy to brag about my weaknesses. Then Christ's power can live in me. For
this reason I am happy when I have weaknesses, insults, hard times, sufferings, and
all kinds of troubles for Christ. Because when I am weak, then I am truly strong"*
(2 Corinthians 12:9-10, NCV).

Back to the *original* ridiculously insane and evil, and strikingly similar,
Middle Eastern justice story. Mrs. Potiphar had Joseph thrown into jail with
a false accusation when she couldn't bring him down (see Genesis 39:13-20),
proving her real motive was using sex for control.  But Joseph won.  **Listen,
when that happened, God was exposing her sin, not punishing Joseph!**
Our theology of "suffering" is often so twisted.  Start praising God when you
have to pay a price for doing what is right!  Testing is temporary.  Truth is eternal.  The Word of God cannot be stopped—it is not limited or *"bound"* (2
Timothy 2:9, KJV).  When your convictions cost you something, you suddenly realize they are worth something!  What an honor to suffer for the name
of wonderful Lord Jesus!  Getting noticed for refusing to deny God gets Him
noticed!  Believers exist to spread the fame of Jesus!  The apostle Peter told
some persecuted believers to suck it up and re-frame their situations: *"Friends,
when life gets really difficult, don't jump to the conclusion that God isn't on the job.
Instead, be glad that you are in the very thick of what Christ experienced. This is
a spiritual refining process, with glory just around the corner. If you're abused
because of Christ, count yourself fortunate. It's the Spirit of God and his glory in
you that brought you to the notice of others. If they're on you because you broke the
law or disturbed the peace, that's a different matter. But if it's because you're a
Christian, don't give it a second thought. Be proud of the distinguished status*

*reflected in that name!"* (1 Peter 4:12-16, The Message). The price tag for Joseph's determination to save his integrity was huge, but the price tag for selling out would have been worse—with her husband and God! His resistance was consistent. No flip-flop in his campaign.

Why? Because this is not a game. It's not just spring break craziness! This stuff is real. People get hurt. Lives are permanently damaged. In Bible framework, what you do with your body is actually a package deal that includes your soul. Every new random, casual, planned, spontaneous, 10-minute or sustained-relationship, protected or unprotected sexual encounter outside of marriage is like committing slow, spiritual suicide. Your soul dies in imperceptible stages. God did not design our bodies for casual sex—any more than for casual calories—but for His bigger, more fulfilling, and more protective purposes (see 1 Corinthians 6:13-17 / 1 Peter 5:23-24). Worst part? Because God made sex so insanely good, the dark side of sex and sin is rarely talked about. But it exists, Sherlock!

### *60 Minutes* and Breaking Silence

February 11, 2011. Cairo. Evening. More than 100,000 people jammed Tahrir Square in the spontaneous and uncontrolled celebration over the collapse of Egyptian President Hosni Mubarak's regime. Boldly pressing through the crowd was South African native, Lara Logan, a CBS *60 Minutes* correspondent, and a seasoned wartime reporter. Two Egyptian drivers and a personal bodyguard served as security, but when their TV camera battery unexpectedly died and the lights went out, Lara was jerked away by a mob screaming in Arabic, "Let's take her pants off." Her resistance and screams didn't work—except to excite and enrage their passion. When someone in the crowd falsely shouted she was a Jew, it was like throwing a match on gasoline. The savage assault turned deadly. In the only interview Lara has given (04-28-11), she talked with Scott Pelley of *60 Minutes* about the nightmare of being repeatedly brutally sexually assaulted for 25 minutes, and her body nearly being torn apart in the frenzy. As thoughts of her husband, 1-year-old daughter, and 2-year-old son raced through her mind, she reasoned: "I had to fight for them. And that's when I said, 'Okay, it's about staying alive now. I have to just surrender to the sexual assault. What more can they do now? They're inside you everywhere.' So the only thing to fight for, left to fight for, was my life...*[there]* was no doubt in my mind that I was in the process of dying. I thought, not only am I gonna die here, but it's gonna be just a torturous death that's going to go on forever and ever and ever." [10]

Lara was finally rescued by some Egyptian women and raced to safety by soldiers. Unimaginable horror. I can't get my mind around it. Everybody ought to be outraged! Why don't we riot for her? But listen to the perspective of this amazing and courageous woman:

*I felt like I had been given a second chance that I didn't deserve....One thing that I am extremely proud of...is...that I'd broken the silence on what all of us have experienced but never talk about....there are a lot of women who experience these kinds of things as journalists and they don't want it to stop their job because they do it for the same reasons as me—they are committed to what they do. They are not adrenaline junkies you know, they're not glory hounds, they do it because they believe in being journalists.*[11]

That's beyond powerful. It strikes at the core of our existence. Lara was powerless to hold off her attackers, but she won because she never surrendered ultimate power over her mind, soul, and response. Her strength is so evident. I pray that God will give her and her family total healing and peace.

What's the point? Simply this. When you hear about these kinds of incidents, in one sense it exposes the real evil and darkness that can happen with uncontrolled sexual desire. Sexual sin is explosive. Joseph could never take a break. His defense had to stay intact against the fresh daily tactics she used. On a sidebar, the very fact that anybody admits this kind of evil exists proves they believe there is some absolute standard of right and wrong, which I personally believe presumes the existence of a source of absolute truth...i.e., God. If you concede that point, or at least agree to keep reading, then in my view, second base would mean we are accountable because there are consequences for how we handle truth. Just another reason consistency with right choices matters.

Hope that makes sense.

No, better yet...hope that starts working for you!

## Chapter 14

# Option-Mania!

American culture is all about options. Consumers demand drive-thru lanes for ATM's and fast food; apps on phones for everything from Angry Birds, voice texting, ebooks, and Skype to Netflix; dating sites from match.com to eHarmony and seniorpeoplemeet.com; cruises with no set meal schedule; online classes and degrees; multiple worship times at churches, mosques, and synagogues; and even 11 different kinds of Individual Retirement Accounts. Maybe we're afraid we're going to miss something. Maybe it's fear of commitment. Maybe it's the rush from the adventure of constantly trying new stuff. Maybe it's the constant obsession with jamming our schedules and maximizing time to make us feel like we're actually in control. Maybe it's a symptom of people trying to fill their souls with security and pleasure in this world, while avoiding God. Maybe it's politics because we can blame anything on Washington, D.C. Or maybe the options exist because of good ol' capitalism, where business pursues profit and the customer *is* god? Maybe it's the independent spirit of Americans who freak out when any one thing threatens to control them. People can resign jobs or repeat driver's tests, switch up or switch out. Nobody in 2012 is buying the idea that they are stuck—whether it's divorce or returning an item at Wal-Mart. We love...*and will defend...* multiple-choice, especially when it equates to freedom. And still...options can be invaluable.

### 5th Right Choice: Use options.

Options work. Especially if you intend to win over temptation. But you have to prepare well and actually use the options to get past the enticements, the sales pitches, the visuals, and the aromas of temptation. Our problems begin when we think options to get past temptation are limited. Basically, there are **5 mistakes frequently made when you are attacked** and under pressure. Peter and John, radically bold followers of Jesus in 1st century

Jerusalem, avoided those 5 mistakes even while under huge stress! They were attacked by the Jewish high court and under threat of punishment if they refused to quit speaking about Jesus (see Acts 4:13-31). Their amazing strategy was to re-connect with other believers and pray. Are you kidding me? No. Prayer helped them avoid disastrous mistakes. Here's the 5 mistakes.

***First, it is a mistake to avoid prayer with other people.*** Rather than kill the story, these guys rallied their network and exposed the spiritual battle. When we area threatened, the natural reaction is to get even, cut off a relationship, quit a job, or spread bad information about the other person. God expects immediate, focused prayer. Not just telling somebody else what happened, but asking spiritually mature people to join you in prayer. When you appeal to God rather than retaliate, you break the power of bitterness and avoid ridiculously impulsive decisions made out of emotion. Praying with somebody else is like protection against trying to fix the problem on your own. It minimizes the anger and confusion, surfaces support, and creates a fresh perspective. You are, in effect, being accountable.

***Second, it is a mistake to think that getting attacked means you are out of God's will.*** Start confessing that God is in control (see Acts 4:24, 28). Listen, attacks are not random. God is in control and is BIGGER than the attack! He pre-determined that people would turn on Jesus and reject Him. So there's nothing weird about being attacked. Expect and embrace it as a part of the process. You are making a difference. Coming under scrutiny, having your motives questioned, being lied about, experiencing opposition, and enduring threats means you are having an impact—the message is getting through your words or lifestyle. Those attacks are like signs, confirming your role until God releases you from it. It means you are doing something right, just like Jesus. If Jesus had to die for some to believe, you are going to have to pay a price to bring people to Jesus! We live in an *entitlement-driven* culture in America. But you can't afford to give in to a *victim mentality*, as though believers are "entitled" to be treated special. Big mistake. If people trash you because of your convictions about honoring Jesus, then God will make His name known through you in a big way! (1 Peter 4:12-14). Here's another disclaimer: if you intentionally violate rules, disrespect people, or initiate controversy—just to be noticed, win an argument, or gain control—then *you* are wrong and God will judge *you* first, not your critics (see 1 Peter 4:15-19). By definition, the gospel message is controversial (1 Corinthians 1:18— *"the message about the cross doesn't make any sense to lost people"*, CEV), so anybody with biblical convictions—like Joseph—will get hammered. But like yo' momma said, "Don't you start any fights!" The other side wants you to believe you have to give up your convictions to please them, survive, and be successful. The subtle message of an attack is that your opposition gives you certain rights—not God! No, God is actually the source and the judge.

MY mistake happened at Panera Bread. After multiple cups of bold coffee, I was really hyper over a presentation to my friend across the table on a potential new facility I was researching for our church. As I flipped my laptop around for him to see the full screen, he asked to take a restroom break. While he was gone, I kept excitedly reviewing the details and rehearsing my talking points as I scanned the laptop screen—so focused that I didn't realize that I was simultaneously drinking his coffee! Not only was I scared I was going to get whatever disease he might have, but now I had a dilemma—would I confess it? None of that was funny, so quit laughing! I was drinking his coffee! Here's the bridge. If you let your attacker dictate how you feel or respond—you are drinking their coffee! You are swallowing their beliefs!

Non-believers may make *you* the issue—accuse you of being intolerant, divisive, difficult to work with, anti-intellectual, or obstructive—but that just confirms something. You are where you are supposed to be. God believes in you so much that He trusts you to be the person to best represent Him and not fold under pressure from an attacker. He has pre-determined that you be right next to the person He has targeted for salvation. He put you in the situation to create enough tension so people who disagree with you or want to disassemble you can see, that like Joseph, you have a bigger agenda than sex, career, partying, or lawsuits. Having to love crazy people is normal! Your unwavering stand is actually an act of love, building a bridge of truth and compassion for the other person to find God. Refusing to surrender what you believe is not crazy. It's consistent! God will use to drive the opposition crazy long enough for them to rethink, repent, or re-connect with Him. But God wants you to show out extreme love to those who speak evil of you or persecute you…all the way through their rebellion (Matthew 5:44).

**The third mistake is obsessing about the attack and the attacker.** The attack is not about you (see Acts 4:25). Normally, you are the innocent bystander. Angry people are striking back at God and you are simply in the way. It's easy to take attacks personally when you are just the convenient target as a believer for that person to reject God. You get attacked because they have a problem! You represent what they don't want to deal with—conviction, control, or change—giving up what they like. Pray for what they could be because when God saves them, they may be sitting beside you in worship. You've been praying for God to kill your enemies instead of killing your pride. Praying for your enemies will change you even if they don't change. There may be nobody else interceding for their soul. 1 Timothy 2:1 jerks self-pitying believers back to reality— *"Pray for everyone. Ask God to help and bless them all, and tell God how thankful you are for each of them"* (CEV). God's love is bigger than both of you. God loves them as much as He loves you. Don't limit God or put boundaries around them. Don't lean into bitterness or the "politics of personal destruction." Believe God can change them, the situation, or you! Do not take Satan's bait to talk about them, or prejudice yourself against them. Don't write them off, but let them see who Jesus is by your reactions.

**Fourth, it is a mistake to focus on winning the arguments.** Peter was praying to have the right response to the threats (see Acts 4:28-29). He didn't even pray to end them. Our role is not to defend ourselves, look smarter, humiliate the other person, get the last word in, or out-argue them.

**Fifth, it is a mistake to ask God for a bail-out, instead of boldness to keep speaking out.** The winning option is to ask God to keep you in the battle where your voice is most needed (see Acts 4:29). Don't quit before God releases you! Don't take His voice that's in you out of the marketplace. Pray for boldness to keep speaking! Joseph stayed. He also stayed strong. But he used options.

## Who Albert Pujols Wants To Be Like

He is the most feared hitter in major league baseball. He won the National League Rookie of the Year award in 2001, has since been selected as an All-Star nine times, has won the National League Most Valuable Player Award three times, has twice won the National League Hank Aaron Award, and has 2 World Series rings with the St. Louis Cardinals—2006 and 2011! He was raised in a campsite-like, poverty-stricken area in the Dominican Republic by his grandmother and other relatives. Sticks were used for bats. He would wad up newspaper for a ball to play baseball, and fold up milk cartons to cover his hands because a glove was an unaffordable luxury. He almost quit playing baseball when he was drafted in the 13th round of MLB. A decade later, The Pujols Family Foundation gives back to assist poor families and children with Down Syndrome like Albert and Deidre's daughter, Isabella. Albert Pujols is arguably not only the best player in professional baseball, but he's what's right about baseball. The bonus for me is his personal story:

> *"Over the last decade my life has radically changed. I went from being a kid with a dream in the Dominican Republic, to playing professional baseball, Rookie of the Year, National League MVP, and winning a Gold Glove and World Championship! What has not changed is my love for Jesus Christ. In the spring of 1998, my soon to be wife, Deidre, began sharing with me the love of Jesus. My most exciting moment came when I asked Jesus Christ to come into my life. If it weren't for Jesus, I would not be where I am today and my life would be without purpose. I've heard kids say they want to be just like me when they grow up. They should know I want to be just like Jesus."* [1]

That passion to be a devoted Jesus-follower is consistent with his passion and performance on the field. But let's get real. Nobody achieves his level of success without an insane amount of preparation. Yes, we'll concede he has a God-given gift, and attributes his success to Jesus. Even then…no way he comes to the plate without having prepared with thousands of swings in batting practice, research on the pitchers he will face, and listening to instruction from coaches on how to adjust to unexpected pitches.

In a similar way, Joseph had to get creative, daily adjusting to the appeals for sex from his boss' wife. He was obviously successful. Briefly. Here's the truth: no option fits all circumstances or lasts forever. You have to change it up or you'll go down.

Entrepreneur and best-selling author, Seth Godin, blogged a response to an idea in Malcolm Gladwell's book, *Outliers: The Story of Success*, that becoming a superstar at anything requires about 10,000 hours of hard work. He proposed an alternative view, referring to the need to get past the predictable *Dip* (the hard moment when you are tempted to quit): "You win when you become the best in the world, however 'best' and 'world' are defined by your market. In many mature markets, it takes 10,000 hours of preparation to win because most people give up after 5,000 hours. That's the only magic thing about 10k…it's a hard number to reach, so most people bail."[2]

He's right. Most people quit rather than finding a way to push through what Godin calls *The Dip*. In his book by the same name, he describes it as "the fifth job interview where they never even call you back….the garage band playing to any empty club in the middle of nowhere….the seventh time you fall…while learning to snowboard….the middle of the marathon, when the excitement of the starting gun is a dim memory, and the joy of the finish line is a distant dream."[3] With no backup but God, Joseph conquered *the dip* in his own life.

### National Treasure and the Semi-Secret Map?

Nicolas Cage and cast were amazing in the *National Treasure* movie series. The history fascinated me and the storyline details in the script were riveting. Yeah, I bought in. It seems totally plausible to me that there could be an invisible treasure map on the back of the Declaration of Independence and that Presidents could compile a *Book of Secrets*. When Genesis 39:10 tells us that Joseph *"kept out of her way as much as possible"* (NLT), we see the REAL overlooked, semi-secret treasure map: Run from what you can't resist.

Despite ratcheting up the pressure, the cougar was unsuccessful in her sexual advances because Joseph used multiple options to create distance: *"She kept putting pressure on Joseph day after day, but he refused to sleep with her, and he kept out of her way as much as possible"* (NLT). Planned avoidance. It's a tacit admission of your own weakness and really wise approach to something or somebody that could overpower your best intentions. Creating and using options implies that you would have to know your limits.

On June 5, 2011, a monster, 50 mile-wide and 10,000 feet-high wall of dust, blasted through Phoenix, Arizona, delaying flights and causing power outages for thousands of people. Like a similar scene from a 1999 movie, The Mummy, the dust storm overwhelmed the city. Nobody could outrun it. In the same way, when temptation accumulates to massive levels, the strategy is to evade, not engage! Stay and be blown away!

Both geography and exit strategies have to be a part of your plan. To avoid something is to abstain or bypass. How do you prepare? Have several comebacks ready, stay near a door, keep your cell phone nearby, make sure there's another appointment conveniently scheduled, have your mate or friend text you at a pre-arranged time, ask a co-worker to interrupt, expect your mate to check your email and browsing, never commit without praying first, or promise never to get in a car or room alone with the wrong person or stuff. When those options aren't feasible or available, just bypass—like driving around a bad accident clogging an interstate during rush hour—the people, or places, or situations where you know you'll be hit with difficult or impossible choices.

There are a couple of girls who have some of this protective "avoidance-style" strategy already provided for them by their daddy. Doug Giles, host of Clash Radio and popular conservative writer, explains in his book, *Raising Righteous & Rowdy Girls*, how he intends to protect his two daughters— 22-year-old Hannah, the journalist behind the ACORN prostitution and tax evasion sting; and, 19-year-old Regis, who hosts the website *girlsjustwannahaveguns.com* and a hunting show called "Primal Urge". In the chapter, "The Ten Commandments for My Daughter's Potential Boyfriends," the 5th commandment reads in part:

> *Thou shall understand that you are a boy talking to a man....I've been in many fights. I've shot at felons. I've spent years in Tae Kwon Do. I've traveled the planet. You, on the other hand, use Proactiv and drive a Ford Focus; therefore you will call me 'Mr. Giles' and my wife 'Mrs. Giles' until we tell you and different.*[4]

That's *gooooood* planning! And good parenting! Every dad with a daughter gets that!

## "Don't go Britney!"

To keep out of her way meant Joseph would be constantly thinking about any job or issue that could bring him into physical contact with this sex-obsessed person. Those would be dangerous intersections, so he would have bypassed it with adjustments to his schedule or responsibilities, possibly by putting layers of people or time protection between them.  Maybe, as house-hold manager, he assigned other slaves to prepare her meals and schedule, or negotiate her business deals.  Whatever options he chose bought him some much needed relief and time.  Every day you have avoided the situation that can kill you is another day of life.

By the way, this is just another prime example of a life-situation where the concept or belief or policy or approach of moderation—whatever you want to call it—fails.  It's like saying, "Party…but don't go Britney", referencing the addiction and meltdown of gifted pop singer, Britney Spears.  Moderation normally doesn't work for drinking any more than using other drugs.  But it absolutely fails the sex-ual temptation test.  Think about the reasoning.  What happens to Joseph if he chooses the "moderation" strategy to dealing with the potential extra-marital affair?  Maybe he reasons, *"I can control the conversation and my feelings.  After all, I've got a job to perform.  I don't want her or anybody else to think I'm a coward or can't handle pressure.  I don't have access to anybody else.  I deserve this anyway for all that's happened to me.  Just some kissing and touching.  I can stop it anytime."*  The sales pitch for moderation emphasizes—and relies upon—your ability to control what you are doing or experiencing PLUS block out what might happen next (i.e., consequences).  The sales pitch for abstinence or purity is based on the belief that you don't have to discuss abortions or STD's or guilt or broken promises if you choose not to have sex outside marriage, plus you'll never kill anybody as a drunk driver if you don't drink.

Listen to a casualty.  She has a name.  It's Alicia.  It might help *you* decide if you're still on the fence.  Check out what she says about "too far".

> *At the beginning of this year, I had a friend named Rick.  Rick and I would talk forever.  We became so close that our feelings developed into more romance than just a friendship.  We started dating, and one thing led to another.  I often wondered how far was too far, but I had decided I could stop whenever I wanted to.*
>
> *Whenever I was at Rick's house, we would always go to his bed-room to be alone.  He had such a large family that his room was the only place we could talk.  Innocently, we would sit on his bed.  After we started dating, it was harder to just sit there with each other.  Kissing came first, and we found it harder and harder to stop there.  Even after we became involved in heavy petting, I still believed I could stop before we actually did it.  After a few months of this, I found that I didn't want to stop.  Then one night it happened—we had sex.  It was worse than I could even imag-ine.  I felt dirty and very separated from God.  I hated myself for doing something I've grown up believing was so wrong.  I had the guiltiest feeling I've ever had.*

*Rick walked me to my car and asked me what was wrong. I burst into tears. I told him that I hated it. I never wanted to do it again. Then Rick told me that he loved me, and the weirdest thing was that I couldn't tell him I loved him back. I had no feelings for him anymore. We sat in front of his house for a long time. We both cried. We knew what we did together was wrong.*

*I didn't see Rick for three weeks because he was out of town. During that time I prayed about it, not knowing what else to do. While we were separated, I realized what a real Christian relationship should be like, and I also realized that the relationship Rick and I had was the total opposite. I learned what was right and reassessed my morals. I asked God for forgiveness and started my life over. I still care for Rick, but I know if we are to have a relationship, it must be based on God.*

*Now I know that "too far" doesn't mean only intercourse, but also the stages leading up to it. Too far is when you crave the physical more than the spiritual. Too far is when sexual thoughts take over your relationship. Too far is when you don't want to stop. It can be different for different people; it can be holding hands, kissing, or hugging. With God's help, I can be pure from this day on.*[5]

What's "too far"? Define it. Because you have to eventually explain it to God, yourself, and others. Define it. Or somebody else will define it for you. Use your options!

## 6th Right Choice: Compare prices.

The Urban Dictionary says "come on" is the single most persuasive phrase in the English language. It can mean things as diverse as to promote a certain image or to encourage someone to change. Or…something more powerful. When the wife of Joseph's boss made her big, final offer, *"Come on, sleep with me"* (Genesis 39:12, NLT), the words were 100% sexual and the offer was "hands on". Typical of these adrenalin-filled moments, it was passionate talk *and* touch. No hidden agenda. There was more. It was like waving a contract in his face. Once clothes are either dropped or ripped, there are few options left. So contracts and price tags matter. To survive, not just win, you've got to know the cost and know what you are willing to pay…and talk about that price tag regularly. Sin is a contract! Know the cost before you sign.

So…2 options…2 prices. Option 1 is **sex.** No limits. No boundaries. No stopping. No thinking. The sex will be *amazing*…and there's no consequences…for a while. Option 2 is **sanity.** Living in the real world, there are built-in results, outcomes, and paybacks for every choice. You can pretend gravity doesn't exist and jump off a cliff. Even if there is a huge rush as you fall, there is an abrupt stop in your future. Gravity exists whether you believe in it or not, or choose to respect or violate it. It's good, sobering, and healthy to be reminded of God's immutable laws of choice and consequences. It cuts through the fog of emotions and stirs fear of God.

Our culture isn't big on advertising real, or even potential, consequences, just choices—usually those promoting indulgence. There's never a photo of a deadly car accident in a beer commercial, or a photo of a broken family in a casino. We've bought in to a culture that exists by feeding on the lie of entitlement. Where's the congressional legislation that guarantees you are protected from really dumb decisions? Where's the fine print that says you don't have to pay? Why should you get a pass?

## America's BIGGEST problem

Contrary to what some well-intentioned advocates of Christianity believe, the biggest problem for an American culture in 2012 and beyond—with all the huge moral slippage already—is *not* homosexuality. It's adultery! Shocked? Shouldn't be if you actually read the Bible. God takes breaking a marriage vow as a personal attack from an enemy directed toward Him and He can't let that go without a response (see Malachi 2:13-17 / 1 Corinthians 6:9 / Hebrews 13:4 / James 4:4 / Revelation 21:8). The core institution of society is the family. The family is supposed to be the basic relationship network that makes God real and promotes a clear moral firewall. As the marriage goes, so goes the family and the nation. Unlike some politicians trying to save their own base, God will have a response.

With the national debt approaching a record $17 Trillion ceiling and unemployment and spending near critical mass, an increasing number of Americans fear our nation could implode. Multiple reasons are offered: economic tsunamis like 2008 that are driven by greed, losing our constitutional compass through an unchecked drift toward socialism, drowning the national budget with entitlement payments, having our identity stolen through tolerance of border violations, lowering of educational standards, selling our landmark institutions and corporations to foreign investors, or being held captive to real terror cells in our cities. If America does go down...and I mean crash like a plane without engines, not just another recession...then it will be the result of God's judgment, not just because of FOX News, Presidential decisions, NBC, Hollywood, CNN, scandals, lack of bi-partisanship, unwise policies, or insufficient planning by our government. Why? Because God has both created and sustained this nation. Even our founding fathers recognized the original idea source for freedom as our Creator, and recorded it permanently in America's Declaration of Independence so it wouldn't be misunderstood, lost, or tampered with by future generations: "We hold these truths to be self-evident, that all men are created equal, that they are endowed by their Creator with certain unalienable Rights".

A national collapse could happen because God, who has the original patent on the ideas that created this 200+ year old experiment in freedom, may check the box called judgment. God's methods of judgment vary depending upon the *scope* (how many people are influenced or impacted), *severity* (how deep you get involved), *sequence* (if you are just starting or have defiantly persisted after multiple warnings and clear conviction), and *saturation* of sin (i.e., frequency in the sense of whether the sin was a one-time deal or is constantly repeated). Scriptural examples of divine wrath cover a broad range on the scale of attention-getting—expulsion from a home, removal from a position of leadership, natural disasters (e.g., earthquakes), disease, famine, death of babies, being conquered by enemy nations, financial ruin, crop failures, plagues, allowing a nation to have the leader it wanted even though it led to disaster, and a simple guilty conscience. It's my personal belief that the worst imaginable scenario of judgment is just God walking away from an individual or nation. I don't know if God physically throws up His hands in disgust or not, but that's my imagery. God's patience and tolerance actually does have both a spiritual ceiling and a calendar "drop dead" deadline.[6] That's what the final book in the Bible, Revelation, is all about. Every nation on the planet, and every person left after believers are taken alive to heaven in the Rapture (the trigger event which unleashes the Anti-Christ, formation of a 1-world government, global currency, the 666 mark of the Beast loyalty and trading test, etc.), will be caught in a 7-year series of escalating judgments of unprecedented proportions to wrap up history as we know it. That's fairly serious and conclusive evidence that God's mercy can be capped and that divine intervention is real.

Being left alone, abandoned by God, totally separated from any hope of deliverance—which is the basic definition of the environment of Hell itself—is worse than all scary movies and real wars combined. Evil left unchecked, without mercy, love, or justice that is sourced in God's presence, only leaves chaos and insanity: *"Since they thought it foolish to acknowledge God, He abandoned them to their foolish thinking and let them do things that should never be done"* (Romans 1:28, NLT). Any judgment will ultimately be the result of indifference to God. Yes, homosexuality is identified as one of the causes for God's judgment and an illustration of extreme abuse of God's perfect design for sexuality, but there is an extensive list of other really destructive behaviors. And all of them are sourced in rejecting the truth about God while re-directing the worship He deserves to every temporary indulgence imaginable (see Romans 1:18-32). The epicenter of the problem is the "de-worshiping" of God. Single out the issue of homosexuality as the *elusive and exclusive* source of our moral confusion and you can rightly be called judgmental. Adultery is actually the larger crisis.

Someone said that committing adultery is actually the only sin that breaks all the other 9 commandments. Why do you think adultery made the cut for the 10 commandments? No commandment directly targets homosexuality. Only adultery. Why the glaring omission? I'm convinced it's because adultery is a *source* sin, not a symptom. Coming in at number 7 (see Exodus 20:14), marital faithfulness is the last wall of defense for family stability. Mostly because it represents trust—a protective barrier around the most sacred intimacy—and ultimately respect for a God who is totally pure and holy. Tear it down and all other sexual sin seems permissible and acceptable in comparison. By the way, it's also a leading source for abortions! Despite my deep respect and consistent support for the pro-life movement, abortion will continue to be an option for some people as long as there is tolerance for adultery.

## The Legend of Jesse James

Once adultery is tolerated in a church, community, office, Congress, Hollywood, or a nation, the floodgates open for any other violation of trust and purity. Then the debate shifts from *"What is right?"* to *"What about **my** rights?"* That's where we're at in 2012 American culture. But the national conscience is not completely seared (see 1 Timothy 4:2), as evidenced by the simultaneous sense of outrage against the role models exposed, and compassion for their victims, in the wake of an epidemic of celebrity confessions about semi-recent sex scandals that includes: golfer Tiger Woods, former President Clinton, New York's former Governor Spitzer, New York Congressman Anthony Weiner, South Carolina's ex-governor Sanford, former Vice-Presidential candidate John Edwards, ex-California Governor Arnold Schwarzenegger, and TV personality Jesse James. Jesse James actually confessed to cheating on his wife of 5 years, Oscar award-winning actress, Sandra Bullock.

Once known as the star of Discovery Channel's *Monster Garage*, Jesse James quickly became hated as the husband who cheated on "America's Sweetheart." In a strange twist, he said he wanted his wife Sandra to know that he was cheating. Listen to Jesse's *mea culpa*:

> *"During the midst of it, it made me feel horrible... I knew I wanted to get caught,"* James, 41, tells Nightline (in a teaser clip shown on Good Morning America Monday morning). *"I know for a fact what it was... it was me trying to self-sabotage my life."* James says he never meant to hurt his wife... *"I never in a million years... The last person I wanted to hurt or harm is her or the kids. I spent my whole life with the kids and with her trying to protect her and protect her from everything. The most hurt she's ever been caused is by the person who wanted to protect her,"* he says. *"It's really terrible and she's going to be hurt for a long time,"* he adds. *"I still really love her and care about her....I*

*think I'm the most hated man in the world now," he says. "I took*
*a pretty amazing life and amazing success and everything and*
*threw it away by my own hands."[7]*

Sad…but predictable. Jesse is right. All of us at some point fail…and feel
miserable…disrespecting the success and blessings given to us by God. It's like
bombing your own home! When we mishandle them, we lose…"by our own
hands!" Like *The Weather Channel* tracking approaching tornadoes, warnings
have been well-publicized in scripture. Jesse's brokenness is eerily rehearsed in
the nearly 3 millennia-old biblical book of Proverbs. In *multiple* chapters,
God provides *multiple* reasons NOT to buy in to an opportunity for adultery,
casual sex, pre-marital sex, or any kind of random sex. For Joseph's situation—
and those guys listed above…and *yours and mine*—here's my summary list
from Proverbs of those really bad consequences:

- ✓ *Strangers take advantage of you*
- ✓ *You lose wealth*
- ✓ *You waste away physically (because most of the time the other*
- ✓ *person isn't a virgin and disease is common)*
- ✓ *A ruined life, full of regret over lost opportunity for happiness*
  *and achievement*
- ✓ *God doesn't miss a move you make*
- ✓ *It leads to multiple bad decisions*
- ✓ *It can kill your body and soul*
- ✓ *You get trapped with no options*
- ✓ *The cheated mate wants revenge*
- ✓ *You do anything the other person wants[8]*

You don't have to be a celebrity or politician to get that reality check. The
truth is that we all face the same temptations: *"The temptations in your life are
no different from what others experience"* (1 Corinthians 10:13a, NLT). We've
all made big or ridiculous mistakes on some level, just like Jesse James. In that
sense, we ALL understand the legend of Jesse James!

## Why I Crossed Over

Actually, that's one of the reasons I became a devoted, life-time follower of
Jesus. I needed an answer—a permanent solution—for my big and ridiculous
mistakes: *"So then, since we have a great High Priest who has entered heaven,
Jesus the Son of God, let us hold firmly to what we believe. This High Priest of ours
understands our weaknesses, for he faced all of the same testings we do, yet he did
not sin. So let us come boldly to the throne of our gracious God. There we will
receive his mercy, and we will find grace to help us when we need it most"*

(Hebrews 4:14-16, NLT). Jesus not only faced the same stress, temptation, desires, and emotions I face but He never sinned one time in His response, AND He broke the power of sin for me through His sacrificial death on a cross. He became my substitute, taking the judgment I deserve and offering me total, unconditional acceptance in return: *"For God made Christ, who never sinned, to be the offering for our sin, so that we could be made right with God through Christ"* (2 Corinthians 5:21, NLT). Amazing! And more amazing to me is that He would give me the undeserved gift of forgiveness for my deliberate, intentional, pre-meditated, shameless rebellion and defiance toward Him and God the Father, plus set me free from those destructive impulses!

Don't miss the PLUS: *"He is so rich in kindness and grace that he purchased our freedom with the blood of his Son and forgave our sins....God saved you by his grace when you believed. And you can't take credit for this; it is a gift from God"* (Ephesians 1:7 & 2:8, NLT). It doesn't end there. He bundled another life-changing gift with forgiveness, by choosing to remove, on His own initiative, the record of my offenses: *"You were dead because of your sins and because your sinful nature was not yet cut away. Then God made you alive with Christ, for he forgave all our sins. He canceled the record of the charges against us and took it away by nailing it to the cross"* (Colossians 2:13-14, NLT). PLUS...the guilt is gone: *"There is no condemnation for those who belong to Christ"* (Romans 8:1, NLT).

That's MY Savior!

*Chapter 15*

# The White House Is Haunted!

British comic Russell Brand used humor to work through his immigration crisis on a trip to Japan in May, 2011 by 'Tweeting' jokes during his detention. When Brand jetted to Japan to join his then pop star wife, Katy Perry, on her world tour, he was allegedly held by immigration officials and subsequently deported due to his prior criminal convictions. Perry alerted the world to her husband's dilemma by writing in a post on Twitter.com, "My husband just got deported from Japan. I am so sad. I brought him all this way to show him my favorite place... It was for priors from over 10 years ago!" Brand also opened up about his situation on the social networking site, posting pictures of himself while in custody and making jokes about escaping. He tweeted, "Planning escape from Japanese custody. It's bloody hard to dig a tunnel with a chopstick...Stockholm syndrome kicking in. Just asked my guard out for (vegetarian) sushi. He giggled... Alcatraz! Shawshank Redemption! And now this! Ah, sweet blue bird of freedom!..."[1] Ha! Nice comebacks, Brand! He just wanted out. There are times when we really get what freedom means. Check out the reaction...better, *the choice*...in what I call the **ultimate escape**, as we continue our investigation of a guy detained in Egypt. He couldn't "tweet" his way out. It was a winning choice, even though it looked really bad. Hmmmm. Lose your job or lose your future? What would you choose?

## 7th Right Choice: Relocate immediately!

It is *impossible* to miss the will of God! I am worn out trying to convince—no, more like mostly comfort—the panicked next generation that believes somehow you can miss God's will. Like it's a well-protected secret and they are begging God to give it up? That's craziness! You can mess it up, but you can't miss it or misunderstand it. Why? There are at least three reasons.

*First, God communicates really well!* If you could totally miss God's will that would mean God failed Communication 101. That implies God could never get your attention long enough or penetrate the distractions well enough to adequately tell you the next step or clarify the big steps like career, marriage, dating, kids, investments, season tickets, home loans, ministry, or Mac vs. PC. God starts with the Bible. His will is revealed there totally. And then He sets up circumstances to get your attention, sends people to advise you, squeezes your conscience in the right direction, loads you up with necessary gifts and resources and contacts, exposes you to multiple experiences, and either gives you a surge of peace or withdraws your contentment to re-direct you to the right decision. God has plenty of options to introduce you to the right decision. And He uses them...in a way you can't ignore or explain the stuff away without looking like an idiot.

    ***Second, God has a specific will for everything.*** Some think it doesn't make any difference to God what career you choose (pick something to make you happy and more money will make you more happy) or who you marry, just as long as you choose somebody compatible that you can trust, believing that any relationship can work out. How ridiculous to assume that the same God who created the precision of the ocean tides and planetary rotations doesn't have a specific will about a life-time mate—i.e., a pre-determined plan that He wants you to follow to give you an amazing life and ministry together. God doesn't have problems coping and never gets confused. Unlike us, He is untouched by sin. We are damaged by sin. He is total Wisdom. Our lack of smart eventually gets outed. Your heart naturally leans toward selfishness and rebellion and you can be easily deceived in any decision (Jeremiah 17:9). That's why guys normally choose a girl's appearance over her college entrance exam scores. God isn't random. The biological mom and name for His Son were pre-chosen. The Bible even asserts that God selected ahead of time the nation, country, city, town, village, mountains, desert, or jungle where every person would originate or migrate; the family, language, and culture He wanted to shape them, and even their DOB (date of birth): *"God, who made the world and everything in it, since He is Lord of heaven and earth, does not dwell in temples made with hands. Nor is He worshiped with men's hands, as though He needed anything, since He gives to all life, breath, and all things. And He has made from one blood every nation of men to dwell on all the face of the earth, and **has determined their pre-appointed times and the boundaries of their dwellings** [emphasis mine], so that they should seek the Lord, in the hope that they might grope for Him and find Him, though He is not far from each one of us; for in Him we live and move and have our being..."* (Acts 17:24-28, NKJV). All of scripture portrays the sovereign God as having a specific plan for everything. For example, in the 60-plus Old Testament prophecies, with more than 300 references about the coming Messiah covering details from His birth city to His crucifixion that could only have been fulfilled in Jesus (see Luke 24:27 / John 5:46), every event was planned and perfectly timed for an eternal purpose. No coincidences. No accidents. Nor does God adjust His plans "in flight", moment-by-moment, based on your whims, choices, failures, flings, or surprises.   Proactive, not reactive.   Like author and bible teacher, John MacArthur, who argued the case against the belief in a God who just reacts to situations when he spoke about God's will for singles seeking dates and mates: "You don't go to an airport and take the first flight anywhere. You have a destination in mind." God's into *control*...not *commentary*.

**Third, God wants you to succeed.** Everything He does in your life is driven by love: *"For I know the thoughts that I think toward you, says the Lord, thoughts of peace and not of evil, to give you a future and a hope"* (Jeremiah 29:11, NKJV).  Thinking God might deliberately withhold information that could make you successful or mislead you so that you make the wrong decision is just...**wrong!**

Our problem is NEVER that we miss or even mis-understand what God expects in any decision.  Our tension is with obedience.  You can **reject** God's will (like Adam and Eve) or **resist** God's will (like Pharaoh in Egypt) or **run** from God's will (like Jonah boarding a ship to avoid going to Assyria), but you cannot say it was never revealed to you.  Truthfully, the more questions you ask, the more you debate a decision, the more tense or hyper you get over what to do...normally means that you don't want to obey what you already know God is telling you to do!  Knowing God's will begins with the source file: Scripture.  And seasoned believers will tell you it's almost never complicated. If you want direction, God will give it.  Most of the time it is black and white clear...and common-sense simple.  If God wanted His name and fame to spread, why wouldn't He make the guidelines, rules, boundaries, principles, and precepts easy to get?  He gives signs.  He sends advice through people.  He creates opportunities.  He opens doors.  He closes doors.  He whispers to your heart.  He shouts through your conscience.

Joseph RAN.  That was his simple solution.  Create distance quickly. EXIT.  Make an escape.  1 Corinthians 6:18 contains the simple, 1-word secret to **WINNNNNING!!!!!** (as Charlie Sheen would say) when faced with sexual temptation: "Run!"  When you are weak or unprepared for the compliments, the offers, the hormone rush, the emotions, or the visuals—GET OUT! These are the moments when GEOGRAPHY IS the issue.  Location matters. Ask Osama bin Laden.

Separation is a *good* strategy.  Bypassing the moment can be the *best* strategy.  Being in the same room or on the same website with your greatest temptation means the situation has the potential to go south...quickly!  *Never be ashamed* of respecting your limits.  Be *careful* about testing them.  Be *totally fearful* of violating them.

### Nelson Mandela Wasn't The First

When it's about survival, like it was for Joseph, give up whatever is required to protect your convictions, health, promises, reputation, purity, or integrity. When his boss's wife grabbed his coat, he jerked away and left it behind (Genesis 39:12). Better to lose a Polo than his purity. Remember, the goal is not to act smart, brave, convincing, or cool when you're about to give in to temptation. The goal is to honor God even if you do it on a dead run in the other direction. Risk-taking may be okay if you are an experienced bull-rider, Navy Seal, mountain climber, day-trader, or pilot, but not when you've done the math and it comes up: *temptation + your mental condition right now of guilt and confusion x your desires at the edge ÷ staying in front of the temptation too long =* **disaster**. At stake was his job *and* his life if he rejected the advances of this cougar, but Joseph knew honoring God was the best…really the *only* legitimate…long-term choice.

Rehearsing some good comebacks and listing ways to withdraw with honor is the ideal. There's really never a good excuse for being unprepared. But when that's not possible, look for the escape route. And look for your personalized escape lane—long *before* you get close to empty—with reasons to relocate. You own a guarantee that God will create and surface a way to get out of the situation: "*….God is faithful. He will not allow the temptation to be more than you can stand. When you are tempted, He will show you a way out so that you can endure*" (1 Corinthians 10:13b, NLT). That's His way of limiting the duration and intensity of the temptation. Because that's His role in temptation, you'll never be able to excuse sin because you won't be able to miss the EXIT sign. God doesn't tempt you or even allow you to be stretched beyond your ability to resist, run, or recognize the right choice (see James 1:13-15). He's for you!

Joseph being falsely accused of attempted rape and sent to prison was not punishment from a negligent or clueless God, but deliverance by a compassionate, attentive God. God honored Joseph's right choices by getting him out of a situation before he reached his limits and would lose the strength to resist.

Technically, prison was a promotion. Yes. Promotion! Don't think the story is impossible or unprecedented. Maybe our generation's version of the Joseph-story is the parallel life of Nelson Mandela, who survived a much longer 27-year political imprisonment near Cape Town, South Africa for his stand against the racially-prejudiced governmental policies of apartheid, to providentially be democratically elected as President. That is a genuine hero enduring for time span beyond what I can comprehend. Fast forward in Joseph's life, post-prison, post-bailout of Egypt's 7-year economic bust, post-reconciliation with his brothers, post-marriage and two kids, and post-rescue of 70 family members. Joseph could connect the dots. Translating his journey to his 11 panicked brothers, the powerful VP of Egypt summarized God's purpose for a life that spanned the hurt of rejection + slavery + prison + promotion: "*You tried to harm me, but God made it turn out for the best, so that He could save all these people, as He is now doing*" (Genesis 50:20, CEV).

Think about it. To create a track for a slave to ultimately land in the role of the vice-president of Egypt, his administrative acumen and insight needed exposure to Pharaoh. Without any normal means of access to Pharaoh for Joseph, if you were God, why not set up a humanly impossible scenario where Joseph is falsely accused so he can be "relocated" to the very prison where two members of Pharaoh's inner circle are housed? At least one of the prisoners from Pharaoh's administration would be prompted to promo Joseph as the smartest guy in to room to consult Pharaoh. Pharaoh was in panic over the bizarre and mysterious dream but was clueless about an impending national crisis of near economic collapse. When Joseph explained the dream to the supreme leader, and gave credit to God for its prophetic content...BOOM! Promotion! So the biblical slant is that God will not only make sure you recognize the **EXIT** sign but that you are rewarded for taking it!

## Brad Pitt and Survivor Guilt

What happens if you don't run? What happens if you STAY? Guilt. Long-term guilt. We've covered...no, we've camped out...on the "make-you-vomit-or-jump-off-a-bridge" type consequences of sexual sin—the typical marriage mess, financial losses, damaged reputation, disappointed friends, etc. But guilt seems to be the "endangered species" of recognized consequences. Maybe because most of our time is spent in denial and guilt-avoidance. Nobody seems to want to admit guilt, much less, guilty feelings or a guilty conscience. Yet there is a lot of behavior—from over-achievement to addiction—that is driven by the desire to make-up for guilt over some past sin, or suffocate the images, memories...or even the persistent voice of God.

In a recent interview, mega-celeb actor, Brad Pitt, admitted he struggles with past choices, providing his own take on the guilt we all experience. "I spent the '90s trying to hide out, trying to duck the full celebrity cacophony. I started to get sick of myself sitting on a couch, holding a joint, hiding out. It started feeling pathetic....It became very clear to me that I was intent on trying to find a movie about an interesting life, but I wasn't living an interesting life myself. I think that my marriage [to Jennifer Aniston] had something to do with it. Trying to pretend the marriage was something that it wasn't," he explained. Now in an established relationship with Angelina Jolie and their 6 children, when asked about happiness, Pitt observed, "I put much more emphasis on being a satisfied man. I'm satisfied with making true choices and finding the woman I love."[2]

I think it's "white shark" important *(most dominant and overpowering image that comes to my mind)* to differentiate here between regret and guilt. Regret and guilt are first cousins, but they shouldn't be confused as twins. When a person sins, both regret and guilt are absorbed mentally and emotionally. Regret is knowing and wishing that you could have done something differently or better. Guilt—from an emotional/spiritual slant—is normally the awareness of actually having done something wrong, sometimes packaged with regret. In a pure legal sense, guilt is confirmed responsibility for some offense or violation. Other varieties of guilt can surface, like the response of "survivor guilt" among some Jewish survivors of the WWII Holocaust, wondering why they deserved to live when others died.[3] Even a child can absorb guilt believing he is responsible for his parent's divorce, or she is to blame for the adult who abused her sexually.

Personal guilt for a sinful choice can only be permanently removed through an intensely personal, spiritual response to God's Spirit that is connected to confession and repentance. Remember, confession is just the starting point for repentance, in which you take full responsibility for the wrong choice.

"I lied" is a simple confession. It's rare, but real. Saying, "I lied because my boss put so much pressure on me" is an excuse or an evasion. Yes, saying "I lied" plus any more words is an admission that you did wrong. But adding a reason, explanation, or defense for what you did invalidates the original intent. No way that you really feel that bad about that lie if you feel it necessary to make a statement with it. No way. Anything less than a stand-alone admission of guilt is a worthless substitute for confession. It's a deceptive attempt to make yourself look better—like the equivalent of saying, *Yes I lied, but if you really understood the circumstances, anybody would have done the same thing because nobody should be treated like that and nobody could have held up under that kind of treatment from my boss. If you got to know me, you'd see I'm really an amazing person that does so many good things. In fact, if I had a better boss, this never would have happened! The attention really needs to be focused on me, and that's not selfish because I am hurting and nobody seems to care about me!*" That's the undercurrent. That's what's really implied. That's why it's really easy to detect a counterfeit confession.

And where there's no real confession, there IS real GUILT! The axiom is: *guilt destroys confidence.* Piggybacking on the phrase above with a little twist, **survivor guilt** can be the emotional residue for the routine circumstance of sinning against God, knowing you should have been hammered but somehow escaped pretty much undamaged, and you can't figure out why, but you haven't changed or got things right yet either. If you have sinned or failed in the past, and never resolved that with God or the people involved, then you are just "bait" for Satan. Under high-pressure temptation, Satan will make sure all you can think about is how you have already messed up your life and disappointed everybody, including God. Those thoughts naturally undermine your belief that you are tight with God and the assurance that you will make the right choice this time around. Under these conditions, you are a convenient target for Satan to accuse…AND…you are defeated *before* the battle with temptation. Only the genuinely naïve would believe *only* God knows what you've done. Satan is aware, so he applauds any decision to hedge your confessions! Like one of my buddies said, "Satan loves darkness." Jesus said we all do:

*This is the crisis we're in: God-light streamed into the world, but men and women everywhere ran for the darkness. They went for the darkness because they were not really interested in pleasing God. Everyone who makes a practice of doing evil, addicted to denial and illusion, hates God-light and won't come near it, fearing a painful exposure. But anyone working and living in truth and reality welcomes God-light so the work can be seen for the God-work it is.* (John 3:19-21, The Message)

## The WHITE HOUSE is Haunted!

Mary Todd Lincoln, wife of our 16th President, Abraham Lincoln, was obsessed with the occult. Mrs. Lincoln claimed to have encountered the ghosts of former residents of the White House, including the spirits of Thomas Jefferson, Andrew Jackson, and John Tyler.[4] After their son, Willie, died in the White House in 1862, the grieving first lady hosted séances in the mansion's Red Room[5] during which she believed she made contact with their two sons, Eddie (who died at age three of tuberculosis), and Willie (who died at age 11, most likely of typhoid fever). Her experiences were shared in detail with her half sister, Emilie Todd Helm, in October, 1863: "Willie lives. He comes to me every night and stands at the foot of the bed with the same sweet adorable smile he always has had. He does not always come alone. Little Eddie is sometimes with him, and twice he has come with our brother, Alex."[6] According to *Lincoln Day By Day*, edited by Earl Schenck Miers, President Lincoln "allegedly attended a spiritualist séance in the White House" on April 23, 1863.[7] The President compared his wife's séances—with their bells, horns, drums and voices—to his Cabinet meetings, where he observed there was always a lot of noise but little agreement on what had happened: "The séances reminded him of his cabinet meetings: the voices of the spirits, he said, were as contradictory as the advice of his secretaries."[8] In November 1860, Lincoln informed his wife he knew he would be elected for a second term but would die in office, claiming to have seen his own assassination in a series of dreams three days before John Wilkes Booth pulled a trigger at Ford's Theater on April 14, 1865. Subsequently, many people reported seeing his ghost in the White House. Grace Coolidge, wife of our 30th President, Calvin Coolidge (1923-1929), was the first person to report Lincoln's apparition in the White House, describing him standing at an Oval Office window, hands clasped behind his back, gazing out over the Potomac.[9] White House staffers have reported the ghost of Abigail Adams, wife of President John Adams, hanging laundry in the East Room. She is the "oldest" ghost still to be encountered in the White House today.[10] The late British Prime Minister, Winston Churchill, refused to sleep in the Lincoln bedroom after claiming to have seen President Lincoln's ghost lurking about. During one of Churchill's visits to the United States during World War II, he actually spent the night in that bedroom. The result?

"Churchill retired late after relaxing in a long, hot bath while drinking a Scotch and smoking a cigar. He climbed out of the bath naked…walked into the adjoining bedroom…[and] couldn't believe his eyes when he saw Abraham Lincoln standing by the fireplace in the room, leaning on the mantle. The two men looked each other in the face, in seeming embarrassment, as Lincoln's apparition slowly faded away." [11] Theodore Roosevelt, Herbert Hoover, Margaret Truman, Dwight Eisenhower, Jacqueline Kennedy, Ladybird Johnson, Susan Ford, and Maureen Reagan have all admitted sensing the presence of the Civil War president in the White House. [12]

**SIDEBAR:** Popular reality investigation shows like the Travel Channel's *Ghost Adventures* and Syfy's *Ghost Adventures* prove there is widespread belief in paranormal activity. Hey, spirits do exist…but not like most people think. The bible clearly teaches that there are real spirits—not ghosts or hauntings by the restless spirits of the departed dead, but demons and/or Satan—that can reside in people, influence thoughts, possess power, create physical problems or suicidal thoughts, have unrestricted invisible movement, assume any form, personality, or voice to imitate or intimidate, but are always subject to the ultimate authority of Jesus. [13] Believer or non-believer, once death occurs, the bible explains you are forever eternally bound to one of two real locations—heaven or hell—and cannot return to communicate with the living, even if you wanted to warn them about hell (e.g., Luke 16:19-31).

And rumors about the White House still persist…as in the following story that started on official White House letterhead.

> **"We are pleased to invite you to join the President as he announces new efforts to improve educational outcomes, provide flexibility to States, and advance reform under the Elementary and Secondary Education Act."**

So began the invitation received by a friend of our extended family, a public school principal, to attend a select East Room meeting in the White House in September, 2011. When this principal, also a young mother, announced the honor to her family, her little boy—who at that moment was consumed with Halloween themes at school and stores—transferred some fear in a 1st-grade style confession, "I heard the White House is haunted!"

His point? Don't go there, mom! That kid's line would get a lot of mileage in late night shows opening monologues, but the confession is priceless—mostly because it we're all afraid of something. And confession is not just a religious word. It can be a scary word.

Confession can feel like putting your most private moments on YouTube. But consider the alternative. Covering up is a bigger scary mistake. A big reason why I love the Bible is because it's God's book of truth, intended to rescue me from destroying my life (see John 3:16). Sometimes I don't like the truth

I read because it makes me uncomfortable, forcing me to re-think what's going on in my head and heart, to re-evaluate my motives and decisions, and re-fresh my relationship with God. But, that's the cost of living in truth—i.e., living in freedom. And here's the corollary, capsule-sized truth to set you free: Hide a sin and the enemy will manipulate your thoughts, constantly reminding you about that incident to exaggerate your guilt and keep you focused on that embarrassment and pain from the past. One of God's labels for Satan is *"the accuser"* (Revelation 12:10, NLT). If Satan succeeds, and you bow down to or give in to his typical, predictable accusations that your sin in the past has made you unworthy, damaged, a failure, unloved by God, or that God is done with you…then you're fried! That's the danger associated with leftover guilt. Leftover guilt…unresolved guilt…makes you MORE likely to bend or fold under pressure.

**SIDEBAR:** Can you see now why God wants you to "take out the trash"? God created you to be in intimate relationship with Him. Guilt is the security alarm, installed by God in your conscience, to make you aware of even the smallest gap in that relationship. Satan's goal is condemnation. Confession and cleansing, not condemnation or criticism, is God's ultimate goal with guilt: *"But if we confess our sins, He will forgive our sins, because we can trust God to do what is right. He will cleanse us from all the wrongs we have done"* (1 John 1:9, The Message). God doesn't beat you up. He wants you out of the bad stuff…and the bad stuff out of you! Conviction of your sin is the work of a compassionate Father in heaven who knows if you don't get righteous— if you don't worth through the pain and humiliation of repentance that you actually owe God for killing His Son in the first place—you will be sucked deeper and deeper into sin and away from Him.

So, when a tempting offer surfaces, relocate immediately…**and don't feel guilty about it!**

# PART FIVE:

# The Wall

*Chapter 16*

# Joseph's ELEVEN

Comedienne Rita Rudner gave the world a funny gift with her "50 Facts About Men" routine. Here's No. 38: "Getting rid of a man without hurting his masculinity is a problem. 'Get out' and 'I never want to see you again' might sound like a challenge. If you want to get rid of a man, I suggest saying, 'I love you...I want to marry you...I want to have your children.' Sometimes they leave skid marks." Ha!

Our guy, Joseph, left skid marks...for all the right reasons...and did it *because* he was being pursued. The amazing truth is NOT that Joseph could give thumbs down on every man's wildest dream, but that he could resist the *other* first real temptation, which far exceeded the sexual adventure offered by Mrs. Potiphar, his boss' wife (see Genesis 39). **What was it?** It's Mistake No. 3 that we've identified in running your God-designed life-race: **Bitterness.**

But since we exited to cover a lot of issues after launching the list of **7 MISTAKES** in Chapters 4 and 6, let's recap:

**MISTAKE No. 1: Wasting your potential.** *God desires to give you an amazing life. Play by His rules in your life-race and you will fulfill your potential!*

**MISTAKE No. 2: Repeating bad choices.** *If you don't discipline your life to give up or separate from the choices that pull you down, you will get sucked deeper into negative attitudes, bad relationships, shaky decisions, and feel more distant from God.*

Now, let's merge back into traffic.

**MISTAKE No. 3: Allowing bitterness to drive choices.**

**Bitterness?** Are you kidding? Surprised? Shocked? Skeptical? Got to feed the dog all of a sudden? Your boss wants to meet with you? I'm not buying those excuses. Got a call on your cell? Press "Ignore". Stay with me. Don't bail! It's not ridiculous. Here we go!

If you don't play by the rules in running your God-designed life-race, you risk blaming God and everybody for the mistakes you'll make and being eaten alive with bitterness as a result. Joseph is proof. Keep reading.

### Kelly Clarkson is Right!

Kelly Clarkson is right. The lyrics from the title track on her 2011 album actually work for us: "What doesn't kill you makes you stronger." Before the young gun, Joseph, faced the predictable risks of sexual favors, he had to process all the emotional garbage from a dysfunctional family and life-shift that could make even a nun question God's existence. Joseph's biggest battle was whether or not to buy in to something more subtle, soul-satisfying, and seductive than sex. According to the backstory in Genesis 37, Joseph's father made a big deal about Joseph being his favorite. That favoritism stirred hatred to the point that his step-brothers couldn't talk to him without verbally attacking him (37:4). The uninterrupted stream of condemnation was probably intended to remind him that he was rejected—no chance of being accepted by his brothers no matter how much he may have wanted a relationship. Like throwing gas on a fire, Joseph had apparently also excelled beyond the "Joseph's ELEVEN" opposition in the family business.

Want a winning principle? Want a good quote for the next meeting or speech? Try this one from me— *"People who get things done make those who don't want to change uncomfortable. People who give up or give in don't like those who succeed. People who don't live pure think people who live pure are insane. People who aren't obeying God resent those who obey God. People who don't want to go forward with God oppose those who want to go forward with God. People who have no faith are convicted by those who do. People who are weak don't like those who are confident. People who won't stand up don't like those who do. Critics will naturally accuse you of their sins, fears, and weaknesses in order to divert your attention away from the stuff in their closet."*

### THE DREAM and THE NIGHTMARE

Apparently the final insult and threat to his brother's plans was back-to-back weird dreams. When Joseph unveiled his dreams full of symbols from God to his brothers (Genesis 37:5-11), they went crazy with hatred. The brothers interpreted their younger brother's dreams accurately—Joseph believed the dreams were a message that God was going to make him this huge leader and they would have to bow down to him one day. That escalated heir hostility to the max. No U.N. resolution needed there for them to act. A plan quickly evolved to kill Joseph. When one brother caved at the last moment and convinced the rest to back the train up on the murder idea, a compromise was reached. Joseph would be stripped of his father's gift—an expensive coat—thrown into a hole or pit in the desert, and eventually sold to slave-traders (Genesis 37:18-36). It meant setting up false evidence, lying to their father about Joseph's death, and sealing the family secret for the rest of their lives, but that's trivial when you are at *terrorist-level* hatred.

So, Joseph had to absorb *the hold on his dream…the hatred…the hole…and the hijacking of his life.* Then WHAM! Another nightmare test…*the habeas corpus suspension.* Even though he landed in Egypt by the mysterious, sovereign hand of God (see Genesis 50:20), and immediately gets promoted to business manager for Mr. Potiphar (head of Pharaoh's secret service detail, Genesis 39:1), Joseph is hammered with unfairness when Mrs. Potiphar pretends to be his rape victim and lies to send him to jail. It's a reasonable defense to argue that he had a right to be bitter. Rejection and abuse qualify, right? Maybe not. However, unthinkable stuff happens. People really do get hurt…sometimes beyond belief.

**"I thought I was having a nightmare."** Those words were spoken by a then 23-year-old Elizabeth Smart on her first day in court, November 8, 2010, for the trial of her accused kidnapper, Brian David Mitchell. In June, 2002, then just an innocent 14-year-old, she was laying in bed beside her baby sister when she suddenly awakened to the feel of a cold knife at her neck, and the sheer terror of the strange man's words: "Don't make a sound. Get out of bed and come with me, or I will kill you and your family." That night, they fled up the hills above her home, with Elizabeth in her red pajamas and tennis shoes, and the knife to her back. Mitchell took her to a tent, had his ex-wife put Smart in a robe, and performed a wedding using words from a Mormon marriage ceremony. "He proceeded to fight me to the ground and force the robes up," Smart said quietly, pausing, "where he raped me." She screamed and he threatened to cover her mouth with duct tape. "I begged him not to. I did everything I could to stop him. I pleaded with him not to touch me, but it didn't work."[1] Elizabeth's nightmare of abuse and rape continued for what she described as "my 9 months of hell,"[2] until she was able to escape. Today, she has overcome the man and the moment that threatened to steal her life by speaking out as she travels across America with her message of hope.

How our hearts break for her! No way to ever comprehend the horror she endured. Only God can heal pain so deep. In an amazing statement that only could have been sustained by God's grace, this bold young woman summarized her emotions and resolve: "I felt like because [of] what he had done to me that I was marked, that I wasn't clean, wasn't pure, wasn't worth the same.…I felt like another person would never love me.…*[then spoken to her abductor]* I also want you to know that I have a wonderful life now, that no matter what you do will it affect me again. You took away nine months of my life that can never be returned, but in this life or next, you will have to be held responsible for those actions, and I hope you are ready for [that] when that time comes."[3]

**HEADLINE: Republicans, Democrats, and Independents AGREE!**

But the incident or experience that produces the hurt than can evolve into the bitterness that consumes your joy and influences your decisions, doesn't have to be something tangible or extreme like the kidnapping, slavery, and imprisonment Joseph never saw coming. Rape, abuse, genocide, divorce, being bullied, going bankrupt, adultery, getting laid-off from your job, losing family in the 9/11 attack, segregation, a soldier losing limbs during the war in Afghanistan, or having your friend killed by a drunk driver would be obvious candidates for bitterness. Republicans, Democrats, and Independents would all come to consensus on that! But bitterness can emerge from the other end of the hurt scale, with things like being passed over for a promotion, getting cheated in a business deal, being lied to, years of unsuccessful attempts to have children, betrayal by a BFF, a break-in at your home, being diagnosed with a disease, failing try-outs for a team, rejection from a college, losing the World Cup, a stylist messes up your haircut, a waiter messes up the order, or just knowing nobody wants to be at your house for the holidays.

Real, hurtful stuff is always in the original stories of bitter people. But bitterness does not occur naturally in nature. It has to be created!

### STD's and Expiration Dates

Hurt is real. Disappointment is normal. Rejection is devastating. Pain is feared. But bitterness is still a really bad option. Yes, it is a choice—as intentional and calculated a response as a presidential campaign speech. Bitterness is not like a virus that invisibly invades your body regardless of how much prevention you do. It's not like hereditary cholesterol that slowly packs your arteries and is beyond your control. Hurt is the email that stings. Bitterness is the reply that wants to match or exceed the damage. Hurt is like a stray bullet. Bitterness is shooting back!

In that sense, bitterness is like an STD (sexually transmitted disease). You get it because you take a risk, entertain the feelings, weigh the options, and enjoy the temporary indulgence.

Here's the insider trading info. *Bitterness is the most under-reported emotional crime, the most frequently committed and repeated relational violation, the most deceptive thought pattern, the most addictive lifestyle choice, AND the most common spiritual negative stuffed into your backpack!* When you import it, you are actually putting a bomb in your spirit (i.e., backpack). That makes you an "emotional suicide-bomber". We'll drill deeper on that soon.

It is the most acceptable drug of choice. If it were a disease, the World Health Organization would label it a Phase 5 global pandemic. If it were a hurricane, it would be a Category 5 (building failures, tidal floods, and mass evacuations—i.e., serious destruction!). If bitterness were a terrorism threat, the USA advisory level would not be low (green), guarded (blue), elevated (yellow), or high (orange). Severe (red) would be the right level.

Recently, I reached into my refrigerator to get some milk to drink with my peanut butter and jelly sandwich. It's was like a state law when I was growing up…or at least a normal Midwestern tradition. If you eat PB&J, then you are required to consume 8 ounces of milk. My taste buds were working big time when I realized there was just enough milk left to make this work. After all, you don't want to have more sandwich bites than you have milk. It's got to come out even. In great anticipation, I unscrewed the cap on the milk and then gagged at a smell worse than a dirty diaper. The milk had soured…gone bad…turned on me. I checked out the container, and it was like only minutes after the expiration date. I don't know how they come up with expiration dates, but not worth the risk to me. I'd tried to drink "expired milk" before and lost it. Never again.

**Bitterness is hurt kept past its expiration date.** Almost nobody confesses to bitterness. MLB players will confess performance-enhancing drug use to a congressional investigation committee sooner. It's just easier to justify or explain away because of how it evolves and takes over your attitude and choices. After all, our culture is all about rights, nor responsibility. Isn't there a "right to keep and bear bitterness" clause in the second amendment of our Constitution?

Bitterness drives choices just like cocaine controls an addict—you do things you never thought you would do. Fast forward in our original biblical reference (below) and get full disclosure. Bitterness is so toxic that these verses represent a **XL** warning label from God:

> *14 Pursue peace with all people, and holiness, without which no one will see the Lord: 15 looking carefully lest anyone fall short of the grace of God; lest any root of bitterness springing up cause trouble, and by this many become defiled. 16 lest there be any fornicator or profane person like Esau, who for one morsel of food sold his birthright. 17 For you know that afterward, when he wanted to inherit the blessing, he was rejected, for he found no place for repentance, though he sought it diligently with tears.*
> (Hebrews 12:14-17, NKJV)

## JFK's Secret

In a recently released explosive tell-all book, *Once Upon a Secret: My Affair with President John F. Kennedy and Its Aftermath*, 69-year-old grandmother Mimi Alford revealed an 18-month affair with the President while she was a 19-year-old intern at the White House. In raw detail, she described how Kennedy seduced her in the first lady's bedroom in the summer of 1962, just a little more than a year before his assassination. Meredith Lepore of *The*

*Thread*, observed, "If young women think Alford is someone to admire for the glamorous factor of having an affair with a famous president, they are wrong. This was her first job and her first sexual encounter with a man. Of course, power is a very attractive thing especially when you are a teenager at your first job and your boss is one of the most powerful, charismatic and iconic men in the world. But girls should not be in admiration of this or hoping that they can be in a situation like this."[4] Nobody should be in a power-play situation like that. Joseph was. JFK's exploits with women are now well documented, but apparently Mimi is still processing the conflicting emotions of temptation, trauma, and truth. It's messy and bitterness hides nearby like a lion crouching in the grass, ready to roar and pounce on unsuspecting prey.

Reverse the players, though, and you understand Joseph's dilemma with the cougar. It would have been easy to become a victim of bitterness because of her domination and decision to send him to prison. Isn't it interesting that sex and bitterness are linked here? Watch this.

**SIDEBAR:** Just like media bias heaps excessive attention on a person or issue to shape public opinion, it was not a coincidence that Esau's name was inserted into a warning about the dangers of bitterness. His character legacy was interestingly labeled in Hebrews 12:16 as a "fornicator or profane person". Basically, he loved sex and hated God. Like JFK, he had a big secret. There were apparently few boundaries for his sexual exploits and even fewer voices of reason to stop him. The crisis came to a head when his twin brother Jacob cheated him out of the family inheritance and God's blessing through their father. Actually, Esau first sold his birthright for a the price of some fast food. But if you have a sense of entitlement, it doesn't matter. Esau's rage exploded in a Mafia-style vow to kill his brother (see Genesis 27:41). Although Esau shed some tears and regretted his casualness about assuming spiritual leadership of the family and failure to take its benefits seriously, he didn't genuinely repent. His heart hardened. He became profane. A classic example of regretting a bad decision but choosing not to change and blaming other people. Under the influence of an enablement-addicted mother who intervened to save both her sons, Esau packed up and left the family. He was drowning in bitterness…and the symptom inevitably appeared—lust! Driven by the unresolved anger against his brother, Esau piled up a history of multiple relationships and marriages (see Genesis 28:6-9). What's the point? Simply this. Lust and casual sex are often the result of symptom of something deeper—bitterness. After all, bitterness has to be released or it will kill you. It's sourced in unresolved sinful anger, which is all about dominating someone to get what you want—e.g., casual sex without commitment. So Esau becomes the poster boy for proving bitterness can create lust. But unlike 24-hour food poisoning, bitterness outlives sex. So what do you do with bitterness?

## Rocky Mountain High!

*You can ruin a life with bitterness, but you can't build one with it!*
That reality consumed the life of Adolph Coors IV, heir to the Coors Brewery empire and a near high-profile casualty. Brandon Dutcher reported the details of Coors' riveting journey in a blog:

> *Young Adolph Coors IV worshiped his dad. And why not? Chairman of the board of the family brewing empire, the rugged cattle rancher Adolph Coors III was also a loving father who always had time for his family. A former semi-professional baseball player, Coors was a private pilot, an architect and engineer, and a pioneer in the development of skiing in Colorado. Growing up in the 1950s, living in the beautiful ranch home his father designed and built, Adolph IV idolized his stern but affectionate father. "I wanted to grow up to be just like him in every way." Adolph said. Like most mornings, young Adolph didn't see his father on the morning of February 9, 1960. As was his practice, Mr. Coors awoke at 5:30 to have breakfast before making the 12-mile drive from the family's ranch in the foothills west of Denver to the brewery in Golden. As he arrived at a bridge outside of Morrison, Colorado around 7:30, Mr. Coors stopped to help what looked like a stranded motorist. What he encountered was a prison escapee who had been planning for this morning for two years. In a tragic moment that would make national headlines for months, Adolph Coors III was shot repeatedly and stuffed in the trunk of yellow 1958 Mercury. The car sped away. All that remained was blood on one of the bridge railings. Mr. Coors's ball cap and eyeglasses were found on the bank of the creek below. For seven months, 14-year-old Adolph cried himself to sleep not knowing whether his father was dead or alive. In September, his father's remains were found in a garbage dump 20 miles south of Denver. For the next 17 years, Adolph Coors IV was filled with hatred for his father's killer, the man who had shattered his world. After a stint in the U.S. Marine Corps, Coors married his high-school sweetheart, B.J., and later they became the proud parents of Adolph Coors V. Adolph Coors IV, the great-grandson of the German immigrant who founded the brewery in 1873, went to work for the Adolph Coors Company of Golden, Colorado with the goal of becoming its youngest president. On the outside, he seemed to be living the American dream. But a gnawing emptiness gripped him on the inside, an emptiness he just couldn't shake. His marriage wasn't terribly strong, he wasn't happy at the brewery, and a consuming anger*

*at his father's killer still tormented him. Not comfortable being alone with his wife, they would spend weekends with friends at their gorgeous mountain home. Living a life of quiet desperation, "I began to bury myself in materialism," he says. "My many futile attempts at covering up this emptiness were useless, because the emptiness always came back." One evening, a friend told Mr. Coors that what he needed was a relationship with his Maker, and that unless he came to know Jesus he would go to hell when he died. Taken aback (that not being the kind of thing one says in polite company), Mr. Coors reassured himself with the thought that he was a good man from a respected family—certainly the kind of man who would make it to heaven. But in 1975 Mr. Coors came to realize that his friend was right. He now understands that there is a "God-shaped vacuum" in every heart, a void that can only be filled by God Himself. "Apart from Jesus Christ—regardless of how good we are, and what family background we have, and what we do in life—we are not going to heaven," Mr. Coors says. "If we could earn heaven through our own good works, our own background, and our own genealogy, then Christ's death would have been meaningless.... There's a void in our lives created by God that cannot be filled with material things. That void can only be filled by a relationship with Christ....There's a saying that 'he who dies with the most toys win.' That's the psychology of materialism: if we can surround ourselves with enough toys, our lives are going to be complete and happy." But Mr. Coors, a member of a family whose company shares were recently worth around $400 million, says "materialism won't do it."[5]*

Following his conversion to Christ, Adolph Coors IV took the radical step of separating from the brewery business, but struggled to separate from the bitterness over the senselessness of his father's death by Joe Corbett that had owned him all those years. Before evil hit the Coors family on that tragic day, Corbett had been a Fulbright scholar at the University of Oregon, headed for medical school, when a fight with an Air Force sergeant ended in a shooting and a prison term. After one of the FBI's largest manhunts, Corbett was sentenced to prison.[6] Coors realized he had created his own spiritual and emotional prison, and he held the key to getting released from the oppression—forgiving Corbett! Coors confessed in a speech, "I knew I wasn't capable of this kind of forgiveness. I knew it was beyond me. But I found the answer in the Bible, the fourth chapter of Philippians, the thirteenth verse, which assured me that I could do all things through Jesus Christ who gives me strength." Adolph discovered that believers can "siphon strength from God to do what we know is right but which we lack the capacity to accomplish on our own."[7] Coors managed to follow-through on the intentional choice to forgive, visiting the maximum security unit of Colorado's Canon City penitentiary where he asked to talk with Corbett. But Corbett refused to see him. So Coors left behind a Bible inscribed with this message: "I'm here to see you today and I'm sorry that we could not meet. As a Christian I am summoned by our Lord and Savior, Jesus Christ, to forgive. I do forgive you, and I ask you to forgive me for the hatred I've held in my heart for you." Later Coors confessed, "I have a love for that man that only Jesus Christ could have put in my heart." Coors was finally free. Healing began. With due respect to the incredible late pop singer, John Denver, that is an authentic "Rocky Mountain High!"

## Forget Harvard!

Almost any injury or disappointment can trigger the startup ("root") of the cancer called bitterness. The side effects are universal...and deceptively powerful. Bitterness is a lethal weapon. That explains the **XL** warning label you just read. Here's **8 side effects**.

**First, it allows unscreened emotions.** Life is a lot about rejection. But rejection doesn't have to own your life. Harvard University accepts only about 7% of the 29,000 undergraduate applications it receives each year. Harvard's list of "successful rejects" is impressive and includes Warren Buffet (Chairman of Berkshire Hathaway and one of the wealthiest people on the planet), Nobel Laureate in Medicine, Harold Varmus (twice rejected by Harvard Medical School), media entrepreneur Ted Turner, NBC News icon Tom Brokaw (rejection prompted him to settle down and stop partying), Columbia University President Lee Bollinger, and former NBC Today Show host Meredith Vieira (rejection redirected her to television journalism). "The truth is, everything that has happened in my life...that I thought was a crushing event at the time, has turned out for the better," reflected Warren Buffett. He commented that unexpected hurts contain "lessons that carry you along. You learn that a temporary defeat is not a permanent one. In the end, it can be an opportunity." His rejection at age 19 by Harvard Business School became a life-changing, not life-crushing, event. When it happened a "feeling of dread" overwhelmed him, specifically, that he feared disappointing his father. To his surprise, his father responded with "only this unconditional love...an unconditional belief in me."[8] It forced him to explore other options which ultimately opened the door to be mentored by investing experts at Columbia University's graduate business school, where he learned the core principles that have made him the most successful investor in history. The ironic twist is the story's footnote. Harvard's rejection was their loss when Buffett donated more than $12 million to Columbia University in 2008![9]

Emotions are God's gift—necessary internal commentary on external conditions. Emotions are not inherently sinful: *"Be angry and do not sin"*

(Ephesians 4:26a, NKJV). Like guns, it's where you point them and fire that can make them lethal. They can save life…or take life. Don't let them go unexamined. The demon of bitterness is looking for cracks in your faith.

### "More faith in that dude than God!"

In his book, *TORN: Trusting God When Life Leaves You in Pieces*, Las Vegas pastor Jud Wilhite challenges some of our most protected and tender expectations about unexpected suffering, teaching that an "important expectation to reframe is that when God puts people, things, and experiences in our lives, He does not give them to us to own" but "as blessings God gives us the privilege to manage."[10] Jud makes the truth personal in the fresh journey of suffering for his staff member, Kurt, wife Kelly, and their son Austin. I've known Kurt and Kelly since they were in high school, so their story is beyond cold, theological "kisses" to me. Kurt updated me in a long phone conversation, letting me know their journey would be chronicled in Jud's book. One ordinary evening 5 years ago, Austin (then 7), sat down with his dad to watch some TV. Suddenly, Austin's body stiffened, his eyes rolled back, and he became unresponsive for about 30 seconds. Kurt helplessly held his son through four seizure episodes in the next few minutes, until panic caused Kurt and Kelly to rush Austin to the hospital. Even the medical team was helpless to stop the seizures. Later, CT scans revealed two sections of scar tissue in Austin's brain—the result of two strokes he suffered while in the womb. Months of prescribed meds failed against ever-increasing numbers of seizures—as many as 100 per day at the worst peak. Mom and dad lived in fear that any one seizure could take his life. Shuttling between doctor appointments across the nation, they ultimately agreed to radical surgery—removing a section of Austin's brain. With thousands praying, the night before surgery, Kurt left the Chicago hospital room alone for the hotel room where he tried to bargain with God: "God, if my son can't come through this healed, alive, normal, take whatever you want from me. It might be selfish. I might sound like a martyr. I just don't know if I can handle him not the being the same kid after surgery as before. I can't live with myself knowing that I made the decision for the surgery to happen and I was responsible for messing up my son's life."[11] Optimism surged post surgery, with no seizures for more than 30 days. Then the day before leaving for home, Austin seized. No worries. It settled into a couple of predictable seizures per week. Austin regained lost weight and returned to school. Then the seizures unexpectedly returned with vengeance. To save his life, surgeons scheduled an operation to remove more of Austin's brain. Kurt told me that when the surgeon promised to take good care of Austin, even though it might sound heretical, at that moment he had "more faith in that dude than God!" I can't imagine the struggle with God's sovereignty when it became obvious God was choosing not to intervene with a miracle. Kurt opened up on his personal struggle: "Do I get angry with God? Do I go places in my mind? Do I question God? Yeah. But have I ever let it go dark? Never! Because I love God. He saved my life. He gave me Austin in the first place. I have never felt that God has shoved my situation off His desk....My wife and I still pray that God will heal Austin and make it better. But Jesus knows what it is like to sit in the garden and beg for His life and hear God say no. So far God has said no. I don't like it, but I accept it."[12] Wow. That's Jesus showing out through my friend, Kurt. Kurt was stand alone faithful to Jesus even during times in high school like when a teacher ridiculed him constantly for his faith. God trusted him so much that He gave this journey...this story...to a couple more surrendered than I am. They have worked through their garden conversation with God. Kurt and Kelly are torn...but trusting God.

Emotions can't kidnap us and hold us hostage. They are controllable. But like an E4 Tornado, emotions can tear us from our moorings, toss us around, and displace us. You can't afford to let the force of hurtful emotions put you in a bad place, where you turn on God. Normally, it's more convenient to blame God for the disasters, disillusionments, and dead ends in our life-journey, because we can enjoy unscreened emotions. It's like, if we can convince ourselves that God has failed, then we feel like we have permission to live in the rush of feelings like revenge, anger, resentment, criticism, sarcasm, or hatred. Besides, we look better to our friends that way, explaining that *"Anybody who's been through what I have has a right to feel this way, because God doesn't care or He would have done something."* In fact, blaming God is actually proof that bitterness exists...and for that matter, that you believe God exists! Once you start down that road, any other emotion seems reasonable. If you believe God has no valid reason for allowing that hurt that you'll never forget, then why believe in God period? Why not just party and go for whatever you want? That's an indefensible position and a scary thought.

In the 2002 movie, *The Count of Monte Cristo*, set in the prosperity and political chaos of France during the exile of Napoleon, a young patriot and ship's officer named Edmond Dantes became a political pawn. To further his own career, Dantes' best friend conspired with authorities and set him up as a fall guy. Falsely accused of treason, imprisoned and tortured for 15 years in the infamous French prison, the Chateau d'If, Dantes claimed he survived only by thoughts of revenge. When a priest who befriended him in prison challenged him to let God take care of vengeance, Dantes firmly announced, "I don't believe in God." To which the priest replied, "It doesn't matter. He believes in you."

Even if you can't feel God's presence...even if you hate God for what happened or didn't happen to you...even if you've threatened to do crazy things...even if you quit church and friends...even if you think you don't believe in God anymore...HE BELIEVES IN YOU! Don't let bitterness kill what God created in you!

## ENDANGERED SPECIES?

**Second, you feel a need to stay in control.** Keeping the hurt alive, like an endangered species in a zoo, becomes a convincing substitute for fixing the problem. Bitterness is a thinly disguised method of rebelling against God. That's why we get the warning in Hebrews 12:15—*"...see to it that no one misses the grace of God"* (NIV). The instant of impact—the moment when you get shocked, upset, hurt, disappointed, damaged, or rejected—God offers you His grace. Grace is the ability or strength to manage the moment of disaster. It is a disaster-management skill that honors God and heals you ultimately. How? God can supernaturally enable you to choose to forgive someone, avoid blaming God or anybody else, steer clear of hatred, trust Him for perspective, and move on. Since the only source of forgiveness is God, bitterness is direction rejection of Him!

That's why bitterness is dangerous—like worse than other sins...even adultery. What? Are you kidding me? Explain! Adultery is reckless indulgence. Bitterness is revenge—emotional payback. It's passing your hurt along, throwing it back in the face of God and any other target that gets in the way. You were rejected and run over, so now bitterness becomes your way of trying to call out God for allowing the undeserved suffering. Bitterness is an intentional choice to SHUT GOD OUT of what's happening to you! Reject His grace and you reject Him. Only God can show you how to respond...to navigate your way through the aftermath of the emotional earthquakes you experience. Bitterness is choosing the comfort zone of your emotions over God. Sure, it's brutal to hack your way through the jungle of emotions in bitterness to move in God's direction, but in the end, living in the jungle permanently without God is worse. What's worse? God forcing you to forgive, to release the resentment and pain, or you protecting the bitterness until it becomes a cancer?

When people do blame or reject God as they try to process the hurt, it's a lame attempt to stay in control of their emotions, decisions, and destiny that simply creates greater and greater distance from God. How do you keep a relationship fresh by blaming the other person? It's not that God abandons you, but you put up spiritual and emotional walls to push back against the injustice and offense you feel.

Bitterness is an intense emotion, dangerously addictive, but providing the rush of energy needed to sustain the inner sense of righteousness and anger. When bitterness moves in, it becomes an indicator that you're trying to build a life and future around getting back at God for things that didn't happen like you expected. Bitterness can own your emotions like an 8th grade bully owns a victim. How bad is it when you want to hurt someone while you are dying, as in the case of the criminal who cursed Jesus while they were both being executed on a cross? (e.g., Matthew 27:44—*"Even the revolutionaries who were crucified with him ridiculed him in the same way"* and Mark 15:32— *"Those crucified with him also heaped insults on him"*, NLT)

## Ted Turner's Questions
**Third, you become increasingly distant from God.** By the way, you can generally tell how far someone is from God by the level of fear displayed in their life. Fear can surface through legitimate disguises like business, entertainment, political, and sports personalities that are ruthlessly driven to succeed. Generally, people can be distant from God for tons or reasons, but bitterness will do it. Sometimes people are distant from God because they believe God has failed them, and they remain suspicious of anything good happening from that point forward. If you detect skepticism or cynicism or even agnosticism in someone, know that it can be real. And despite their protests or denials, it is normally linked to a specific incident in their past, where in their mind, God didn't come through for them. In that sense, bitterness is the subtle process of rejecting God's love and plan for your life-race to sculpt a bizarre idol out of that unexplained hurt.

Media entrepreneur and CNN founder, Ted Turner, had to endure his own private struggle with suffering that had a negative outcome. At one point as a teenager, Ted felt drawn to be a missionary. When his sister, Mary Jane, contracted lupus, Ted prayed for her healing an hour each day. Her unexplained suffering and untimely death left residual anger against God in Ted, causing him to label himself an "atheist" or an "agnostic". Having lost his faith, Ted explained, "I was taught that God was love and God was powerful, and I couldn't understand how someone so innocent should be made or allowed to suffer so."[13] Suffering is universal and unending. Everybody has to deal with the same questions as Ted Turner.

As I write this chapter, the national media is focused on the alleged abduction in Kansas City of an 11-month-old baby, Lisa Irwin. Parents Jeremy Irwin and Deborah Bradley have wept and pleaded for the return of their daughter. Deborah failed a police lie detector test, and was caught on video buying diapers and wine in the hours before her husband came home from work at 4:00am and discovered the house in disarray and Lisa missing from her crib. Three witnesses have now come forward claiming to have seen a suspicious man in a t-shirt, walking down the street in the cold morning darkness, carrying a baby that was dressed only in a diaper. How would you cope? From stealing a child to the 2011 storms that leveled Joplin, Missouri and Tuscaloosa, Alabama, tragedy is a fact of life.

In *The New Answers Book*, featuring 15 authors breaking down the Creation/Evolution debate, Tommy Mitchell asked the hardball questions: "Is God responsible for human suffering? Is God cruel, capricious, and vindictive, or is He too weak to prevent suffering? If God truly is sovereign, how can He let someone He loves suffer? Each day brings new tragedy. A small child is diagnosed with leukemia and undergoes extensive medical treatment only to die in his mother's arms. A newlywed couple is killed by a drunk driver as they leave for their honeymoon. A faithful missionary family is attacked and killed by the very people they were ministering to. Thousands are killed in a terrorist attack. Hundreds drown in a tsunami, while scores of others are buried in an earthquake. How are these things possible if God really loves and cares for us? Is He a God of suffering?[14] Where is God in this stuff? The normal response to tragedy is to blame God, like evolutionist Charles Darwin did following the death of his beloved daughter Annie: "Annie's cruel death destroyed Charles's tatters of beliefs in a moral, just universe. Later he would say that this period chimed the final death-knell for his Christianity....Charles now took his stand as an unbeliever."[15]

As the late pastor Adrian Rogers observed, "First the man shapes the idol. Then the idol shapes the man." Choosing to worship the "idol of undeserved pain" and fall down before the "altar of lingering questions" separates you from God's mercy and comfort like the Great Wall of China. Intense emotions can create a hard heart. Bitter people tend to speak less and less about God in general and become more focused on what's happened or not happened to them. The longer you hang on to your perceived right to feel the way you do, regardless of whether anything or anybody changes, the harder it becomes to hear God's voice. The more time spent insisting on your rights, the less you are aware of how far from God you have drifted, and how your passion for worship has faded. Then life becomes all about how you define "good", so you begin to substitute your level of goodness for a real salvation experience with God. Then you fall into the trap of demanding this constant, air-tight proof that God loves you, that He is real, that the Bible is true, that people can be trusted, that you will never be hurt again, etc.

The tragedy is that you end up not fearing God, but fearing everything else will go wrong—your plane will crash, you'll get cancer, you'll lose the baby, you won't make the team, you won't get the job, or you will never meet the right person or if you do, you'll never have a happy marriage. Instead of buying a t-shirt that says, "Life is good", you want one that's more real, one you can relate to, that says, "Life stinks." After all, it's true. Life is unfair. At least that feels true when you're distant from God.

### Muammar Qaddafi is Dead!

**Fourth, you become defensive.** Under the influence of bitterness, a defensive spirit typically emerges. It's a survival tactic. Intensely bitter people develop an approach to life that carries a determination to never be hurt again. Bitterness evolves from self-righteousness and survives on selfishness, in the sense that you tend to believe what happened to you should not have happened, you deserved something better, and you are going to hold out until God and everybody else agrees.

**Fifth, bitterness deceives.** The hidden power of deception in bitterness makes you believe you are right and God and everybody else is wrong. It is pride on steroids. The core is a rebellious, defiant attitude disguised and protected over time by a lot of stories about how you've been wronged or hurt. Repeat the stories long enough and you will believe your version is real!

**Sixth, you get stuck spiritually.** If you are bitter over a past hurt, that's where your life with God got parked. When your identity becomes linked to a hurt in the past, spiritual progress is impossible. Growth stopped the moment you chose bitterness over forgiveness. God can't change anybody that doesn't want to give up what's holding them back. If you don't let it go, then God can't let you go. When you hear someone repeat their "hurt stories" over and over again, they are stuck spiritually. In a conscious choice, they parked their life and emotions at the point of impact. Somewhere in their past they erected an historical marker to where the battle for their emotions and future took place, that's just a real to them as the Battle of Gettysburg was to the Civil War. It's where normal life shut down and dysfunctional life emerged. That's why you shake your head at some 40-year-old professional that shocked everybody by acting like a college student. Why? They never grew past that moment in college—when their parents divorced, frat brothers lied to them, sorority sisters cheated on them, professors jumped on them, or med school rejected them. The same scenario is repeated at random ages and circumstances in everybody's life. Maybe you really didn't deserve what has happened. But that doesn't justify trashing God, giving up on yourself, dumping anger on others, or running from responsibility for your reaction.

That's why we need God's Word. If you haven't explored the issues surrounding suffering in the Bible, no way you would know that scripture is actually "fair and balanced." For example, there is no definitive causal link between suffering and guilt or innocence. Some really bad people seem to escape the consequences, while thousands of innocent people are killed in tsunamis. But bad things that happen to you don't automatically mean you are being judged for some sin. Muammar Qaddafi's 42-year regime of terror as Libya's unpredictable dictator ended in a riot and execution on November 20, 2011. With Qaddafi's convoy in escape mode, NATO planes fired, and the bloodied, once-feared leader was found cowering in a drainage pipe. Revolutionary forces could not restrain their bitterness and put a bullet behind his left ear after beating him with their shoes. Crowds in the streets cheered, "The blood of martyrs will not go in vain."[16] Scenes like this are used to sustain the argument that God eventually gets it right and the universe gets back in balance—i.e., suffering finally makes sense when bad guys get it! But why did he get away with it for so long?

You may be totally innocent and still suffer. Check out John 9:1-3. Passing by a man born blind, Jesus' disciples asked Him if the blindness was caused by the man's sin or his parent's sin. Jesus explained that neither of those traditional Jewish interpretations of suffering were valid, and took their thinking in a fresh direction: *"This happened so the power of God could be seen in him"* (NLT). It was like a lecture in THEOLOGY 101 by Professor Jesus [my label and translation]: *God actually has a right to allow innocent people to suffer because the most important thing to God is making His name and salvation known.* Then Jesus calmly healed the blindness! Wow. But, after all, the most innocent person who ever lived, Jesus, was falsely excused, tortured, and executed for our sins. His death is the explanation for all suffering: God designs, allows, manages, and uses suffering with the innocent and guilty both, to point people to salvation through His Son. One of the thieves dying on a cross beside the suffering Jesus did finally abandon the hype and come to terms with his own bitterness by admitting he had messed up (see Luke 29:41—*"We deserve to die for our crimes"*, NLT).

**Seventh, expectations spin out of control.** When bitterness owns your spirit, expectations balloon. Demands for people around you to perform and please you seem normal. Bitterness inflates expectations to abnormal proportions. The mindset is that God and everybody else owes you. You argue that he whole world is supposed to revolve around you because nobody's ever experienced the level of pain exactly like what you endure. Then, you double up on the whining, complaining that God didn't come through and meet your expectations, so He doesn't deserve your belief and worship. You wanted God to save you from something, but you really didn't want Him. It's not about changing, but getting what you want. Those are the powerful forces that propel your thinking, ultimately driving all your relationships, and controlling the level of your passion for worship, work, and wealth. If you actually believe God has failed you in some way, then you reason that you have a right to do what you want, including hurt Him or anybody that represents Him. As an emotional response or attitude, it tempts you to demand others back away, create a lane for you, and show you respect or special treatment at impossible levels. That approach makes you feel like you are staying in control, getting God on your terms, like the criminal who cursed Jesus while on the cross, demanding that Jesus prove He was God by saving Himself and the two dying criminals (see Luke 23:39b).

**Eighth, problems become more complicated.** Rather than immediately revealing the hurt, and resolving the pain through confession and/or reconciliation, people normally tend to repress the dark stuff. *It's crammed deeper into their backpack of emotions*, hoping it will go away. After all, in many cases, bitterness is simply repressed anger over an unhealed wound. You've never really closed the case. And people who hang on to hurt just get weird. You can become dysfunctional trying to cover up the leftover emotions from the "accident", rather than just confessing your resentment before God, getting released, and moving on. People around you know something's not right, either by the sharp edge in your tone of voice, the victim-mentality you display, a negative or critical attitude, a change in performance, or the general sense of depression—like you've resigned from life. Sometimes co-workers, classmates, children, clients, and church members begin to avoid you because they fear some innocent remark will trigger an explosion of anger. Even dogs run when they don't know if their owner is going to beat them or stroke them. Unpredictable responses complicate relationships. You can look crazy trying to manage the disconnect between what you're feeling inside and the "normal" life everybody else seems to enjoy. Resentment can build when you feel that those closest to you aren't giving you enough attention, don't appreciate you, or don't understand you.

Bitterness **exaggerates** the pain.

**Bitterness** complicates **the solution.**

*Chapter 17*

# Devolution

It took decades for Bill Gates to learn it. Hey, I'm not making this up! Read closely. In his June 8, 2007 Commencement Speech at Harvard University, Microsoft founder Bill Gates spoke with humor about his campus life before becoming what the student newspaper, *The Harvard Crimson*, called "Harvard's most successful dropout." But he quickly shifted to confess his biggest regret that he has transformed into his greatest passion:

> *"I do have one big regret. I left Harvard with no real awareness of the awful inequities in the world....And I knew nothing about the millions of people living in unspeakable poverty and disease in developing countries....Imagine, just for the sake of discussion, that you had a few hours a week and a few dollars a month to donate to a cause—and you wanted to spend that time and money where it would have the greatest impact in saving and improving lives. Where would you spend it? For Melinda and for me, the challenge is the same: how can we do the most good for the greatest number with the resources we have? During our discussions on this question, Melinda and I read an article about the millions of children who were dying every year in poor countries from diseases that we had long ago made harmless in this country— Measles, malaria, pneumonia, hepatitis B, yellow fever. One disease I had never even heard of, rotavirus, was killing half a million kids each year, none of them in the United States. We were shocked. We had just assumed that if millions of children were dying and they could be saved, the world would make it a priority to discover and deliver the medicines to save them. But it did not. For under a dollar, there were interventions that could save lives that just*

*weren't being delivered.…If you believe that every life has equal value, it's revolting to learn that some lives are seen as worth saving and others are not. We said to ourselves: 'This can't be true. But if it is true, it deserves to be the priority of our giving.' So we began our work in the same way anyone here would begin it. We asked: 'How could the world let these children die?' The answer is simple, and harsh. The market did not reward saving the lives of these children, and governments did not subsidize it. So the children died because their mothers and their fathers had no power in the market and no voice in the system. But you and I have both. It took me decades to find out. **The barrier to change is not too little caring; it is too much complexity.** [emphasis mine] To turn caring into action, we need to see a problem, see a solution, and see the impact. But complexity blocks all three steps. Even with the advent of the Internet and 24-hour news, it is still a complex enterprise to get people to truly see the problems.*[1]*

He's right on the issue of reversing global health deficiencies. But on another level his wisdom is transferable to the perennial battle to get past bitterness. The barrier is not lack of desire but the confusion that results from bitterness that makes life seem impossibly complicated…too messed up to change! People need to see the problem first.

So it's time to trace the *devolution* of bitterness. If evolution is the theory that a species gradually develops toward increasing complex and more adaptable forms, then I'll use the term *devolution* to describe a process of going backward. Spiritual *devolution* is about slippage from a previous solid spiritual position, hope, and forward development. Bitterness is a condition, a response, a place, and always…a downward movement, creating a lower functioning level spiritually…the opposite of survival of the fittest.

Bitterness is like conviction in the sense that there is totally predictable process and direction. In the process of conviction, the Holy Spirit slowly and systematically reveals truth to us about our sin, God's righteousness, and a final judgment (see John 16:8), even though we move through stages of understanding and awareness about spiritual reality at different rates of speed. For example, sometimes a person can move from skepticism to openness in one dramatic life-crisis. In the other extreme, a person may resist for years admitting the truth that they are accountable to God for their sin and there is a place of eternal separation from God. In a similar way, it's possible for someone to move slowly through the stages from hurt to fully developed bitterness, or to embrace it minutes after some huge disappointment. It's not about speed but direction. Where are you going with the hurt?

### The Village People?

How does bitterness develop? (Check out the diagram) Here's my take.

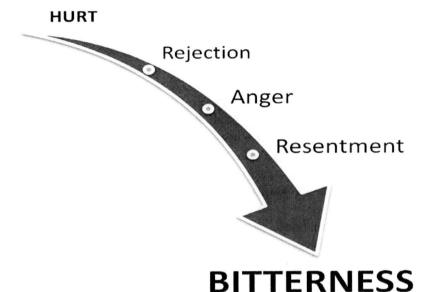

**HURT**

Rejection

Anger

Resentment

# BITTERNESS

**Level 1: HURT.** Bitterness has a beginning point, just as it has a destination. There is always a real, specific, historical moment in time when your life gets interrupted by an unexpected event. Wherever there is disappointment, disillusionment, injury, an accident, harassment, loss, persecution, a wound, a crime, a wrongdoing, rejection, broken promises, or crashed expectations, hurt can emerge. You feel wronged and owed something. You are not content with who you are, what you have, and what has happened to you. Regardless of whether or not there was a real offense, perception wins. It's how you *feel* you were treated in traffic today, how you *feel* about last weekend's fantasy football results, or how that remark by your dad, girlfriend, teacher, boss, co-worker, the media, teammate, or coach *felt* to you that colors your story. That's why God's counsel in Hebrews chapter 12, verse 14, is front-loaded with urgency—all about being proactive.

Believers are supposed to "pursue" peace—meaning that God expects you to pour some energy and passion into resolving the anger, confusion, or hurt **the moment it happens**. Responsibility is assumed. That's a mega-truth. Everybody gets *run over* emotionally...sometimes even physically (e.g., suicide-bombers, drunk drivers, sexual abusers, etc.) and spiritually. In fact, sometimes people run over you, then put it in reverse and *back up* a couple of times to make sure they got you. But not everybody becomes bitter. It's how you process what happens to you—not what happens—that makes the difference.

Technically, nobody "makes" you mad. You are the *only one* responsible for your attitude toward the perpetrator.

Want a good definition of radical? Here's radical. The verse says to pursue peace with ALL people. No exceptions because certain people might be more deserving of your anger and hatred. Serial haters are eventually going to be busted by God. In fact, the "pinheads"[2] that you dislike the most should be the first targets of the peace process. You don't have to like it—just do it. The Jesus you claim to follow did it while dying on a cross. With his executioners and critics celebrating the blood flow, He responded: *"Father, forgive these people! They don't know what they're doing!"* (Luke 23:34, CEV).

No boundaries or exclusions. Don't think you can draw dotted lines around your life—like nations on a world map—to define your borders (i.e., deciding in advance the people who get to live in your nation or village). That's "nation-building" in the worst sense. You can't control the people who come into your village but you can control the reception.

### "I'm already in your head."

At the 2010 Chick-fil-A Leadercast, leadership guru John Maxwell observed that we have to expend more energy "connecting" with people we don't like. His cited proof is those funny but awkward moments when we round a grocery store aisle only to see that person that we can't get along with, and we reverse direction, hoping they never caught a glimpse of us. When you can't get your enemy out of your head when you go to bed, watch a movie, get on your iPad2, romance your mate, go to work, walk through your subdivision, watch a movie, lay out on the beach, go to church, pray, open your locker, or take a test, you have waited too long to deal with the hurt.

Actually, some motivation is required to get past the hurt beyond just realizing that a negative reaction is not good for you and will enslave you. Yes, bitterness eventually owns you…takes over your life… as we'll see. Corrie Ten Boom, a Dutch Christian woman, whose story of saving Jewish refugees was told in the book, *The Hiding Place*, survived a Nazi concentration camp during the Holocaust of WWII, and said, "Forgiveness is to set a prisoner free, and to realize the prisoner was you." ***Bitterness makes you the prisoner.***

And frankly, that's why I'm personally not into bitterness. I don't like anything other than God controlling my life.

In the 2012 movie, *Safe House*, Denzel Washington played Tobin Frost, the most dangerous former CIA ops man. Frost, the ex-intelligence officer turned renegade, had been on the run for a decade, giving up assets and selling U.S. military intel to any cash buyer—everything from trading secrets to North Korea to supporting splinter cells. Captured, taken to the Cape Town, South Africa CIA Safe House and "interrogated", Frost manages to protect a secret. A bored rookie CIA operative, Matt Weston (played by Ryan Reynolds) was then assigned to protect the fugitive. When mercenaries attacked Weston's Safe

House, Frost and Weston barely managed to escape. Realizing security had been compromised, the unlikely allies took on a mission to stay alive long enough to uncover who wanted them dead. Was it terrorists or an insider? So Weston had to figure out who he could really trust. At one point in the chaos, Weston pushed back against his suspected partner: "You're not going to get in my head." Frost coldly replies, *"I'm already in your head."* Nobody else should get into your head! Your thoughts should not be consumed with the name or image of someone who has hurt you. The missionary entrepreneur Paul captured it like this: *"Everything is permissible for me—but not everything is beneficial....I will not be mastered by anything"* (1 Corinthians 6:12, NIV).

Just because it might be technically legal or culturally acceptable doesn't mean it is **spiritually smart**. You might have the freedom to get away with using the *"it's-okay-because-I'm-over-21-and-I-can-do-what-I-want"* line, but just because she's available, you've got the money, or you haven't been killed yet, doesn't mean that it is right. And that's not freedom. **Freedom is the power to do what's right, not permission for, or protection from, risky behavior.** Bitterness is emotional and spiritual suicide. It's like drinking poison and hoping the other person will die. It's like putting a pistol to your head, pulling the trigger, and hoping the bullet will take out your enemy.

## That Black Creepy Thing in Spiderman 3

So God explained that 5-word expectation for pursuing peace with all people. He tagged it with the best reason: it's about *"holiness"* (Hebrews 12:14, NKJV). Holiness is simply choosing to live a life that best reflects the character of God. It packs the idea of an intentionally exceptional lifestyle, of living "separated for a purpose"—i.e., responding differently than the culture so that people realize your reaction can only be explained in terms of God showing up and creating supernatural responses of tolerance, compassion, love, and forgiveness. Running your life race successfully is linked to God's core character value of forgiveness. Remember...lifetime devoted followers of Jesus are obligated to chase God's purpose. That's the believer's best optic. So God knows that the best image of Him is the one where you are rejecting bitterness and choosing forgiveness. The only reason that the "pursue peace" stuff is going to hold up—the only motivation that is bigger than the emotional-high that bitterness brings—is the holiness factor. **Living bigger than bitterness makes God real.** It brings Him into the rearview mirror for your friendly neighborhood skeptic.

Bitterness is a rush but it takes *more and more* energy to consume it for the same high. So the formula is simple. Play by the rules. Please God and get past hurt. Fight God on this and hurt takes you down and takes over, like the symbiote black suit in Spiderman 3 that controlled Peter Parker's behavior.

And the worst news? Without holiness, you don't see God. Back up for a moment. The only way you can pursue peace and holiness in the first place is if you have actually experienced forgiveness. Without the personal acceptance

of Jesus Christ as Savior and exclusive sacrifice for your sins, you are not officially "clean" in God's eyes (see Hebrews 10:14, 22).  A dirty heart never
cleaned up anybody's mess.  You can't give what you don't have.  You can't
answer with what you don't know.  You can't set somebody else free if you are
in prison.  You can't rescue anybody when you are drowning.

### Shock my brother!

Refusing to forgive continues the downward spiral toward **Level 2:
REJECTION.**  Not in the sense of someone rejecting you, or you categori-
cally rejecting someone, but you rejecting God when the tsunami of hurt hits
your unprotected heart.  Classic example?  A powerful Jewish religious/political
leader named Saul, consumed with rage and obsessed with his personal vendetta
of persecuting Christians to their death, was blinded by a crushing, mysterious
light while traveling to Damascus, Syria.  Behind the light came the voice of Jesus:
*"Saul! Saul! Why are you persecuting me?....I am Jesus, the One you are persecuting!"*
(Acts 9:4-5, NLT).  Jesus exposed a wounded and threatened man, whose real
war was with Him.  For whatever reason, Saul's cover-up for lack of forgiveness
was destroying the lives of people who disagreed with him.  Either way the
result is the same.  If you choose not to forgive, it's a Level 2 life for you.

Rejecting the option to bury the offense by accessing God's resources embeds
you in that offense.  You become an unsuspecting prisoner of that hurtful offense,
handcuffed and bound by unforgiveness.  One Greek word translated "forgive" in
the Bible actually means "to set a prisoner free".  Four unique words are used in
the original Greek New Testament to describe slices of the concept of forgiveness:
to forgive a debt (*aphiemi*, 1 John 1:9), a pardon of punishment or guilt (*aphesis*,
Matthew 26:28), release a prisoner from repaying a debt (*charizomai*, Colossian
2:13, Luke 7:42), and set a prisoner free (*apoluo*, Luke 6:37).

According to Hebrews 12:15, God can resource the strength and resolve
you need to forgive someone at the moment of impact ( *"lest anyone fall short of
the grace of God"*, NKJV).  Repeat it out loud:  God and only God!  And the
timing is amazing—up front!  It's like your dad giving you a no-limit credit card
when you begin college, not *after* you've maxed out your cards with pizzas and
parties, 6 years and zero degrees later.  Believe it or not, since God is fair, the
expectation to avoid hiding bitterness in your backpack is covered by an
implicit promise to fund the journey.  The ability to forgive is captured in the
phrase, "grace of God'.  He'll provide the grace—the ability to navigate the
pain—at the point of impact.  Neither your buddy, boss, blogging, burgers, or
a beer is going to get you pumped up enough to feel like forgiving.  Even if you
say that Jesus has changed you, that's inadequate.  It takes *case-specific grace.*

Remember the audience?  This passage was written to people who had
already crossed-over to belief.  The recipients were the Jesus-people who were
under threat...real disciples...serious followers...*believers, but* they were apparently struggling with the first generation issues of persecution—hurt, forgiveness,

and bitterness. Forgiveness is baseline in that relationship. At the core, forgive-ness is surrender. That's right. It's a choice of the will. Not just giving up in frus-tration because "that's the way things are and we've got to deal with it", or some random forced compliance. That's not surrender because there's no purpose...no target. Surrender to *Jesus*. Surrender all your rights...all the "settings" you have already checked for your life...and illusions about control...and emotions...and what you hoped your life would be all about. Believers are supposed to be really good at surrendering, but severe hurt creates severe tests—will you pull back or give back? Forgiveness is the "classic" surrender.

How do you know if you've forgiven someone? By first knowing what for-giveness is *NOT*! Forgiveness is NOT:

✓ *Denying reality by ignoring a sin, wrong, or hurt*
✓ *Pretending the hurt didn't happen*
✓ *Avoiding the person or situation*
✓ *Excusing the wrong or the damage*
✓ *Reducing the severity of the wrong*
✓ *Condoning the actions that were wrong*
✓ *Removing guilt from the person's conscience*
✓ *Allowing the offense recur again and again*
✓ *Reconciliation*
✓ *A process, but a choice that has to be repeated*
✓ *A one-time act, but a repeated attitude*
✓ *Random, because the hurt is specific*
✓ *Dependent upon a person's attitudes*
✓ *Offered depending upon a person's response*
✓ *Trying to play the victim*
✓ *A power play to control another person*
✓ *Forgetting just to "move on"*
✓ *A positive feeling or good thoughts*
✓ *Vacationing with the offender*

Forgiveness sets **YOU** free first! That's why God's strategy is rational. Pass along the same grace (i.e., tolerance, acceptance, love, etc.) you received when Jesus forgave you. The ultimate reason to forgive is because you too needed forgiveness from Jesus (see Ephesians 4:32)...AND because God said do it! Jesus said truth sets you free (see John 8:32). This is truth, not hype. If you doubt it, maybe it's because you haven't really ever bought in. Failure to take advantage of God's strength at the moment of hurt—in order to forgive—pushes you deeper into bondage (i.e., deeper into an emotional obligation to the hurt and a spiritual blindness to the real issues). Hebrews 12:15 removes all excuses like: "God didn't show up when I got hurt" or "Nobody could for-give what was done to me" or "They don't deserve forgiveness". All of that is a rejection of grace, which is a tacit rejection of God, which itself is an attempt to get even with God by withholding the one action that makes God real to another person: forgiveness!

Choosing not to forgive at your first opportunity usually means you have decided to take God's place as Judge of every word, motive, incident, and circumstance. Or it can mean you've had enough pain and can't take it anymore. Or it might mean you want to stay in control. Whatever the reason, refusing to forgive immediately is technically a rejection of God. You really don't believe that He exists or that He can replace hatred with love.

Here's my update on Aesop's Fables—*Taser Tales.* A police officer, who spoke to one of our children's groups at church, compared his police uniform and equipment to a believer's spiritual armor. When he mentioned his Taser, a little boy in the back shouted, "Shock my brother!" We laughed, but that shout-out was way too quick! There had to be a lot of history and not much forgiveness between those brothers. Are you still secretly hoping somebody you know gets "tasered"? Then here's the diagnosis: YOUR biggest enemy right now is yourself!

## TAKE OUT THE TRASH!

Continuing to reject the idea of forgiveness or God's grace as necessary to survive moves you deeper into the pit at **Level 3: ANGER**. Anger is the "I don't have to take this"-impulse. Anger is connected to survival instinct. Anger is a defensive reaction...*and*...Anger can be a convincing disguise for rebellion against God. That raw emotion is good cover for the real issue of refusing to resolve the hurt. It's the logical, irreversible progression of protecting yourself and postponing the pain of releasing the offender.

Luis Palau, Argentina-born international best-selling author of nearly 50 books, broadcaster, and evangelist from Portland, Oregon, told the story of a friend of his who went through a massive emotional breakdown. After his recovery, they went for a walk. "Luis," he said, "don't ever allow anyone to make you bitter." He gave the background on his breakdown which proved very embarrassing. "My problems began when I got so worked up about the contractor who didn't build my basement and driveway right. I hated what he'd done to my home. And since he lived next door, I saw him almost daily. Each time I saw him, my anger and bitterness grew even more intense until I finally cracked."[3]

Still skeptical about the risks associated with anger? Researchers have reported serious data suggesting connections between anger and health risks. According to researchers, chronic anger is so damaging to the body that it competes with cigarette smoking, obesity and a high-fat diet as a powerful risk factor for early death. Dr. Redford Williams at the respected Duke University Medical Center summarized: "Our studies indicate that hostile, suspicious anger is right up there with any other health hazard we know about."[4] In another study, Dr. Mara Julius, an epidemiologist at the University of Michigan, analyzed the effects of chronic anger on women over a period of 18 years, discovering that women who had answered initial test questions with obvious signs of long-term, suppressed anger were three times more likely to have died than those who did not harbor such hostile feelings.[5]

That's why forgiveness is a life and death issue. Bitterness never dies. It has to be killed. Bitterness never fades. It grows. It grows because it is fed and protected. Think of every inappropriate angry thought as a piece of trash that needs to be discarded. Every time you think of what you lost, who hurt you, or how your life changed, the pile of *trash thoughts* grows. Chasing that analogy, the longer you leave stinking trash in your house (i.e., heart and mind), the more it takes over. You can admit you have trash piled high, apologize for the odor and disorder of your life, wake up every morning feeling guilty about it, or even make plans to take it out soon. But if you don't, it decomposes to the worst—bitterness. Basically, anger survives as long as you protect your perceived right to be in control. After all, if you live in a 2-dimension world—intellectual and emotional—it seems right and feels right to fight this thing. But we exist in 3rd dimension—spiritual—as well, so the intellectual poisoning, emotional spoilage, and spiritual garbage piles up!

Anger is really driven by fear—the feeling that there will be no relief, no fairness, no cap on the suffering, no solution, no resolution, no answers, no improvement, no healing…**OR**…the fear that we might be exposed for who we really are!

## PEPPERONI, EXTRA CHEESE, and SAUSAGE

If the hurt is still unresolved, you get your ticket punched on the emotional roller coaster ride [or "slide" might work better] downward to **Level 4: RESENTMENT.** Resentment is the first layer of protection for the hurt. It hardens your heart toward God, the offender, and everybody else in your life.

Jackie Huth published a story in *Reader's Digest* about a late night phone call. Sometime around 2:00am their phone rang, waking her and her husband out of a sound sleep. "Wrong number," her husband growled, and slammed down the phone. A few minutes later it rang again. She heard him say, "One with pepperoni and extra cheese and one with sausage. Pickup in 20 minutes." "What was that?" she asked. "I took his order. Now we can sleep."

Resentment wears you out trying to sustain even the justifiable anger and weak arguments that God and the world owe you big time. Resentment is the "creative" phase of this process, when you constantly search for new ways to frame what happened. Normally, resentment drives you to discover innovative ways to keep on rehearsing the offense and defending your right to your feelings. Eventually, though, you reach the tipping point and it flavors how you talk and respond. Because it is an addictive emotion, the assumed right to judge people and situations and motives takes over. Normally, offended people develop a critical attitude to cover up the sin of refusing to let God help them forgive. When you can't confess this basic sin, the resentment, you are not going to be confessing other sins. And unconfessed sin has its own down-side—your prayers don't get answered by God (Psalm 66:18), Satan gets into your family (Ephesians 4:26), discouragement surfaces in your speech (Ephesians 4:27), and you lose peace and confidence (Ephesians 4:3, 30 / Romans 15:13).

### You say you want a DEVOLUTION?

Beatles John Lennon and Paul McCartney collaborated in writing *Revolution*, their legendary commentary on the social protests that were rocking America in the 1960's (first version released in 1968). The lyrics begin with a simple statement, *"You say you want a revolution."* When it comes to resentment, we can tweak it into a question: "You say you want a DEVOLUTION?" Unresolved hurt that devolves into an unwillingness to forgive, that devolves into anger, which devolves into resentment, is ballooning into an unresolved resentment creating the final level of emotional and spiritual bondage. That final level? It's fully-*devolved* and lethal. It's **Level 5: BITTERNESS**. Say the word and it sounds like you are taking a bite of something. The Greek word translated "bitterness" in Hebrews 12:15 means "cutting or biting, irritable, harsh". It's the TRASH of your spirit—emotions that have spoiled. There's only one way to survive. TAKE OUT THE TRASH!

### Legalizing Pot

*Hoarders* is a reality show on A&E television, documenting the crisis of people who simply can't get motivated to remove anything, including trash, from their homes. In one episode, a woman confessed her obsession with keeping everything and parting with nothing. After she had made her way through the path of trash in the kitchen, her take on her addiction was: "I have three coffee pots. It's easier to buy a new coffee pot than it is to clean." That's a crazy version of "legalizing pot". Pun intended.

That's the way some people manage bitterness. Just buy another coffee pot. Get a socially acceptable substitute. Use a diversion. Find another way to cope or get through. After all, it's easier to start something new than resolve the problem. Bitterness is simply hurt or disappointment that has never been cleaned up, dumped, or discarded.

### The BIOLOGY of BITTERNESS

Hebrews 12:15 is scary, because bitterness is described in almost biological, bacterial, or botanical terms. It *"springs up...causes trouble...and many become defiled"* (ESV). "Springs up" is like breaking through the surface. And it is non-stop—no closing for holidays, family crisis, vacations, economic slowdowns, or school. Bitterness is progressive. It never gets better, only worse, stealing your energy, creating a darker negative lens through which you view others, choking and squeezing out your joy, and suffocating your desire to obey and believe in God, with constantly increasing power. No way you manage, contain, hide, disguise, or repress bitterness. God did not design your spirit to contain or cap such poisonous and explosive mega-emotions. If you don't get rid of it, you'll hurt other people, pull them down, and make it easier for them to sin. Former Notre Dame football coach and now ESPN analyst, Coach Lou Holtz observed, "If you burn your neighbor's house down, it doesn't make your house look any better."

Bitterness can never be isolated to one segment of your life. No way it can be successfully contained. Saying you are bitter about one person or incident and cool with everybody else is naïve at best, and risky at worst. Bitterness takes over your entire spirit like AIDS affects your entire body and can be spread to others (cf., "many become defiled"). You can't be one person at work and display personality 2 at home long-term. What you are emotionally and spiritually is what you are, regardless of geographical location. Bitter at work equals bitter at church or bitter at home.

## You Want That Coffee to Go?

Bitterness is like a constant stream of coffee pouring into a small cup. As soon as it reaches the fill line capacity and surges past the rim, the overflow begins. Because God did not design your spirit (mind, emotions, or soul) to contain this toxic stream of bitterness, you have to dump it somewhere—shift or transfer it to others. When your cup is full, it will spill on whatever you bump into. And remember, whatever is in the cup is what spills out. If you have coffee in the cup, then it is coffee that splashes around, not juice or milk. Using that analogy, whatever is in your spirit (i.e., your "cup of emotions") is what spills out in your words, conversations, and reactions. Fact. You can't stop it. What you say is really what you are! Jesus said, *"Your words show what is in your hearts"* (Matthew 12:34, CEV). If you keep rehearsing the details of an offense, consistently have a critical and negative edge to your words, are hyper-sensitive to how people should treat you, are insensitive to their feelings, have difficulty apologizing, find yourself constantly thinking about payback, refuse to talk to some people, expect others to cater to your demands, secretly celebrate when somebody else has problems, or get angry—*fast, loud, and frequently*...you are showing signs of BITTERNESS! The ultimate result is that you are caught in a cycle of beating up on yourself because you are getting whipped by this deeply embedded hurt and anger, and then taking it out on somebody else. But you are not in control for long. Bitterness evolves into something like a demon possessing you, taking over inside of you. This emotional "demon" spirit seems to force you to manage its agenda with increasingly sharper remarks, quicker paybacks, skillful manipulation, and dominating others like you are being controlled internally. Frankly, God routinely catches the blame because it's easier to attack God for His unfairness, failure to come through for you and protect you, instead of owning up to your responsibility in processing the initial hurt.

People controlled by bitterness experience *and* deliver emotional terrorism. They bounce back and forth on an emotional scale from hostility to depression. And normally that hostility or depression can't be easily traced to the real, historical source moment or incident that is causing the bitterness. Even those closest to bitter people—whether family or inner circle or teammates or staff—can't seem to believe it or connect the unpredictable behavior to anything consistently.

A bizarre scene was captured in 2011 on the security cameras of the downtown Sears store in Seattle, Washington. An elderly man calmly hand-delivered an envelope containing a $100 bill and a note, hand-addressed to the Sears manager. The explanation? The note was a confession from this man who wished to remain anonymous, that he had stolen between $20-$30 cash from the store in the late 1940's, and wanted to repay it with interest. Store manager Gary Lorentson believed the man's conscience "has been bothering him for the past 60 years."[6]

Just like the invisible guilt over a singular bad choice that haunted this man for over six decades, the covert cancer of bitterness in your spirit cannot be removed until you deal with the source. It owns your thoughts. No statute of limitations on murder…or bitterness.

### It wasn't Nemo he found!

In the huge 2003 Disney classic movie, *Finding Nemo*, a daddy clownfish in the Great Barrier Reef starts a high-risk search for his son, who was captured, taken to Sydney, and placed in a dentist's aquarium. After life and death encounters with sharks, jellyfish, deep sea creatures, sea gulls, and a trawler's fishing net, the dad's love is rewarded when he is reunited with his son. In another fish story, something bigger than Nemo was found!

It is my conviction, from more than three decades of counseling exposure to diverse and dysfunctional family profiles, that most depression—except physically or chemically-induced depression—is rooted in unresolved bitterness. Take just one Old Testament example—Jonah. Jonah, a respected Jewish prophet, is mentioned in II Kings 14:25 as serving during the reign of Jeroboam II (786-746 BC) of Israel (the Northern Kingdom). Running from God's direct command to go and offer forgiveness to the hated Assyrian nation, Jonah boarded a ship to escape, only to be caught in a storm, thrown overboard by the crew, swallowed by a giant fish, and vomited out in enemy territory. It's worth noting that since God actually created the jet streams, geography, marine life and its metabolism, and ocean currents, He can override any route you've planned. Jonah reluctantly moved forward with God's plan and walked through the huge metro area, preaching forgiveness in the streets of the capital city, Nineveh. Jonah fully expected the people all across the city to do just what they did—repent (i.e., turn from their sins). Even the king asked for God's forgiveness. The final chapter

of this brief adventure shows Jonah on a hillside, overlooking the now spiritu-
ally-changed city, asking God to take his life!

God's reply was classic: *"Why are you so angry?"* (see Jonah 4:1-4). God
knew the deeper issue was not the assignment but the attitude. Jonah was bitter and his bitterness led him to suicidal depression. The Assyrians had a reputation for extreme brutality in war, the terrorist nation in their segment of
history. It's highly probable that some really bad history existed; that Jonah
either had relatives or friends that had been killed in exchanges with this rogue
nation. Unresolved hurt plus rejection of forgiveness could easily have devolved
into anger, resentment, and ultimately bitterness. So extreme and entrenched
was this apparent bitterness that Jonah wanted to die rather than deal with the
hatred. Ironic, huh? Jonah had wanted the Assyrians dead. Now, because he
doesn't get his own way and he's not in control, and his hatred looks worse than
the Assyrians' hatred, he wants to end his own life? No. Not really. Bitter people rarely take their own lives. They want the other guy to die. Jonah was a big
chicken. God didn't talk him off the ledge because he never really intended to
jump. His bitterness was exposed. Jonah was still consumed with hatred. People who hate normally fight to live because they want to win, to crush their enemies, and they have to have hatred to survive. To give up the bitterness that
protected some deep hurt was too much to ask, even when God closed the book
by asking Jonah if he even cared about the 120,000 innocent children living in
the city that was about to be destroyed. That, friends, is the power of bitterness…on record! But the Jonah stories haven't stopped.

One day, a teacher was talking to her first grade class about whales when
a little girl had a question, "Do whales swallow people?" The teacher
responded, "No, even though they are much bigger than a person, they have
throat pleats that filter their food of krill and plankton. "But my Sunday
School teacher says Jonah was swallowed by a whale." In a tense voice, the
teacher stated, "Blue whales cannot swallow people." "Well, when I get to
heaven I'll just ask Jonah if he was really swallowed by a whale," the girl
insisted. With obvious frustration, the teacher posed, "What if Jonah went to
hell?" Undeterred, the girl challenged, "Well then, you can ask him."

You've been there. You've thought life wasn't worth living. Even CSI
probably could not uncover the victim story that has been buried in your spirit
and memory for so long. But it's real. After years of denial, explanations, and
attempted changes, you want to give up. Are you going to let that original
hurt or disappointment finally take you down? I pray not. It's time to change.
A new life is possible. That's what God does. All you have to do is ask Him
for forgiveness. Let Him take over your heart…and life changes…immedi-
ately!

**UNPACK the BACKPACK!** Re-think how you've been living. Are you
good with where you're at? Like who you've become? Beware of Jonah's mistake. Believe God knows what He's doing. It just might save you.

*Chapter 18*

# EXIT Strategy

### They Did It On A Bike

Brides and bridegrooms are "reinventing the tradition of a grand entrance or exit," said Millie Martini Bratten, the editor in chief of *Brides* magazine.[1] It's big time theater with recent newlyweds arriving for their weddings by helicopter, school bus (teachers), hot air balloons, or elephants, and departing their ceremonies on things like a Jet Ski, ice cream truck, or bike. Cycling fans Hanne and Brian Duncan of Philadelphia, met at a race, had a second date on a 60-mile ride, and left their wedding on a tandem. The bride was still in her formal white gown, sporting three inch pink-and-orange heels. "I practiced beforehand," she said.[2] Exits are now trendy. Satan knows that.

### Satan's Exit Strategy

Believe it or not, running your life-race requires an effective defense against Satan's substitute plan—an exit strategy. **An exit strategy is a plan to get out of a situation, either because you have met a goal or reached your capacity to handle what's going on. It is not intended to be a cover-up for failure!** If you don't have a plan to finish the race, and walk away when Jesus says that you've done all He expected, you will follow Satan's exit strategy.

Protecting a hurt or offense is actually buying in to Satan's strategy, because ultimately it will make you want to quit! His strategy can always be reduced to one word: EXIT! *The believer's invisible enemy knows that you cannot carry a backpack full of bitterness and be effective.* Tolerate the bitterness sourced in the past and you'll eventually question everything from your sanity to your status with Facebook. Then you'll decide there is less stress in fearing God's going to strike you dead than the stress of trying to live right…and you'll take the first exit from commitment. So, if you don't deal with the junk that's piled up in your emotional/spiritual backpack, what's the next risk exposure? Check it out: *"…let us strip off every weight that slows us down, especially the sin that so easily trips us up. And let us run with endurance the race God has set before us....So take a new grip with your tired hands and strengthen your weak knees."* (Hebrews 12:1, 12, NLT).

## Hitting The WALL

Running with endurance means pushing through the pain, the setbacks, the pressure, and the mounting physical stress that makes you feel like death or a total collapse is not only imminent, but needed. When you just want relief...when you just want it to be over...when the race has become so threatening that you can't remember why you chose to run in the first place...and your body is screaming at you...God is saying in those verses that *you've got to energize—not exit!*

The challenge is to *re-energize* from the effects of a brutal race by getting rid of excess weight by getting a "new grip" and strengthening the "weak knees". Translation? Just flip that expectation upside down and you get: Don't quit! Long-distance runners or cyclists know what it means to *hit the wall*. During competition, mostly in endurance sports, glycogen reserves in the muscles or liver can become depleted, resulting in sudden fatigue, loss of energy, and/or collapse. Without proper nutrients in the system or ingested when you near empty, recovery is slow or impossible. At some point in their life-race, every person will *hit the wall*—cap out on stamina under intense stress. You will want to quit!

## MISTAKE No. 4: Thinking quitting is a good option.

That's Mistake No. 4. . .that you will resign, walk out the door, or just mentally and emotionally check out. There's no acceptable reason *to stop believing* in Jesus. There's no good reason *to delay obeying* Jesus. No excuse for bailing on Him survives because He took it all the way to the cross for you! The winning argument is that not only do we know Jesus made it through this life without quitting, but since our "race" (i.e., our God-designed life plan) is His idea, then He's in it with us. Hebrews 12:2 states both personal strategy and promise— *"We do this by keeping our eyes on Jesus, the champion who initiates and perfects our faith"* (NLT). We don't have to stress about our capacity to believe or finish because Jesus Himself protects our entire belief journey. That's huge! Our part is to dump the crushing weight of the negative stuff we've accumulated in our emotional/spiritual backpack (i.e., spirit), and His role is to make sure nothing hits us on the journey—hard enough or for a long enough season—that could actually take us under. We control the choices. He controls the pressure.

In *Outliers: The Story of Success*, author Malcolm Gladwell examines the diverse forces behind success, like family, culture, friendship, childhood, and accidents of birth, history, and geography. He argues, "It is only by asking where they are from that we can unravel the logic behind who succeeds and who doesn't."[3] Gladwell presents his theory through the anecdotal case of "Christopher Langan, a man who, despite an IQ of 195 (Einstein's was 150), wound up working on a horse farm in rural Missouri. Why isn't he a nuclear rocket surgeon? Because of the environment he grew up in: there was no one in Langan's life and nothing in his background that could help him capitalize on his exceptional gifts."[4] Gladwell concludes, "He had to make his way alone, and no one—not rock stars, not professional athletes, not software billionaires, and not even geniuses—ever makes it alone."[5] True. Believers know life isn't random and we are never doing it alone! Jesus controls the journey—the intersections, the conditions, the destiny, and the outcome.

Quit worrying about whether you are going to make it through all the junk. You *will* make it NOT because you have an awesome support network, read the right books, or choose to think positive, but because Jesus created faith in you and will complete that faith—i.e., get you through life and to heaven (see Philippians 1:6).

### Nobody ever drowned in sweat!

Called by some *"the best football coach in 50 years"*, Lou Holtz was inducted into the Hall of Fame in 2008. Now a popular ESPN analyst known for his ability to motivate, Dr. Lou said, *"Nobody ever drowned in sweat! Motivation is simple. You eliminate those who are not motivated."* The belief that you can't get through your trials is like choosing to eliminate yourself because you've let somebody or something steal your motivation and you know it! Former Arkansas governor, 2008 candidate for the Republican presidential nomination, best-selling author, and host of the FOX NEWS weekend hit, *"HUCKABEE"*, Mike Huckabee was asked by Fox News whether former House Speaker Newt Gingrich should get out of the 2012 Republican presidential primary race after losing to former Massachusetts governor Mitt Romney by 15% in the Florida primary. He humorously responded, "Getting out is the only way you know what the outcome will be!"[6] Don't quit!

Your attitude will determine your success. As best-selling Christian author and pastor David Jeremiah said, "God called us to be runners, not judges!" Just run your race. Don't act like a judge, being critical of every mistake you've made, obsessing over how much time you've wasted, or beat yourself up over the hurt you may have caused. No matter how easy and tempting it would be to just walk away from trying to honor Jesus with your life, it's not worth it. That would be a bigger sin. The truth is that letting the negative stuff pile up is what creates discouragement.

Quitting can really look good when you reach the limits of what you think you can handle, carrying all the stuff around, even though you know it needs to be put down. Endurance is simply consistently doing the hard things you don't enjoy at the time. Endurance doesn't just create success—it *is* success. The Greek word in our text (*hupomone*) translated as "endurance" does not mean trying to stay positive in a negative world, resigning yourself to a life of rejection and failure. Nor is it passive tolerance, letting people mistreat you because you think you deserve it and things will never change. Endurance is not trying to do your best even though you believe you're not going to win and it won't make a difference. It's the opposite of the depressed attitude or feeling of being stuck that leads to bitterness, resentment and complaining. Endurance is both an attitude and an approach to your life-race. It's a strong determination to get something done AND become what God has called you to be, regardless of all the temptation and pressure to slow down or give up. Jesus expects you not just to finish, but finish big! Not just to cross the finish line, but to have done something with your life that counts. You were NOT created to be ordinary.

Denny Coates, creator of an online coaching service for developing personal strength and people skills called ProStar Coach, blogged that success could be explained in part by motivation and personal strength.[7] His comments were in sync with the success theory popularized by Malcolm Gladwell, the "10,000 Hour Rule", that in order for a person to master any complex skill, from brain surgery to playing the cello, a minimum of 10,000 hours of focused practice are required. Coates friend, a West Point classmate who became a plastic surgeon, captured it well: "You gotta want it. You really gotta wanna."[8]

Someone has accurately warned, "It's always too soon to quit!" Your God-assigned life-race is an intense contest, a struggle with conflict and competition. It implies there is something worth fighting for! But the race believers commit to run AND win, is not a sprint or a 100-meter dash. In fact if you try to run like the race was short, you will soon be "sidelined". One of the greatest mistakes we can make in this agonizing race is not to pace ourselves properly. Many rookie followers of Jesus start out intense, emotional, pumped, dancing and strutting, but they quickly begin to fade for multiple reasons. Typically they become disappointing casualties—just statistics because they've underestimated the pressure and overestimated their capacity to handle it. Sometimes unseasoned believers get discouraged enough to quit because they flip-flop and go back to their previous lifestyle for "just a taste" of what they remember as good. It's convenient to believe we can take a quick break from our commitment to Jesus without impacting our resolve to endure or any negative slippage back into the old, self-indulgent lifestyle.

Coach Holtz created a reality check for one of his football teams: *"On this team, we're all united in a common goal—to keep my job."* Funny. Probably true. At least that's the way I would coach! And some people actually use that approach as a substitute plan for their life-race. They live that way, thinking it's all about self-protection—survival at all costs. But what if you treated your mate or kids that way? What if you decided not to come home for days or weeks at a time so you could "have a life" too and enjoy a few things? That would do major damage to the trust in your family. Try to name something good that comes from quitting. Outside of temporary relief from some stress, the consequences are devastating. When you fail to do the things that build endurance, you are vulnerable to walking away from the amazing opportunities Jesus has planned for you. Even if it's only temporary, you lose big time. Most opportunities come disguised in difficulty.

Here's reality: *The more you invest in a relationship or goal the less likely you are to bail for something that competes with it.*

Want to get serious about endurance? Focus on just one specific goal. It reduces the fear factor. And quit repeating your failures and weakness to other people. You can't survive long by looking backward. Keep moving. Deal with sins and move on. Your past is not who you are. Your identity is in Jesus and what He is doing for you right now! Refuse to let all the dark and dumb things in your past to define your future.

Repeat this out loud right now: "Quitting is NOT an option!" Shout it like you are getting pumped for a championship game. You need to hear yourself saying it. Now…live that way.

## African-American in the White House?

In 1862, after the death at the White House of her 11-year-old son, Willie, President Lincoln's wife, Mary, turned for comfort to a former slave—a skilled seamstress—who had become her constant companion. Oddly enough, Elizabeth Keckley once worked for the woman who became the First Lady of the Confederate States of America, Mrs. Jefferson Davis. In a PBS documentary, *Abraham and Mary: A House Divided*, historian Margaret Washington surfaced the details of this unusual and deep friendship: "Keckley dressed her, made her clothes, fixed her hair. And Keckley listened, empathized. And Mary felt she could talk to Elizabeth in a way that she could not talk to the gossiping jealous women of Washington. So they became confidantes."[9] Elizabeth had also lost a son during the Civil War, and comforted Mrs. Lincoln with the story of how she had kept grief from overwhelming her: "To assist the thousands of ex-slaves now crowded into camps behind the Union lines, Keckley had helped form the Contraband Relief Association, dedicated to providing food and clothes and finding them jobs."[10] Keckley bridged the social divide with her famous friend by reminding Mrs. Lincoln of a universal truth nobody could take from her: "I know what liberty is, because I know what slavery was."[11] That perspective meant Keckley was never really "owned" by anybody.

Knowing Jesus means you don't have to be bound, addicted, enslaved, entangled, or *owned* by any sin! In fact, if you are captured, in bondage to or addicted to any habit or choice, it's your fault, not His or anybody else's fault, and it is an embarrassing contradiction of what life in Jesus is all about. Surrendering to Jesus sets you free from the power of sin, and making the right choices keeps you free! Check it out in Romans 6:

> 6 We know that our old life died with Christ on the cross so
> that our sinful selves would have no power over us and we
> would not be slaves to sin. 7 Anyone who has died is made free
> from sin's control. 8 If we died with Christ, we know we will
> also live with him. 9 Christ was raised from the dead, and we
> know that he cannot die again. Death has no power over him
> now. 10 Yes, when Christ died, he died to defeat the power of
> sin one time—enough for all time. He now has a new life, and
> his new life is with God. 11 In the same way, you should see
> yourselves as being dead to the power of sin and alive with God
> through Christ Jesus. 12 So, do not let sin control your life here
> on earth so that you do what your sinful self wants to do. 13
> Do not offer the parts of your body to serve sin, as things to be
> used in doing evil. Instead, offer yourselves to God as people
> who have died and now live. Offer the parts of your body to
> God to be used in doing good. 14 Sin will not be your master,
> because you are not under law but under God's grace. (NCV)

God gives every believer access to ALL the resources for freedom—things like the presence of the Holy Spirit, strategies of resistance and spiritual warfare from the Scripture, and the ability to identify the things that defeat you.

But for now, the truth is that the power to change habits and the strength to refresh choices comes from your new life source—Jesus. The verses just listed are the contractual language that guarantees you can still be an untested rookie follower of Jesus totally surrounded and captured by sin—AND STILL BREAK FREE! That's why sin eventually makes you feel awkward, empty, and helpless. Because you were designed by God for freedom, not captivity. Sin creates a prison cell that can only be unlocked from the Person who was the first to defeat it—Jesus. Jesus broke the power of sin to dominate your life and infused that power in you the moment you invited Him into your life (Romans 6:10-11). Technically, spiritually, and theologically, you *are* already free when Jesus lives in you. It's just that it has to become practical daily reality by your choices.

## Dick Vitale and the "Trifecta, Baby!"

One of my favorite all-time basketball color analysts is Dick Vitale. His passion, voice inflection, and unique terminology describing plays can make "Duke Crazies" or just NCAA basketball fans out of anybody. When I hear him say, "Trifecta, Baby!" I know the season is on! According to the previous verses, there is actually another trifecta—a trifecta of freedom:

separation, surrender, and substitution (see Romans 6:12-13). It's both a progression and a package. Let me explain.

### A Few Good Men?

Tom Cruise, Demi Moore, and Jack Nicholson starred in the 1992 Oscar-nominated film, *A Few Good Men*. When a rookie Navy defense attorney (Cruise) demands that a power-drunk Marine Colonel Jessup (Nicholson) on the witness stand give the truth about his role in the cover-up of a soldier's murder, Col. Jessup shouts, "You can't handle the truth!" Can only *a few* handle the truth?

It may be difficult for some believers to face the truth. Yes, living the life God has designed means **separation** from the sins that dominated the "before" photo of your life. Dump them. Walk away. Get upset about what those sins did to you and break away. But that's incomplete, inadequate, and insufficient. You're not where you need to be yet. Verse 12 carries a tone of insistence and verse 13 repeats it like the double ads you see in some magazines. The thrust is unmistakable. Quit giving yourself up to that stuff, and sin won't control you. That's **separation**. However, it's not over.

You have to develop a consistent discipline of **surrender**, offering your body, mind, will, desires, and energy for God's purposes (6:13b— *"Offer yourselves to God"*). Surrender is all about ownership, compliance with God's purpose for each day, pursuing His next adventure. Without intentionally stepping up to accept God's control moment by moment—in effect admitting that He's God and you're not and He's actually smarter than you—you won't be able to impact people or penetrate the spiritual darkness around you. Translation? You are going to look stupid and won't be able to win a single argument with the non-believing crowd.

Complete the trifecta with **substitution** (6:13c— *"Offer the parts of your body to God to be used in doing good"*). Get aggressive. Substitute good choices for the old bad choices. Following Jesus has never been a defensive strategy. Unless followers are strategically assuming an offensive position, nothing changes. We've got to bridge a culture to Jesus that has swallowed every lie and chased every offer about what brings permanent happiness.

***Our destiny cannot be reduced to simply creating a life free of sin.*** It's bigger than moral success. Besides, we never really conquer all desires this side of heaven, and framing our new life just with the separation noun is a pathetically weak argument for conversion. Would you support your favorite college sports team just because they have promised "no more NCAA recruiting violations"? Not enough, right? You want more if you're going to shell out for season tickets, paint your face, head, or chest with their colors, sit next to obnoxious people in a crowded section, and give up your day off! Fans prefer to brag about conference and national championships. Point taken.

There's more to life. It's about replacement. **Substitution.** Remove sinful choices and entanglements, but don't stop there. **Pack your life with good stuff.** Replace the sinful stuff that messed you up and threw your life off course with really healthy, God-pleasing choices to make a difference before your time runs out. Footnote: If you don't start making the right choices, you'll fall back to the wrong choices. Just like body weight, nobody can maintain the same weight forever. You are always gaining or losing, depending on what you choose. Allow the life of Jesus to flow through you to touch and transform people around you. Be that vessel of hope and healing. Look for the opportunity to do good and point people to the only One who can deliver them.

Summary? Do **more** than avoid sinful stuff. Daily surrender to the process of recycling—throwing out the repeated mistakes and cycling-in better choices to create a new, more God-honoring and people-friendly life.

### It's a Rookie Mistake!

It's the way non-believers look at believers. It's a frequent mistake of rookie believers. C'mon, man! What is it? It's assuming that being a lifetime devoted follower of Jesus just means that you've committed to giving up the fun stuff that both sides know down deep is bad (casual sex, getting drunk, cheating, fighting, lying, etc.). It's a traditional misconception—defining Christianity in just moral categories. Following Jesus cannot be limited to a list of what NOT to do. Big deal. I know plenty of people who are NOT buying in to Jesus that live sexually disciplined lives, abstain from alcohol and drugs, give to charities, show up at their kids' ball games and recitals, stay faithful to their mates, never cheat on their taxes, vote in every election, and pay all their credit card bills on time.

In fact, that one twisted definition of Christianity is why non-believers are relieved down deep inside, if not totally giddy, when a believer messes up morally. A single mistake in judgment—which believers know will happen because we're not perfect—we know is regrettable, but forgivable. Yet it gives non-believers the ammo they think they need, not just to ridicule or isolate or marginalize believers at the office or in the media, but to excuse themselves from dealing with God on His terms. For that debate, know that just because a politician takes a bribe, a policeman is abusive, or a preacher is a bigot, doesn't exempt you or me from playing by the rules, obeying the law, or being ultimately accountable—not just to a mate, judge, or the electorate—but to God. You'll be laughed out of the courtroom if your only defense for a speeding ticket is that the cop who stopped you got drunk once, because that's not the issue. We cannot come to God on our terms. We are not the final authority. That's belief "over-easy". Works for a breakfast order at Waffle House, but God says, "Not in MY house!"

For a non-believer to justify ignoring Jesus and believers on the basis of the imperfection they see in a professing believer is a lost cause, because it's Jesus, not believers, that is perfect.  I know, believers are supposed to accurately and consistently represent Him, like a defense attorney does for a client or a U.N. Ambassador does for their country.  And I know that a consistent, God-honoring life doesn't change anybody's beliefs . . . but it does remove their excuses.  And, next to living holy because God is holy, that's basically the secondary reason for living consistently—to remove convenient excuses and real hindrances to belief on the part of skeptics (see 1 Corinthians 8:9-13).

The lyrics of Avril Lavigne's song, *Complicated*, describe the disillusionment and frustration with inconsistency and hypocrisy:

*Why do you have to go and make things so complicated?*
*I see the way you're*
*Acting like you're somebody else gets me frustrated*
*Life's like this, you*
*And you fall and you crawl*
*And you break and you take*
*What you get and you turn it into Honesty*
*Promise me I'm never gonna find you fake it*

Just like the song, non-believers can detect a fake a mile away.  In reality, they're looking for somebody who is real, not perfect.  A believer—*who can talk about how their belief in God has survived the same unexplained suffering that everybody universally experiences, that can admit there is a real struggle to discover truth, and can relate with remarkable candor the tension in making right choices when tempted*—will never lack anybody to discuss Jesus at Starbucks, on the golf course, during lunch, at the gym, at the ballpark, on the boat, in the pickup, or at the office.

### *THE* Top Ten

Besides, only having a default moral standard is not a very impressive or an extremely compelling stand-alone argument for a non-believer to crossover to life with Jesus.  Think about it.  When I was a skeptic, I didn't seek out people who said they were Christians just because they weren't into all the other stuff on the campus.  Whether your friends, family, teammates, or co-workers are tolerant of religion, or hostile to the hyper-spiritual, why should they care?  The tendency would be for them to interpret remarks like, "Hey, I don't party" as a rejection of them—that you are superior or want to impose your beliefs—not build a friendship.  Or at a minimum, it conveys the image that you're out-of-touch, leading a boring life on the same level as how the Amish are wrongly perceived.  Some immature believers mistakenly think that they are doing good or maximizing their influence for Jesus by merely avoiding

destructive habits and lifestyles that owned their former life. Simply announc-
ing, "I don't do that stuff anymore" communicates arrogance, not truth. That
genre of statements smacks of elitism and provides no good reason for a non-
believer to flip their life. Because that approach has been overlaid on the Ten
Commandments for centuries, the original law looks like the constitution for
an oppressive religious regime, packed with "don'ts", prohibiting a fully-lived
life and promoting a negative, intolerant life-perspective.

It's actually quite the opposite. God's purpose in the world's most concise
societal legal and moral agenda (the 10 Commandments) was to *protect* families. How? By putting boundaries around what is valuable and vulnerable in
life, educating us on priorities of everything from worship to relationships, and
pointing out the need for God and forgiveness through the obvious impossi-
bility of perfectly achieving all ten of those commandments (see Romans 7:7).
There's a simple explanation in Galatians 3:24:

> *Until the time when we were mature enough to respond freely*
> *in faith to the living God, we were carefully surrounded and*
> *protected by the Mosaic law. The law was like those Greek*
> *tutors, with which you are familiar, who escort children to*
> *school and protect them from danger or distraction, making*
> *sure the children will really get to the place they set out for.*
> (The Message)

Although intended for another issue, author Donald Miller's analogy
about being obsessed with a single approach seems to hit home:

> "I've also found that the more I trust in Christ's redemption
> to be sufficient, the less overtly religious I am. And, quite
> honestly, the more suspect overtly religious people become to
> me. When I'm with somebody who talks zealously about
> faith, about Jesus, about the Bible, after a while, I find myself
> wondering whether or not their faith is strong at all. For
> instance, if I were with somebody who kept talking about
> how much they loved their wife, going on loudly and pro-
> fusely, intuitively I would wonder whether or not they were
> struggling in their marriage. I would wonder whether they
> were trying to convince me they loved their wife, or if they
> were trying to convince themselves."[12]

Pressing the issue of moral superiority or success by definition means you
are not talking about other issues and may be reaching for reassurance.
Describing your life as a believer simply in terms of "not getting high anymore", or something similar, falls ridiculously short of winning an audience.

A non-believer is left with more questions than answers. Limiting their pro-file of Christianity to a narrowly defined list of obligations is at best confusing, and at worst, scary.

It's a relationship, not a set of rules! Why would a non-believer want to take on something that seems to guarantee failure? If you *know* you're going to crash, only an idiot gets on that plane! A non-believer compares lifestyle and happiness scales—not just results—and concludes that keeping rules, even if morals are a good thing, is oppressive and impossible. It's like a different lan-guage that requires an interpreter. When I surrendered to become a life-time Christ-follower, my buddies argued, "Who's to say that your rules are better than mine?" Obviously the right answer is, "It's not about rules. It's about a relationship—a life of freedom. Check out the results." The counter-argu-ment is that every belief has a consequence, and things like peace trump guilt, and love is actually superior to hatred or bitterness. Jesus framed it in practi-cal images: *"every good tree bears good fruit, but a bad tree bears bad fruit....a tree is known by its fruit"* (Matthew 7:17, 12:33, NKJV).

I remember what life was like for me as a college student, as a hostile non-believer at times, trying to tread water in the flood of ideas and beliefs. No way that I wanted to hang out with believers or listen to their sales pitch. The last person I wanted near me in college was somebody who would ruin my party. As a finance major, going "religious" was the equivalent of "going Amish", checking into prison, registering for another English course, or doing over a fraternity initiation. No interest. Irrelevant. Totally unappealing. Waste of time. Wouldn't ever use it. Didn't fit my lifestyle. My primary goal thought was to get as far away from restrictions and anything that represented confining me to any one belief, location, job, or even restaurant. Well, that's not entirely true. I had 3 serious commitments. One to my girlfriend, who became my wife. One to the University of Nebraska Cornhuskers. And one to Valentino's restaurant in Lincoln, Nebraska. In that order. No confusion there.

So, why would a non-believer get pumped about another list of rules or becoming friends with someone who couldn't talk about anything else? Believers are obligated to answer a sticky question then. What is it that you do that is positive, that builds bridges of friendship, that gives purpose to your life, or that makes a difference in the lives of other people?

Bottom-line, it's up to you. Strip off the hindrances and the break way from the entangling sins—so that you can create a life with impact!

A guy walked into a warehouse on his first day on the new job, and asked if anyone wanted to hear a good truck driver joke. One guy said, "Before you tell it, you should know that I am 6-2 and weigh 225 and I'm a truck driver. See that guy? He's 6-4 and weighs 250 and he's a truck driver, too. And see the guy across the warehouse? He's 6-6 and weighs 280 and he's a truck driver, too! Now, do you still want to tell your truck driver joke?" The guy said,

"Nah." To which the truck driver smiled and said, "What's the matter? Are you chicken?" The guy says, "Nah. I just don't want to have to explain it three times."

I've explained it three times already. Ready?

Wait. It's still probably essential for us to investigate what happens in the vanilla-plain, white-bread, ordinary, no substitutions, unremarkable, universal experience called a "choice".

*Chapter 19*

# The DNA of a CHOICE

### Young Lovers, France, and Accidents

He was an 18-year-old high school senior. She was a sophomore. They fell totally in love. With his new found romance, he lost motivation for his post-graduation summer international mission project. Although she didn't yet share his religious beliefs, she spoke against his new plan to go to college and marry her. She said, "No, you must go on your mission. That's your family heritage." He backed up on his dream and obediently spent the next 30 months in France, surviving on a little more than $100 in monthly support from home that had to be stretched between rent, food, and transportation. He lived in an apartment complex where the toilet was shared and the shower consisted of attaching a hose to the sink faucet and holding it over his head.[1] But at the age of 21, an even greater life lesson was imminent. His life would be forever altered through a car accident on a winding road in southwestern France. He was behind the steering wheel of a stylish low-riding Citroën DS with his supervisor, his supervisor's wife, and three others crammed into a car made for five people. Another car, driven by a speeding priest who appeared drunk, struck their car head-on. Police who arrived on the scene initially assumed that the young man was dead. A photo of him in the hospital later showed him with only a cast on his arm and a black eye. But his supervisor's wife tragically died in the crash.[2]

In a 2012 interview with David Gergen for PARADE Magazine, he recalled the "spiritual and emotional impact": "It brought a seriousness to my life—a recalculation of what was important and a recognition of life's fragility. Young people think bad things won't happen; I recognized that bad things can happen to me and those I love."[3]

That near-death experience changed the thinking of 21-year-old Mitt Romney. It has obviously influenced his entire family life and business/political career, as he openly discussed it during the 2012 Presidential campaign.

Although nobody could control or predict the accident, Mitt and Ann together made choices as teenagers that ultimately placed him in that moment—that life intersection. By what choice or destiny did Mitt survive? How does anybody explain it? How did you get to where *you* are?

What drives our choices? If such seemingly small choices, such as keeping a commitment to a mission project, have lasting effects that shape our destiny, then the choices we make are important. Let's break down the components of a choice as we drill deeper for insight on **how our backpacks get overstuffed—mostly with negative emotions and consequences—and how they get unpacked and repacked with the right choices and experiences.**

## A Coma, 5 Slices of Pizza, Lee Strobel, and Abortion

Choices are not made while you are in a coma. *Choices are real-time events!* So there are always external forces and internal feelings. Nor can a choice be defined as just a single, decisive word or thought, frozen in time. Every choice has a history and a personal flavor that keeps the taste alive for long past the moment.

Just to stay relevant, let's look at a choice as though it were a 5-slice pizza, and label each slice with its specific ingredients. According to our verse in focus, a choice is totally **INDIVIDUAL.** You, as an individual have complete responsibility for your level of success—or failure—in life. Specifically, the challenge is that because you put the negative and sinful experiences, emotions, and consequences in your own backpack, by yourself, choice by choice—you alone are the one who has to get rid of them. An accurate translation of Hebrews 12:1 goes like this: *"You yourself get rid of what's wearing you out, right now, once and for all".* It's like God saying to you: "Quit making excuses and get serious." There's no way you can blame somebody else for your attitude, for getting involved with the wrong person, for indulging in something that leads to sin or destructive habits, for buying into wrong beliefs about God, the church, Christians, the Bible, or for the way you invested your money, or whatever! Neither is it anyone else's obligation to bail you out or clean up your mess. Whatever mistakes have been made are your responsibility. Working through the consequences—the embarrassment or hardship required to separate from the "weight" or "sin"—is totally your property. Whether it's a bad mortgage, a bad ministry, a bad merger, a bad move, or a bad marriage, you must do what you can to make things right. Atheist-turned-Christian-turned-apologist Lee Strobel, the former award-winning legal editor of *The Chicago Tribune,* is a *New York Times* best-selling author of more than twenty books and has been interviewed on numerous national TV programs, including ABC, Fox, PBS, and CNN. In his book, *God's Outrageous Claims,* Strobel discussed three categories of circumstances where people find it hard to forgive themselves, including: exaggerated reactions to mere mistakes. His personal story kicked in at that point as he described a moment of decision in his pre-Christian college days. One of his fiancé's friends got pregnant and asked him what to do. "No problem. I've got the perfect solution. It's easy. No pain. No regrets. Just get an abortion." He helped her get to New York where abortion was legal. The guilt eventually kicked in: "Years later, when I came to understand the magnitude of what I had done, I tortured myself with remorse. How could I have been so cavalierly irresponsible about that kind of decision?"[4] After coming to know Christ, Strobel reversed the self-anger he had placed in his "backpack", forgiving himself because Jesus had forgiven him, and now uses the memory as motivation to speak out for the pro-life position.

The choice is clearly also **INCLUSIVE**—get rid of EVERY weight. You cannot handle the weight and be effective simultaneously. What's implied is that everybody has unnecessary stuff in their lives that makes them spend extra energy just to survive, and that approach doesn't work. You can't keep carrying the same old lifestyle, praying for God's strength, and expect things to improve. *You will get worn out and be discouraged with God, not yourself!* The word "every" really does mean "all", with no exceptions, regardless of how normal it seems for you even if it is a problem or sin for others, how long you have been doing it, how many of your friends think that way, how much you enjoy it, even if you can't see or haven't experienced any bad results or consequences, or even if you think you can handle it and run at the same time!

Another slice of a choice reveals that it is **INTENSE.** There is REAL competition for your energy, passion, abilities, influence and resources. To make the right choices, at some point you will offend some of your friends, have to reject some appealing offers, fight through really strong desires and feelings, choose the right priorities, and make bigger commitments than you ever thought about before. One Olympic athlete said she intentionally chose to give up dating in high school in order to give 100% attention to training for her sport in the Olympics, and would not have succeeded had she compromised. There will always be tough choices that cost you something to achieve God's best. Either you control your calendar or somebody else will!

The choice presented here additionally carries the meaning of being **IMMEDIATE.** There is NO NEGOTIATION, as in waiting for a less crowded schedule, more stable emotions, improving circumstances, or greater responsiveness or understanding from people. An athlete doesn't wait until the day before a game to get in shape. Life is not going to get less complicated. Options and people competing for your worship, money, and energy will just get bigger and more frequent in the future. Making the right choices NOW lowers the tension and prevents mistakes…AND GUILT later.

Finally, an underreported component of a choice is that it has the power to **INSPIRE.** Commitment to doing the right thing builds confidence and boldness to do more. It energizes. It builds discipline to achieve more. Boldness creates boldness. Not only are your choices going to ultimately be reviewed by God, they will be on display to influence more people than just your Facebook friend list or family.

## More Like Falling In Love

When you *choose* to dump the negative choices destroying your life and complicating your relationship with God, you are demonstrating a radical belief: *obedience is the first priority of any life-time devoted follower of Jesus.* Genuine obedience is like a teenager engaged in a disagreement with a mom or dad, saying, "Even if I don't agree or understand why you are expecting me to do this or making me do this, I trust you enough that I'll do it." Obedience is a response normally based on trust and not fear-based. If you don't trust the person asking you to do something, you definitely won't follow through. If you are being forced to do something, especially deny your beliefs—like a believer arrested and threatened for teaching the Word of God, or a soldier captured and tortured for information by the enemy—withholding obedience to your captor is the normal and sane response, though costly.

It's the opposite with God. If your relationship, approach, worship, obedience, generosity, or prayer-life with God is obligation-driven, then the motivation will die a slow death. Jason Gray said it best in his song, *More Like Falling In Love:*

> *Give me rules, I will break them*
> *Show me lines, I will cross them*
> *I need more than a truth to believe*
> *I need a truth that lives, moves, and breathes*
> *To sweep me off my feet*
>
> *Its gotta be*
> *More like falling in love*
> *Than something to believe in*
> *More like losing my heart*
> *Than giving my allegiance*
> *Caught up, called out*
> *Come take a look at me now*
> *It's like I'm falling,*
> *It's like I'm falling in love*
>
> *Give me words, I'll misuse them*
> *Obligations, I'll misplace them*
> *Cause all religion ever made of me*
> *Was just a sinner with a stone tied to my feet?*
> *It never set me free*

*Its gotta be*
*More like falling in love*
*Than something to believe in*
*More like losing my heart*
*Than giving my allegiance*
*Caught up, called out*
*Come take a look at me now*
*It's like I'm falling*
*It's like I'm falling in love*
*Love, Love*
*Deeper and deeper*
*It was love that made me a believer*
*In more than a name, a faith, a creed*
*Falling in love with Jesus brought the change in me.*

Religion is about **obligations**—obligations that leave you miserable, frustrated, and lifeless. Following Christ is all about **obedience** born out of love, because His love motivates us, controls us, compels us to this radical obsession (see 2 Corinthians 5:14). Jesus is all about freedom. CAUTION: You can lose your heart to a Savior like that! You will want to do insane things like walk away from bitterness and forgive people.

Fred Smith, the late corporate consultant to Fortune 500 firms like Ford Motor Company, said:

> *Years ago a psychiatrist helped me as I was dealing with the issue*
> *of lagging loyalty among senior plant employees. In figuring out*
> *a solution, I looked for the reason. I knew if I could see the basis*
> *for their thinking, there would be a logical explanation. My*
> *friend, the eminent psychiatrist, spoke two words to me ——*
> *Hostile Dependence. Their livelihoods were at the mercy of the*
> *company. They knew it and they were mad about it. He said he*
> *saw this in marriages, in adult children who returned home,*
> *and in work environments. "I want you, I need you, I love you"*
> *turns to "I need you, but I am not sure I want you, and some-*
> *times I hate you."*

> *I believe many of us experience hostile dependence on God. We*
> *know intellectually, morally, even spiritually that we are totally*
> *dependent and yet our self-love rebels against this. Instead of*
> *surrendering ourselves unconditionally to the love of God, we*
> *hold ourselves in a state of hostile dependence. We miss the joy of*
> *His love. When we try to reason out our relationship to God, we*
> *fail miserably. Divine grace is impossible to measure through*

*human rationing. "If He knew me like I know me, He wouldn't love me" was the answer I received once when asking the "Do you believe God loves you?" question. How pathetically foolish.*

*If the truth of God's love broke into our life, it would revolutionize us. My friend, Ray Stedman, once told me, "Fred, my life completely turned around when I discovered God was for me."*

*Hostile dependence denies the power of this love. We know He is in control and we thrust our fists heavenward, waiting for His retribution. What if we waited for His love and extended our arms to receive it? How few experience that freedom.*[5]

## 2.7 Seconds

Wow. He was so right. Stripping your life of the stuff that is destructive is really all about surrendering to loving God, even if you enjoy the stuff that is bad for you and don't see how it competes with accomplishing God's purpose. It proves you trust God. It's a *shout-out* that you believe God is **FOR** you! Confidence surges like a 5-hour energy drink when you realize God is NOT against you. Yes, we give up bad stuff to gain freedom…and freedom is not permission to live without boundaries, but *the power to live without bondage.* But that's still weak. It's not just about avoiding being a slave to sin. **We give up the bad choices messing up our life-race because we want to know and honor God!**

So, let's summarize. If you don't run your life-race by God's rules, you are assuming significant risk. That includes the potential of repeating bad choices that dig you a deeper hole spiritually. It's more bad risk than the good "capture life"-kind-of-risk in Tim McGraw's song, "*Live Like You Were Dying*":

*I went skydiving*
*I went rocky mountain climbing*
*I went two point seven seconds on a bull named Fu Man Chu*
*And I loved deeper*
*And I spoke sweeter*
*And I gave forgiveness I'd been denyin'*
*And he said some day I hope you get the chance*
*To live like you were dyin'*

Yet, it *IS* possible to dump the excess weight of negative and sinful choices. If we get locked into that cycle of carrying around the bad experiences, then the next big **MISTAKE** pops up like a video game monster. Let's take it on in the next chapter.

# PART SIX:

# The Finish

*Chapter 20*

# Click on FINISH

### The "Fades"?

In the 2011 BBC supernatural drama television series, *The Fades*, a teenage boy named Paul is haunted by apocalyptic dreams that nobody can explain, and begins to see spirits of the dead, known as the Fades, all around him. The Fades can't be seen, smelled, heard or touched by other humans, and are actually the residual of humans who died but have not been accepted into heaven. As one of the few humans who can actually see the Fades, an "Angelic" named Paul is on a mission to prevent the Fades, who are now embittered and vengeful against the humans race, from breaking back into the world and destroying humanity.[1]

How this for a bridge? For our purposes, the "Fades" are real in another spiritual sense. Use the word to describe a new lower level of energy in pursuing Jesus. These "invisible, rarely detectable" emotions can take over your attitude, draining your passion to run your life-race by God's standards.

"Fade" can mean to gradually move away from or incrementally decrease something. The word captures a sense of losing freshness, strength, or passion. Fade is frequently used as a term in movie production describing the shift from one scene to another, usually with the picture becoming darker before the next scene emerges—basically losing something or merging into another perspective. But it can also graphically describe what happens to your view of chasing the next adventure or accepting the next challenge in obeying Jesus. The original romance can become routine. Worship can FADE…real easy…real fast. Or as John, the disciple of Jesus imprisoned on an island called Patmos[2] for preaching that Jesus is Lord, heard in a Sunday morning revelation about a once-famous and strong church in Ephesus: *"…you have left your first love"* (Revelation 2:4, NKJV). For believers, "winning" in life is about sustaining love for a person—Jesus Himself! So, Mistake No. 5 becomes real.

## MISTAKE No. 5: Neglecting worship.

Worship in 2012 America is like bungee jumping—big risk, big rush, and big results. Cultural worshipers treat worship opportunities and venues like an escape to the Mall—shopping, swiping credit cards, and seeing friends. Get there. Get something on sale. Go back to real life. Life really is all about worship. Everybody worships something. The generic definition of worship covers the scale from respect to reverence, but really means loving something so much you begin to give it priority and exclusive devotion. With that street explanation, you can worship everything from Jennifer Lopez to Dr. Oz to a Porsche. But there is huge spiritual movement underway in 2012 American culture. Whether it's always biblical worship or not is still up for a vote. From mosques to mega-churches, people in record numbers are bowing, raising hands, jumping up and down at Christian concerts, holding hands in prayer at flagpoles and government buildings, cheering sermons at packed baseball stadiums, and filling former shopping malls to watch holograms of their favorite speakers. But what about the majority who prefer to stay on a bridge rather than have a cord with a Velcro strap wrapped around an ankle and dive from nauseating heights at high speed toward the ground? Do we need some legislation here? Doesn't Congress need to step in and define worship or something? Who's in charge of worship, anyway? Wow. Good question. Let's back up.

## ANALYZE THIS!!!

Ever try to define "worship"? Try doing it without using standard, rehearsed, pre-owned words like band, lights, stained glass, organ, keyboard, choir, church, preaching, singing, prayer, saints, mass, communion, readings, or religion. Hard, isn't it? Worship is ultimately *more captured than comprehended* but never divorced from loving God with all your mind (Luke 10:27); *more dynamic than static* because God is both constant and mysterious (Isaiah 6:1-5). God never changes but He is constantly changing things around us. Worship can be as natural as a child's uncensored prayer and as elusive as describing a child's laugh. But real worship could not possibly be dictated, designed, or owned by any leader, culture, generation, or religion. Why? Because worship is all about God—not you! Worship exists because He exists. And because He is eternal, worship for the believer should be an uninterrupted stream that begins the moment of conversion to Jesus and just "uploads" or continues, when we enter heaven. God created you to worship. He has never apologized for being THE only God…expecting to be THE exclusive target of worship (Isaiah 44:6). He scared the daylights out of an entire nation when He used a fire, light, and smoke show on Mt. Sinai in the desert (Exodus 19:16-20) to introduce a law *[the first of the Ten Commandments given to Israel]* that could never been overturned by any court: *"You shall have no other gods before Me"* (Exodus 20:3, NLT).

Here's my big-tent, big-package definition of worship, derived from merging a lot of scripture research: ***Worship is the intentional choice to honor God in all circumstances regardless of the cost.*** If you buy in to that biblically-driven statement, you get the universal nature of worship. That means worship is not weird. It can be planned or spontaneous, passionate or structured, loud or quiet, expected or unexpected—but always tied to recognizing and reacting to the presence of a Holy God in your moment! Authentic biblical worship will be as diverse as a New York City public school and as de-centralized as a Disney World crowd. For example, worship was the natural overflow...the irresistible impulse...the spontaneous reaction...the visceral emotion of a tear-covered prostitute who was forgiven by Jesus (Luke 7:36-48), of the shocked parents of a 12-year-old girl who was raised from the dead by Jesus (Mark 5:40-42), and of the innocent political prisoners who survived torture and an earthquake while they worshiped Jesus (Acts 16:25-34). But worship of God also emerged through the planned dedication of a national monument (2 Chronicles 6), in the aftermath of a near-death experience (Exodus 15), and when a national leader was threatened by a terrorist nation and later learned he was dying (Isaiah 37-38). Because worship is specifically focused on pleasing God and fulfilling His purpose, nobody has exclusive rights on how to do it. Worship is a dynamic experience with God which cannot be limited, controlled, or defined by circumstances or a set order, specific preferences in style, location, appearance, participation, or tradition. Because worship is inseparably connected to the eternal God, it can evolve or explode anytime or anywhere because God has no limits. Jesus can be worshiped in the halls of the Capitol or during lunch in the school cafeteria...during chemotherapy at Children's Hospital or over coffee at Starbucks...in secret home gatherings in China and Egypt or in a prison cell in Iran...through a post-game interview with Tim Tebow or when a contestant falls off the stage at an American Idol audition. Nobody can control it because you cannot control God. Worship is the deepest response to God. It's heart...soul...strength...and mind consumed with Him. Everything you are and have surrendered to all you know of Him (see Romans 12:1). ***You can experience worship, but never really totally explain it because you cannot absolutely explain God and His ways*** (see Isaiah 55:8-9). Check out this story.

## Jungle "Booking"

In his book, *Prayer: The Great Adventure*, David Jeremiah sets up my premise of a broader-based definition of worship: "Have you ever thought about what God could do in you if you were fully, totally, completely, unreservedly, immediately available to do whatever He asked you to do? You may be thinking, *Well, I've been trying to do that. But it doesn't look like God's doing anything in response. It doesn't look like God's even hearing my prayers.* You know, the King doesn't always have to tell His subjects every detail of what He's up to. But God is always up to something. You've got to trust Him." He shared this amazing story from a worker with the Overseas Missionary Fellowship:

> *While serving at a small field hospital in Africa, I traveled every two weeks by bicycle through the jungle to a nearby city for supplies. This requires camping overnight halfway. On one of these trips, I saw two men fighting in the city. One was seriously hurt so I treated him and witnessed to him about the Lord Jesus Christ. I then returned home without incident. Upon arriving in the city several weeks later, I was approached by the man I had treated earlier. He told me he had known that I carried money and medicine. He said, "Some friends and I followed you into the jungle, knowing you would camp overnight. We waited for you to go to sleep and planned to kill you and take your money and drugs. Just as we were about to move into your campsite, we saw that you were surrounded by 26 armed guards." I laughed at this and said, "I was certainly all alone out in the jungle campsite." The young man pressed the point, "No sir, I was not the only one to see the guards. My five friends also saw them, and we all counted them. It was because of those guards that we were afraid and left you alone." At this point of my church presentation in Michigan, one of the men in the church stood up and interrupted me. He asked, "Can you tell me the exact date when this happened?" I thought for a while and recalled the date. The man in the congregation then gave his side of the story. He stated, "On that night in Africa it was day here. I was preparing to play golf. As I put my bags in the car, I felt the Lord leading me to pray for you. In fact, the urging was so great that I called the men of this church together to pray for you. Will all of those men who met to pray please stand?" The men who had met that day to pray together stood— there were 26 of them!*[3]

Dr. Jeremiah posed the obvious questions that frame my simple definition of worship: "What might have happened to that medical worker had the man back in the United States chosen to ignore God's call to pray? What might have occurred had he said, 'Well, Lord, this just doesn't make any sense to me. I'm getting ready to golf, anyway. I'll pray when I get home.'"[4] ***Worship is not just an overflow of love for God, it is obedience out of love for God.***

## Ten Hands, a Blonde Chick, and a Guitar

Worship is bigger than religious ceremony or traditions, regardless of how respectful, dignified, or emotional you feel in some public service. At baseline, it is encountering the living God. It's not just mental. It's not just visual. It's not just emotional. It's not always that feeling you get when your team wins on the last play of the game. It's spiritual. Jesus clarified it for a confused, marginal, cultural worshipper in Samaria: *"But the time is coming—indeed it's here now—when true worshipers will worship the Father in spirit and in truth. The Father is looking for those who will worship him that way. For God is Spirit, so those who worship him must worship in spirit and in truth"* (John 4:23-24, NLT). Even for one person, worship varies from confessing sin to celebrating forgiveness…recognizing an answer to prayer over your daughter's illness to recalling an unexplained check in the mail. Why? Because worship is spiritual—experiencing a living Savior who does something fresh and real in your life every day to bring hope. Under our scenario, you can actually worship your Savior by achieving excellence on a project at work or giving to a charity that finds clean water for African children. Writing this book has been an act of worship for me. Authentic worship doesn't happen exclusively in a religious building but can overtake you in the car or be a daily plan in the privacy of your bedroom. Worship can happen wherever and whenever God shows up or you want Him! Worship changes you when the circumstances don't change. But worship doesn't have a life of its own. Like the YouTube video, *"Ten Hands, a Blonde Chick, and a Guitar"*, it only works if you hit on it. It works…it's addictive…it's new every time you experience it. Worship has to be sustained. And you can't ask your buddy or momma to do it for you. You have to stay focused!

## Best-Selling Author

Running your life race, according to Hebrews 12:2, is sustained by that singular focus: *"looking unto Jesus"* (NKJV). Why? Without a commitment for a serious, moment by moment, intense dependence on the God who designed your life-race, you will become casual about Him. Worship fades. Like a weak canned energy drink, after making only a few confrontations with your own sin and a dark culture, a divided heart will CRASH! You will lose the energy to sustain commitment at the highest output level. Allowing desires that compete with Jesus' plan for your life to hang out in your heart will kill your original passion…the hunger…the edge…the drive…the internal spiritual tension to consistently honor God publicly. You just can't date two people simultaneously with the same degree of love for both.

That phrase *"looking unto Jesus"* translates to giving Jesus your undivided attention. It implies that you have to quit looking at other things that appeal to you *AND* that hold the potential to choke your commitment to death. Interestingly, in the original Greek language, the word is in the present tense, indicating continuous action—i.e., **keep** looking at Jesus. No breaks. No gaps. No vacations. No excuses...*and* no "combo-commitments" where you worship sex, friends, wealth, career, food, power, celebrity AND Jesus. It's a command for exclusive devotion. Frankly, there's risk whether you follow Jesus wholeheartedly or chase something else. I've chosen the security of making God responsible for my protection because I'm pursuing Jesus. It's not Jesus that makes life complicated. We do. Non-compliance creates confusion. Maintain an uninterrupted pattern of depending upon Jesus to get it done!

So, God knew your next logical question and added the answer in the rest of the verse: But what about Jesus is so inspiring? Why should He deserve or own our undiluted energy? Look at how Jesus and His journey is described in 12:2-3—*"the author and finisher of our faith, who for the joy that was set before Him endured the cross, despising the shame, and has sat down at the right hand of the throne of God. For consider Him who endured such hostility from sinners against Himself..."* (NKJV).

The word "author" basically means "leader". How awesome is it that the One we have chosen to follow deserves our uncompromised allegiance because He *was* and *is* the perfect Leader! He not only preceded us—perfectly finishing God's plan for us first, complete with suffering—but He remains in that same role of undefeated leadership to guide us through all life's challenges! We don't live and die for a religion, a philosophy of life, gold, blue or black credit cards, secure portfolios, corporate dominance, a political agenda, a moral code, a culture, nationalistic pride, patriotic zeal, or a just causes like world peace and fighting hunger. We follow a Person!

And He's not a mere historical footnote or anecdote. Jesus, God in the flesh, perfectly completed the most challenging life-race imaginable. Hating the shame of our sin, He never wavered from His mission to give His life up to satisfy God the Father's full anger and punishment for those sins that separated us from God by dying on a cross. Completing that purpose was possible by keeping His eyes focused on the pure joy that was promised to Him after defeating death and returning to take His rightful place at the right hand of the throne of God in heaven. There Jesus was crowned! Initially rejected by the majority while on this earth, His suffering was fully validated by heaven. His life is now—and can be in the future—glorified, vindicated, and explained by those who follow Him through similar suffering to fulfill and finish their God-designed life-race and purpose.

So, how do you know what owns your heart, spirit, and attitude right now? How do you know if you are compromised and real heart-worship is threatened? Easy. Just listen to what you talk about the most. Whatever owns the most words is what you currently worship. When we allow our lives to become so jammed with things that demand our attention and we lose sight of our first love, we get confused and God's life-plan doesn't seem as critical as the other stuff. That's why the ONLY possible way to persevere successfully is to keep believing, trusting, worshiping, and focusing on Jesus, who led the way and totally achieved all that God expected of Him in His race. Because He did…and because He is in you…YOU WILL MAKE IT!

### "You don't recognize my voice!"

Recently, I took a risk and answered an incoming call on my smart phone when it was displaying a number that I didn't recognize. I heard a guy say, "I bet you don't recognize my voice! This is the first time you've heard it. It's Chad!" Wow! It was really him!

More than a year before the call, I had been asked by a friend who works for a major grocery store chain to visit a fellow manager who had been suddenly hospitalized. Without warning, in a matter of hours, this *"healthy—married with a baby—athletic—charismatic—20-something high-achiever popular with all his peers"*-guy became totally paralyzed from the neck down, unable to speak and fighting for his life and every breath while attached to a ventilator. The diagnosis? Something his frightened wife had never heard: Guillain-Barre Syndrome. Guillain-Barre is an autoimmune disorder in which the body's defense system gets confused—your own immune system inexplicably attacks your own nervous system. It's like your body decides to kill you! Research has been unable to definitively isolate what triggers the reaction that may keep a person down for years. Most victims survive and eventually recover completely, but live in a state of sustained weakness. Imagine the fear Chad felt when he couldn't breathe or move, unable to do anything but talk to God.

After 11-months, Chad miraculously recovered and walked out of the hospital to try and get his life back. He was calling to thank me for all the hospital visits and prayers: "Thanks for speaking to me like my life was not over!" he said. I had joined Chad's wife and many others, intentionally choosing to believe God for Chad's complete healing, and spoke that out loud in ICU—through all the tubes—whenever I leaned over close to him in those unresponsive days, and squeezed his motionless hand. The times when Chad was alert and his eyes followed me, blinking understanding or appreciation, and sometimes leaking a tear, were enough encouragement to keep me praying. I remember those tender moments like when Chad's wife placed their baby on his chest to keep hope alive, even when his precious newborn had not heard daddy's voice or felt the comforting warmth of his touch.

When he couldn't lift a finger to scratch his nose, hug his baby, kiss his wife, go to work, drive, or utter a word to express pain or go to the bathroom in his 11-month ordeal, life came into perspective. He told me that he really hadn't taken God's plan for his life seriously until Guillain-Barre, the life-threatening syndrome he had never heard of, took over.

Translation? Worship didn't just fade. It died, man! Chad confessed his choice to substitute other stuff for his original pursuit of Jesus. Now it's reversed. Like a campaigning politician, he unashamedly explained that he was working "one-on-one" to tell anybody who will listen about how God gave him his life back and how important it is to get serious about the one chance we get to get it right. Chad is now committed. He's not turning back for any reason. He means it.

When unexpected trials take over your life, and threaten to take you down, everybody gets **convicted**, but not everybody gets **committed!** Will you allow yourself to be permanently changed in the direction that Jesus is moving?

Whenever you feel like you've made a mistake and your commitment to Jesus is not working—costing you more than you can handle or wanted—think about Jesus. When you are tired, beat up, alone, hurting, and have nothing to show for trying to do it right and honor Jesus...remember He did it for you first!

Want a fresh couple of truths to re-energize you? He's finished the race and He's waiting for you! Those verses told us that Jesus *"sat down at the right hand of the throne of God,"* meaning that Jesus didn't collapse or compromise—He finished what God wanted Him to do! It's not your effort, endurance, or excitement that saves you—it's JESUS who has ALREADY FINISHED! He is more than just the One who started your faith. He is more than just the One who became the perfect example of how to live out your faith. He is the One who FINISHED all that is required of faith...FOR YOU!

The key question is scary: *Is Jesus enough for you?* Every time you chase stuff that doesn't matter for eternity—giving up irreplaceable days, weeks, months, or years of the only life you will get—you are shouting back to God, your family, and everybody you have the opportunity to influence, that Jesus is *NOT* enough for you! Jesus endured the suffering and shame of rejection, hatred, and disappointment all the way THROUGH the cross...FOR YOU!

Conclusion? Jesus is worthy of more than your *praise*...He should be your total *purpose* in life. When you realize fatigue and discouragement are taking over...when you realize desire to worship Him passionately is fading...when other things seem more appealing...do what Hebrews 12:2-3 says—research again what and how Jesus put up with for you: *"Keep your eyes on Jesus, who both began and finished this race we're in. Study how He did it. Because He never lost sight of where He was headed—that exhilarating finish in and with God—He could put up with anything along the way: Cross, shame, whatever. And now He's there, in the place of honor, right alongside God. When you find yourselves flagging in your faith, go over that story again, item by item, that long litany of hostility He plowed through. That will shoot adrenaline into your souls!"* (The Message).

## What would you do for $10,000?

"Husband Combs Florida Landfill to Find Wife's Engagement Ring".[5] Even the headlines make you cringe. Only the threat of an angry wife and having to replace a $10,000 diamond ring could make a husband dive headlong into a giant garbage dump and sort through tons of filth, disease, and choking odors. The ring story started on Halloween Day, 2011, when Anna McGuinn, 31, of Margate, Florida, was in the shower and handed her husband, Brian, 34, her $10K engagement to put in the jewelry box. He realized later he tossed it out in the trash along with a disposable razor his wife had handed him at the same time. Bad news? The trash had already been picked up that morning. Anna said, "I was saying to myself, 'OK, no one died, get a grip.' Then I started crying again." In desperation, she contacted the trash company, which gave them permission for a search. Brian volunteered, not just because he was guilty and wanted to live, but because she was a medical practice administrator and five months' pregnant with their first child. Anna said Brian suited up "like an alien" and sorted through feces and dead animals for about an hour when he saw her hot pink frozen yogurt cup from the night before that was lodged close to her barely visible ring covered in sludge. He pulled off a glove and grabbed the ring that was now the focus of their marriage. Brian commented, "It was like hitting the lottery." Brian's second mistake? He went home and stuck the stinking, sludge-covered ring on her finger! Funny…and it's real life.

What would you do for $10,000? Obviously, we would give our lives to save a family member or close friend, but what else is of ultimate value? For whom or what would you sacrifice, take on significant risk, endure with, fight for, cry over, pray about, or believe in, without hesitation? Or, asking the same question from the opposite slant, who or what could make you abandon an important commitment? That can actually be **Mistake No. 6** for not seriously engaging in running the life-race God has handed you.

## MISTAKE No. 6:  Avoiding commitment.

A man and his wife were having some problems at home and were giving each other the silent treatment. The next week, the man realized that he would need his wife to wake him at 5:00 AM for an early morning business flight to Chicago. Not wanting to be the first to break the silence (and lose), he wrote on a piece of paper, "Please wake me at 5:00 AM." The next morning the man woke up, only to discover it was 9:00 AM and that he had missed his flight. Furious, he was about to go and see why his wife hadn't woken him when he noticed a piece of paper by the bed. The paper said, "It is 5:00 AM. Wake up."

If you're married (or used to be married because of stuff like that), you totally have a moment like that on your marriage resume. Not that it's right, but somebody will frustrate the life out of you and the "fight back" mechanism is triggered. Yes, it's a defensive reaction…*normally* driven by fear, fatigue, or failure. But it's still real. Sometimes emotions win. They override commitment. Getting somebody else's bad behavior dumped on you can make your commitment to them seem unreasonable. And people who walk away from original commitments either misinterpreted what was involved or intentionally planned to misuse the label and perks for a while and then move on to the next gig.

**Our commitments not only define who we are...they change us. We become like what we commit to.**

**So choose carefully.**

## Quid Pro Quo

Yes, it is possible to have underestimated the pressure and abuse that results from becoming a devoted, lifetime follower of Jesus. Here's the giant truth: Real commitments to Jesus last only because believers *"are kept by the power of God through faith for salvation ready to be revealed in the last time"* (1 Peter 1:5, NKJV). Salvation, as originally gifted by Jesus, includes sustaining us even at our worst or weakest moments. But it is assumed that trials are part of the package. It's universal truth. You can't follow Jesus, who was rejected and killed, without being identified with Him and targeted because of Him: *"...everyone who wants to live a godly life in Christ Jesus will suffer persecution"* (2 Timothy 3:12, NLT). **So...Deal with it!**

Commitment simply means that you believed in something or someone so much at a given moment that you chose to wrap your life around it. Other things become secondary once you chose to obligate yourself. But our culture has become schizophrenic on real issues like this. Commitment is now defined by what we feel and what our goals happen to be at the moment. If something better comes along, then the previous commitment is no longer valid. AND...under the new terms—the updated Commitment 2.0—it's possible to still define yourself as a "committed person" by simply transferring your commitment to the next relationship, coffee flavor, political party, Face-book friend, or attorney whenever convenient. Then, we expect the FDA to be committed to truthful research to protect us on everything from e-coli in raw chicken to diabetes risk in statin drugs; and the CEO's of Freddie Mac and Fannie Mae to be so committed to lowering interest rates for new homeown-ers that they give up crazy big salaries. But society as a whole doesn't seem to question partial-birth abortion or divorce because of "incompatibility" issues at the same level of intensity—and both of those issues are all about commit-ment. Gary Busey gave it the typical humorous slant: "Marriage is the only war where you sleep with the enemy." A PsychPage contributor said that divorce occurs at "5-7 years due to high conflict" and at "10-12 years due to loss of intimacy and connection".[6] Either timing is regrettable but both surface the commitment issue. It's not just about unrealistic expectations, crazy in-laws, poor financial decisions, personality conflict, control issues, or different career goals. It's the "C" word! Commitment means you work through stuff even if you don't like it and it takes forever. Ministry, marriage, model-ing...whatever...you name it...it's all leaning away from commitment and toward *quid pro quo* ("You do something for me and I'll do something for you"). Obligate is a scary word to a 2012 American culture that "freaks out" if they can't "back out" of something—whether by lawsuits, lying, or just leaving. One business owner told me he has had employees just fail to show one day and never hears from them again. Biblical commitment, as in "doing it like Jesus did for us", may require you to give what you don't feel like giving, love somebody even if they reject you or never reciprocate, or serve without recognition or reward. Why? Because a life-commitment to Jesus means He assumes responsibility for the outcome, sees what you have to endure, and rewards it big His way. Ultimately, the only sanity is in living for Him—not yourself or even the other person.

From the way these 1st generation believers got blasted in Hebrews 12:4—*"After all, you have not yet given your lives in your struggle against sin"* (NLT)—they were apparently at risk of giving in to self-pity, fatigue, and discouragement (see verse 3). Nobody had lost any blood in this resistance movement. Protesting against the evil in their culture had only resulted in minimal pushback—but it probably *felt like* it was killing them. Losing jobs or friends, or facing threats of jail just because you speak up for Christ, can overwhelm anybody. But they needed a reality check. They were facing opposition and rejection—not death. It's the difference between the U.S. Secretary of State in heated negotiations with the President of Afghanistan versus the American soldier who actually engaged enemy fire.

Under war conditions, every part of your commitment gets questioned. Comedian Don Rickles once described a prison riot as "a difference of opinion with injuries." If a husband-wife argument escalates, each starts to question whether they made a big mistake in choosing the other. Often, the mistake a couple will make is to say, *"I shouldn't have to live this way. I don't have to take this."* It's natural. To be expected. *But that's NOT where God wants you to stay.*

When believers are trying to work through their own maturity issues, sorting through all the bad choices they have crammed into their emotional/spiritual backpack…AND THEN get hit with the stress of being rejected at work or home or school simply for trying to live a Jesus-pleasing life, **commitment begins to seem unreasonable**. Questions like, *"Why is this happening to me?"* surface…and can own you if you don't have a response. Ridiculous statements of defiance like, *"Nobody understands what I'm going through"* fall short of getting God's attention. Why? Take your worst day and try to explain to Jesus why He couldn't possibly understand your suffering. Name a situation, issue, problem, or crisis you face right now that explains why you can't be faithful to Him! Swap stories with Jesus. Who wins every time?

Everybody needs perspective at some point. When you are hurting or disappointed from lack of change, lack of results, or lack of approval, it's just easier to quit or bail out. ***Don't grow weary no matter how strong the spiritual warfare appears, how long you have to fight, or how much stuff you have*** *to unpack from that overloaded backpack!* Get a reality check. Every believer has to fight against discouragement and fatigue, wondering if it's all worth it. You will face exhaustion. Don't be surprised...and don't walk away. You'll always wind up doing something stupid...something you will regret. Worst case scenario? Jesus comes back and catches you doing it! (see 1 John 2:28).

**WARNING:** Remember this too. What you do in moderation, your children will do in excess! Whoever is watching you will be more likely to back down on their commitment if you do!

### Do You Have Any Tattoos Or Piercings?

On the *girlsaskguys.com* website, there is a list of "20 Random Questions To Ask A Girl" to keep a conversation moving naturally while on a date. The questions range from "Ever broken any bones?" (No.1), and "What is your biggest fear, except for spiders?" (No. 8), to "Do you have any tattoos or piercings?" (No. 17).

Questions can surface reality.

The spiritual-momentum question you should ask is, "Jesus, how can I make you known through this trial?" That question should not be driven by *obligation* but *obsession*. Fake commitments will fail and be exposed under intense pressure and scrutiny. A person who loves Jesus exclusively will want to embrace the opportunity to honor Jesus in every act of persecution, and the trial will serve to validate who is genuine. Own the trial or be overcome by it! Why should you apologize or shut-up, much more quit, if you have been doing what is right? Here are 3 categories of legitimate questions about pushing through doubts about God's will and your level of commitment:

1.  **What happened to my Original Commitment?** *Did I have a word from God to do what I'm doing? Did God originally tell me to get involved in this or did I get into it based on emotions or selfish goals? Has He revoked that call or confirmed that He released me from that call with the same level of clarity?*

2.  **Why do I have this Oppressive Feeling?** *Am I wrestling with a sense of feeling overwhelmed or threatened? Would Satan like to see me give up? Is the impact of my prayer, commitment, witness, or giving creating enough of a threat to the enemy that it costs me something now?*

3.  **What is my Opportunity Cost?** *What would be the cost if I don't follow through with what God told me? Who and what would be negatively impacted and might use me as an excuse not to consider the reality of Jesus?*

These believers either decided they had maxed-out in effectiveness with their witness or that the lack of results were a sign that it wasn't worth it to invest more or keep doing it. Everybody claims they want answers. So, here's the answer. Hebrews 12:3 says, *"Think of all the hostility He endured from sinful people; then you won't become weary and give up"* (NLT). "Think" means to be totally consumed with what Jesus endured. Translation? **Discouragement comes from focusing more on our hurt than Jesus' hurt.** Compare your hurt with what Jesus endured. Think constantly about the hostility directed against Him by organized opposition—hatred, lies, betrayal, physical beatings, ending His ministry, destroying His closest friends, removing all His possessions, setting Him up in court, refusing to believe Him, and turning others against Him. The words translated *"hostility He endured from sinful people"* describe the opposition Jesus could never escape—He couldn't do anything without having somebody who hated Him speak out against Him!

In the larger meaning, looking at the "why" from 30,000 feet, the word "endured" emphasizes that Jesus persevered through the pressure of unbelievable hostility, more than we will ever feel, for one purpose—to save us! How about that perspective? **What you are going through is intended by God to make Jesus' sacrifice known in a way that will create both interest in knowing Him and disillusionment with sin.**

Rewind to the real heart of the missionary preacher, Paul, in a sound bite from his impromptu speech to a group of next generation leaders in Miletus (on the coast of Turkey) about *his* life-race: "I consider my life worth nothing to me; my only aim is to *finish the race and complete the task* the Lord Jesus has given me—the task of testifying to the good news of God's grace" (*emphasis mine*, Acts 20:24, NIV).

**Will you endure so somebody else might come to know Jesus?**

*Chapter 21*

# Misunderstood God

## The Blizzard and The Bakery

Richard Silberlust told a crazy story about trying to run an errand in a raging blizzard. He made it the half-mile to the local bakery, where he asked a guy behind the counter for six rolls. "Your wife must like rolls," the guy said. "How do you know these are for my wife?" Richard asked. "Because your mom wouldn't send you out in weather like this."

He got it. Sometimes people don't get God. He typically gets blamed for most of the bad stuff that happens in the world and in our lives. With all the misrepresentation circulating about God—plus the inconsistency of some people who claim to be Christians—it's not surprising that God is misunderstood. I know He is quite capable of defending His own reputation, but our scripture text does provide a solid explanation for the biggest question marks over His character.

## MISTAKE No. 7: Mislabeling God's character.

Mistake No. 7 when you opt out of your God-designed life-race and/or start choosing your own rules, is that you can begin to misinterpret God's actions toward you—which ultimately means you put a question mark over God's trustworthiness...His character...His love! When you are struggling through a trial, it's convenient to believe that difficult circumstances mean God is against you and wants to make life miserable for you. Most of the time, the reason people buy into that convenient answer is because they are already miserable, fearful, and angry over some unresolved or undisclosed sin. If you are covering up sin, the tendency will be to think that when suffering crashes your life it has to be driven by a God who is getting even. God is not evil or arbitrary, waiting for your next misstep. He is merciful. If He really wanted to make you pay for your sin now, you'd already be dead.

## God Was In Bangkok?

In his book, *An Unstoppable Force: Daring To Become The Church God Had In Mind*, Erwin McManus related one of a parent's worst nightmares that turned out to be what he described as "a miracle in Bangkok".[1] Erwin, his children Aaron and Mariah, and 42 team members were enjoying a day off, shopping for last minute family gifts in the markets of Bangkok, after having just completed a week of ministry in Kanchanaburi.[2] Despite his repeated warnings to the group about the traffic, as a light turned red, his 8-year-old daughter, Mariah, ran into the street before he could restrain her. In a surreal scene, Erwin said, "I could almost feel the weight of the car as it hit her head-on. Just a few feet away, I watched helplessly as her body bent around the hood of the car before it was thrown like a rag doll onto the streets of Bangkok....Under the ominous cloud of the birds, on the busiest street, at the heavily populated intersection, and admist the multitude of cars, my little girl lay crumpled on the hard concrete. I rushed over to her, and bent down to pick her up, but before I could do so, she stood on her own. Not a bone was broken. As I held her in my arms, the police arrived and insisted that we rush Mariah to the hospital. The driver of the car implored us to come with him for medical care as a large crowd gathered around us. Somehow, all I could say was, 'Mariah is a follower of Jesus Christ. God has protected her. She's fine.' Rather than uttering the words, I felt more as I was hearing them. It was if someone else was saying them, and I was simply observing....My little girl is my miracle from Bangkok—proof that God has a significant purpose for her life."[3]

That moment is just one more evidence that God desires to merge all circumstances together to create something good...something that makes you better reflect the Jesus who gave up His life for you...because He is FOR you![4] God was in Bangkok...and He'll be there for you. Don't doubt me...or Him!

## 1 Hour After You are Dead and Buried

But a just and fair God cannot ignore flagrant, willful defiance by His kids—there has to be a response. God is DANGEROUS! He wants to radically change your life! And if it means messing with your life to get you to abandon the choices that are killing you, God will discipline without hesitation or apology. Tony Campolo, Professor Emeritus of Sociology at Eastern University and author of more than 35 books, addressed the hidden pride issue during a speech: "Don't think too much of yourself. One hour after you are dead and buried your family and friends will be eating potato salad and telling jokes." Life goes on without you, and God is bigger than you. Multiple stories in the Bible recall moments when God reached the limits of His patience, and people reached their full capacity for sin. From the biggest global judgment—Noah's flood—to the Dispersion of the 12 tribes of Israel, nobody ever suffered at the hands of an unjust God. God doesn't joke about sin or justice. But He is NOT a terrorist, either.

Comic Craig Sharf confessed, "I was diagnosed with antisocial behavior disorder, so I joined a support group. We never meet." Funny. But apparently the original recipients of our text, who were under duress, bought in to the enemy's lie that God was *antisocial*...and more...that He was looking for ways to make their life miserable. So they needed the following update to correct their misinformation about their suffering. Read this:

> *5 And have you forgotten the encouraging words God spoke to you as his children? He said, "My child, don't make light of the Lord's discipline, and don't give up when he corrects you. 6 For the Lord disciplines those he loves, and he punishes each one he accepts as his child." 7 As you endure this divine discipline, remember that God is treating you as his own children. Who ever heard of a child who is never disciplined by its father? 8 If God doesn't discipline you as he does all of his children, it means that you are illegitimate and are not really his children at all. 9 Since we respected our earthly fathers who disciplined us, shouldn't we submit even more to the discipline of the Father of our spirits, and live forever? 10 For our earthly fathers disciplined us for a few years, doing the best they knew how. But God's discipline is always good for us, so that we might share in his holiness. 11 No discipline is enjoyable while it is happening—it's painful! But afterward there will be a peaceful harvest of right living for those who are trained in this way.* (Hebrews 12:5-11, NLT)

God is like a good father—He disciplines because He loves you, solely for the purpose of moving your life in the right direction—holiness. God is holy and expects His children to embody, display, reflect, and promote a separate, distinctive and righteous character and lifestyle. When you exit that direction, even for a moment, God will get your attention and jerk you back toward sanity and responsibility using varying methods of discipline. God's disciplinary methods are custom-fitted to factors like your *level of maturity* (1 Corinthians 3:1-4), *level of resistance* (1 Corinthians 5:1-5), *level of damage* (2 Samuel 12:10), *level of knowledge* (Acts 5:1-5), *level of responsibility* (Acts 9:17-18), or *level of potential* (1 Peter 5:10). All those verses remind us that disciplinary action is never fun, but the long-term benefit is protection from the tendency to quit or go crazy with rebellion. It's about keeping you pure. It's about keeping your perseverance. It's about keeping you positive about God. The more you understand His character, the more you will love Him and accept whatever disciplinary method He uses.

The original audience for these words needed to understand that God was using the hostility they faced as a tool to discipline them—in effect, to make them more energized and effective. In context, the explanation for their stress was that God was allowing the opposition in order to force them to replace sloppy theology and the immature, irresponsible attitude that they could serve Jesus effectively while blatantly participating in sin (cf., Hebrews 12:1—*"...let us lay aside every weight, and the sin which so easily ensnares us..."*, NKJV). Getting angry at God for persecution was wrong. Buying into theology that God was trying to kill them was off limits as well.

### Why Did This Happen?

God wants us to buy in to His perspective. He's totally all about eternity. What happens on this planet, in this ridiculously short life, has to be interpreted through the heavenly grid of what matters for an eternal agenda. It does make a difference in the whole dedication/discipline argument. An eternal perspective shifts the "I-don't-know-why-this-is-happening-to-me" attitude to embracing a bigger picture of "What-is-God-saying?". What if God was actually supervising your universe in a way to create maximum attention on heaven and the need to be prepared?

Bruce Goodrich was being initiated into the cadet corps at Texas A & M University. One night, Bruce was forced to run until he dropped—but he never got up. Bruce Goodrich died before he even entered college. A short time after the tragedy, Bruce's father wrote this letter to the administration, faculty, student body, and the corps of cadets: "I would like to take this opportunity to express the appreciation of my family for the great outpouring of concern and sympathy from Texas A & M University and the college community over the loss of our son Bruce. We were deeply touched by the tribute paid to him in the battalion. We were particularly pleased to note that his Christian witness did not go unnoticed during his brief time on campus." Mr. Goodrich went on: "I hope it will be some comfort to know that we harbor no ill will in the matter. We know our God makes no mistakes. Bruce had an appointment with his Lord and is now secure in his celestial home. When the question is asked, 'Why did this happen?' perhaps one answer will be, 'So that many will consider where they will spend eternity.'"[5]

God bless you, sir. That's maximum trust. God wants all the attention no matter what is happening to us...and He deserves it. By the way, heaven is reward...not punishment. So suffering and death are only temporary and can't diminish the hope of being with God in heaven...unless you let it.

### Don't Mess With That Teacher!

Following an injury, a public school teacher had to wear a cast around his entire upper body. He concealed it perfectly under his shirt so nobody would notice when he returned for the first day of the new semester. To his surprise, he learned some of the toughest students were assigned to his class. Walking confidently into the rowdy classroom, he opened the window as wide as possible and then sat down at his desk. Every time the wind blasted in, his tie would flap. Then the students started acting out, unintimidated by his multiple warnings. Finally, frustrated with both the tie and the students, without thinking he stood up, grabbed a big stapler off his desk, and stapled the tie to his chest in several places. Discipline was never a problem after that.

Discipline is not a problem with God either. As an option, discipline is actually just as much a part of God's character and His motivation/teaching tools as is a miracle healing. So, based on our key verses, if we know "why" God takes His kids through a training regimen—developing our purity and perseverance through opposition—"how" does God discipline His children? Remember, the strategy He implements will always be *driven by love, defined by limits*[6] (you may be crushed but God will never abandon you because He knows what you can take before losing it), and *developed for life* (so you can experience freedom and bring eternal life in Jesus to someone else). Here's my interpretation, categorizing a huge God-response into 3 simple strategies.

Entry level discipline is simply **disturbing your conscience**[7] when you start thinking like the non-believing culture, giving in to wrong desires, or acting out wrong behavior.[8] Tension in your conscience could happen in one of three ways when God: (1) withholds His strength from you so that every task becomes more difficult;[9] (2) allows you to experience partial or full consequences and/or guilt of what you've done to wake you up;[10] or, (3) stops restraining you so you can get what you want without Him which will ultimately make you feel empty.[11] For example, despite the godly influence of his uncle Abraham, Lot chose to move his family to the edgy and prosperous city of Sodom only to ultimately be daily conflicted with guilt and lose his wife and sons-in-law to the lure of immorality.[12]

If you are unresponsive to those subtle reminders of *whose* you are and His purpose for your life, then expect to have the discipline repeated (because God is total grace!), and escalated to the next level of attention-grabbing moments. In His sovereignty, God will operate—get His point across—through **designing unexpected circumstances**. Why? Again, to save you. It's that simple. God is FOR you, not against you. If a father really cares about his children, he will love them enough to discipline them so they won't self-destruct years later. Famous examples of God specifically designing challenges or disasters, inserting ongoing problems, stirring up opposition, or disrupting your plans include: Jonah being thrown overboard and swallowed by a giant fish for resisting God's call;[13] Joshua losing a battle for tolerating pride, theft, and deception;[14] or King David losing a baby, having his daughter raped, and enduring the murder of one son and the rebellion of his oldest son because of his adultery and murdering someone.[15]

If all other interventions are ineffective, God will not hesitate to begin **disabling your control**—i.e., shutting down your life in some degree, from illness to death. Again, what's up with that extreme approach? Why would

God respond at that level? First, because you didn't! That's right. When you don't respond, it's not just a "relationship issue" with God...it's that you've doubled-down on defiance. You don't negotiate with terrorists or toddlers, so why would God dumb-down or bend His standards for a rebellious follower? Second, because His holiness is at stake (not at risk). God will never allow His holiness to be prostituted or His glory to be put up for sale. So, sending radical stuff like pain or suffering happens if we push the limits of God's grace and self-trigger it, but it basically becomes a last resort measure. God doesn't initiate suffering. He never did. But He'll use it if your actions are a threat to yourself or His plan. Don't challenge God. You will lose...every time. The Rx? Take two examples and go to bed. James explained to first century churches that sickness could be the result of sin.[16] One wealthy couple was actually struck dead for their attempt to deceive a new church by misreporting finances in a land deal.[17]

The options for discipline are as infinite as God and as diverse as the 7 billion people on our planet. God will use what fits your attitude and His plan. Accept it. You'll get it over with quicker. You'll have more peace in your life. You'll be more believable to skeptics. You'll be stronger...and smarter.[18]

**So...what's in your backpack?**

# ENDNOTES

ENDNOTES

*Chapter 1*
1. From a broadcast of *NBC Nightly News*, August 16, 2011, http://www.msnbc.msn.com/id/3032619/ns/nightly_news/#44167629
2. Ibid.
3. Josh Levin, "Will LeBron James' First Title Make Sports Commentary Less Dumb? Or will ESPN and everyone else just find new dumb things to say?", *Slate*, slate.com, June 22, 2012, © 2012 The Slate Group, LLC, http://www.slate.com/articles/sports/sports_nut/2012/06/lebron_james_2012_nba_title_will_the_heat_s_championship_win_make_sports_commentary_less_dumb_.html (sourced 06-29-12).

*Chapter 2*
1. Rick Reilly, "Go Fish" Blog, *ESPN The Magazine*, espn.com, December 2, 2009, © 2012 ESPN Internet Ventures, http://sports.espn.go.com/espnmag/story?id=4707070
2. Cal Fussman, "What I've Learned: Merle Haggard," *Esquire*, August 23, 2007, © 2012 Hearst Communications, Inc., http://www.esquire.com/features/what-ive-learned/whativelearned 0907 (Sourced 05-29-12).
3. Jenna Bush-Hager interview of Merle Haggard, TODAY Show, 05-28-12, Video, © 2012 TODAY, http://today.msnbc.msn.com/id/ 2618 4891/#47588947
4. Ibid.
5. Greg Hardesty, "Girl In Famous Picture Speaks", *Orange County Register*, July 16, 2007, © 2012 Orange County Register Communications, http://www.ocregister.com/articles/phuc-72437-vietnamese-pain.html, (Sourced 05-29-12).
6. Ruth Schenk, "Napalm Attack Begins 36-year Journey to Faith and Forgiveness," *Southeast Outlook*, PreachingToday.com, September 11, 2008.
7. Ibid., Hardesty.

8. "History", Kim Phuc Foundation International, http://www.kimfound ation.com/modules/contentpage/index.php?file=story.htm&ma=10&s ubid=101, Retrieved May 18, 2010 as quoted in the article, "Phan Thi Kim Phuc", Wikipedia, Wikipedia Foundation, Inc., http:// en.wikipedia. org/wiki/Phan_Thi_Kim_Phuc (Sourced 05-29-12).
9. Ibid., Schenk.
10. Ibid., Schenk.
11. Ibid., Hardesty.
12. Liz Tomas, "Facts About Carrying Backpacks in School", eHow.com, March 22, 2011, © 1999-2012 Demand Media, Inc., http://www. ehow.com/how_18333_wear-school-backpack.html

*Chapter 3*

1. Tess Weaver, "Recap: Shaun White's Perfection and More From Day Four of the X Games", *On The Snow*, January 30, 2012, http:// www.onthesnow.com/news/68/a/105978/recap-shaun-whites-perfec- tion-and-more-from-day-four-of-the-x-games
2. "Shaun White. biography", bio.com, A&E Television Networks, LLC, © 1996-2012, http://www.biography.com/people/shaun-white- 201311
3. Quoted from Blog by Kevin Pounds, http://serveburlington.com/ vent- ing-knowledge-vs-experience-4
4. From a sermon by Dr. David Jeremiah delivered October 29, 2009 at a Pastor's Leadership Breakfast, Greenville, SC.
5. The original phrase "chariot of fire" is from 2 Kings 2:11 and 6:17 in the Bible.
6. Quoted from Christianrunners.org, "Running To Further His King- dom", Toronto Memorable Quotes, Roswell, GA, http://www. christianrunners.org/torontoquotes.html

*Chapter 4*

1. Daniel Gross & the Editors of Forbes Magazine, *Forbes Greatest Busi- ness Stories of All Time*, (Byron Preiss Visual Publications, Inc., and Forbes Inc., Published by John Wiley & Sons, Inc., © 1996), 180.
2. From a presentation by Seth Godin on the Chick-fil-A LeaderCast, May 6, 2011
3. Gross, Ibid., 181.
4. Ibid., 182.
5. Eric Pfeiffer, "CNN Producer Third Person This Year To Win Georgia Lottery For Second Time", The SideShow, A Y! News Blog, February 16, 2012, Yahoo! News, © 2012 Yahoo, Inc., http://news.yahoo.com/ blogs/sideshow/cnn-producer-third-person-win-georgia-lottery-sec- ond-173440037.html

6. Ibid.
7. Ibid.
8. Taken from galottery.com, http://www.galottery.com/games/instant-games/instant-games/11865-50x-the-money
9. Pfeiffer, Ibid.
10. Used by permission.
11. Peter Emerick, Senior Writer, "Jeremy Lin: 5 Characteristics of Linsanity That Make Him Such a Special Player," *Bleacher Report*, February 20, 2012, © 2012 Bleacher Report, Inc. http://bleacherreport.com/articles/1072309-linsanity-5-things-about-jeremy-lin-that-make-him-such-a-special-player
12. Ibid.
13. Ibid.

*Chapter 5*
1. Mark McDonald, "North Korean Prison Camps Massive and Growing", *The New York Times*, May 4, 2011, © 2011 The New York Times Company.
2. "Human Rights in North Korea", *Human Rights Watch*, July, 2004 http://hrw.org/english/docs/2004/07/08/nkorea9040.htm (Retrieved August 2, 2007).

*Chapter 6*
1. Ray Stedman, from his sermon "The Race of Life".
2. SFC Robert J. Ehrlich, "Soldier's Load and Combat Readiness", © 2000-2012 GlobalSecurity.org http://www.globalsecurity.org/military/library/report/call/call_01-15_ch11.htm
3. Dave Ramsey, *EntreLeadership*, (New York: Howard Books, © 2011), 81.
4. Ibid., 82.
5. Michael Hyatt (Chairman of Thomas Nelson Publishers), "The Momentum Theorem", Intentional Leadership Blog, October 10, 2009, © 2009 Michael Hyatt, http://michaelhyatt.com/the-momentum-theorem.html
6. Being "underwater" as a homeowner means to owe more on your mortgage loan than your house is currently worth on the market.
7. From an interview with Don Imus aired on *FOX News*, March 31, 2010.
8. Shane Bacon, "Tiger Woods' Ex-Wife Bulldozes $12 Million Home", Devil Ball Golf, YAHOO! Sports, yahoo.com, January 5, 2012, © 2012 Yahoo! Inc., http://sports.yahoo.com/blogs/golf-devil-ball-golf/tiger-woods-ex-wife-bulldozes-12-million-home-232405259.html

9.   "Woods Says He'll Continue To Get Help", ESPN.com News Services, February 19, 2010, © 2012 ESPN Internet Ventures, http://sports.espn.go.com/golf/news/story?id=4927694

10.  From a sermon delivered at the Pastor's Conference of the Missouri Baptist Convention, 1980's.

## Chapter 7

1.   Derek Kravitz, "Number Of Underwater Mortgages Rises As More Homeowners Fall Behind", Huffingtonpost.com, March 8, 2011, © 2012 The Huffington Post, Inc., http://www.huffingtonpost.com/2011/03/08/number-of-underwater-mort_n_833000.html

2.   TATTOO IDEAS HUB, http://www.tattooideashub.com/cover-up-tattoos/

3.   Interview with the Boot, http://www.nextnewmusic.net/the-band-perry-if-i-die-young-story-behind-the-lyrics/. At the time of this writing, the song has sold over 2,000,000 digital copies in the US alone, making it the 11th country song to do so, and only the 4th time that a band reached this plateau, following Lady Antebellum, Zac Brown Band and Rascal Flatts.

4.   "Tebow Laughs at Hurricanes Bounty Report", FloridaToday.com, August 18, 2011, © 2012 www.floridatoday.com, http://www.floridatoday.com/article/20110818/BREAK-INGNEWS/110818020/1002/SPORTS/Tebow-laughs-Hurricanes-bounty-report

5.   "Hawaii's Love Affair With Canned Item Continues", *Associated Press*, msnbc.com, February 22, 2009, TODAY Food, © 2009 Associated Press, http://today.msnbc.msn.com/id/29301750/ns/today-food/t/hawaiis-love-affair-canned-item-continues/

6.   Credited to James Michener, from his 1955 book, *Hawaii*.

7.   YAHOO! Answers: Resolved Question from a person with label "Eminem" by "StayHappy", © 2012 Yahoo! Inc., http://answers.yahoo.com/question/index?qid=20110219173537AA4BtDG

## Chapter 8

1.   Doctor Jokes: "Unattractive", http://laughs.rd.com/clean-jokes-and-laughs/unattractive-joke/article82506.html

2.   "Science Proves It:  Men Lie More Than Women", *CBS News* broadcast, May 20, 2010, © 2012 CBS Interactive Inc., http://www.cbsnews.com/stories/2010/05/19/health/main6499561.shtml

3.   Ibid.

4.   For detail, see Genesis 16:11-12; 17:20; 25:12-18.

5.   Lee Strobel, *God's Outrageous Claims*, (Grand Rapids, MI: Zondervan, © 1997), 204-205.

6.   Dr. Joyce Brothers, "7 Lies Men Tell Women", *Reader's Digest*, © 2012 The Reader's Digest Association, Inc., http://www.rd.com/family/7-

lies-men-tell-women/

7.   "Memorable quotes for Fireproof", Internet Movie Database, © 1990-
     2012 IMDb.com, Inc., http://www.imdb.com/title/tt1129423/quotes

Chapter 9

1.   Definition for "entangle", *Merriam Webster Online*, © 2012 Merriam-
     Webster, Inc., http://www.merriam-webster.com/dictionary/entangle

Chapter 10

1.   Quoted from the homepage of his website: tuckermax.com, © 2012
     Tucker Max, http://www.tuckermax.com

2.   "Tourism Minister Takes Bungee Leap of Faith", *ABC News*, Sydney,
     Australia, January 12, 2012, © 2012 ABC, http://www.abc.net.au/
     news/2012-01-12/minister-jumps-after-australian-woman27s-bungee-
     cord-snaps/3769318/?site=sydney

3.   "How To Succeed In New Surroundings", johnmaxwell.com, © 2011
     The John Maxwell Co., http://www.johnmaxwell.com/products-
     resources/leadership-on-demand/articles/how-to-succeed-in-new-sur-
     roundings/

4.   Mark Koba, *"Facebook's IPO: What We Know"*, cnbc.com, May 23,
     2012, © 2012 CNBC LLC, http://www.cnbc.com/id/47043815/
     Facebook_s_IPO_What_We_Know_Now

5.   Julie Appleby, *"Many Who Lost Savings, Jobs Pleased"*, USA Today,
     usatoday.com, May 26, 2006, © 2011 USA TODAY,
     http://www.usatoday.com/money/industries/energy/2006-05-25-en
     ron-workers-usat_x.htm

6.   "Scott Harrison", *Wikipedia*, Wikipedia Foundation, Inc.,
     http://en.wikipedia.org/wiki/Scott_Harrison_(charity_founder)

7.   Jessica Root, "Meet Scott Harrison, Founder of charity: water", *Planet
     Green*, August 13, 2009, © 2009 Discovery Communications, LLC,
     http://video.planetgreen.discovery.com/work-connect/change-makers-
     scott-harrison.html   (Retrieved November 14, 2010).

8.   Scott Harrison, "Scott's Story" (Founder's Story), charity: water, chari-
     tywater.org, video, March 20, 2012, © 2006 – 2012, http:// www.char-
     itywater.org/about/scotts_story.php, (Retrieved November 14, 2010).

9.   Jeff Slobotski, "Scott Harrison shares the charity: water story, discusses
     best practices", *Silicon Prairie News,* April 26, 2010, http:// www.sili-
     conprairienews.com/2010/04/scott-harrison-shares-the-charity-water-
     story-discusses-best-practices, (Retrieved November 14, 2010).

10.  Seth Doane, "Party Promoter's New Campaign: Clean Water", *CBS
     News,* August 18, 2009, © 2009 CBS, http://www.cbsnews.com/2100-
     18563_162-5250639.html, (Retrieved November 14, 2010).

11.  Nicholas D. Kristof, "Clean, Sexy Water", *The New York Times,* July 11,

2009, nytimes.com, © 2009 The New York Times Company, http://www.nytimes.com/2009/07/12/opinion/12kristof.html (Retrieved November 14, 2010).

12. "Scott Harrison, Photojournalist", *Gothamist*, August 31, 2005, © 2003-2012 Gothamist LLC, http://gothamist.com/2005/08/31/ scott_harrison_photojournalist.php (Retrieved November 14, 2010).

13. Ibid., "Scott's Story" (Founder's Story), charitywater.org video.

14. Kristof, "Clean, Sexy Water", Ibid.

15. Ibid., Root, "Meet Scott Harrison, Founder of charity: water".

16. Kristof, Ibid.

17. Ibid.

18. Ibid.

19. Root, Ibid.

20. Stanley Bing, "How To Deal With Your Crazy Boss: The Bully Symptoms", CNN.com, © 2012 CNN, http://money.cnn.com/galleries/ 2007/bing/0705/gallery.bosses_types_bing.fortune/index.html

21. Randall S. Hansen, Ph.D., "Dealing With a Bad Boss: Strategies for Coping", quintcareers.com, © Quintessential Careers, http:// www.quintcareers.com/bad_bosses.html

22. "Jim Collins Quotes", Goodreads.com, © 2012 Goodreads, Inc., http://www.goodreads.com/author/quotes/2826.Jim_Collins

23. T. Scott Gross, Karyn Buxman, and Greg Ayers, *The Service Prescription: Healthcare The Way It Was Meant To Be*, (Self-published, © 2009), 31. Survey data by BIGresearch.

24. Ibid., 36.

25. Howard Schulz, *Onward*, (New York: Rodale Books, © 2011), 23.

26. Ibid.

27. Ibid., 27.

28. Ibid., 40-41.

29. Ibid., 57.

30. Ibid., 61.

31. Ibid., 63.


*Chapter 11*

1. Chuck Colson, *Being the Body*, (Nashville, TN: W Publishing Group, © 2003), 205-206. Quote originally taken from transcript of *60 Minutes* 15, No. 21, as broadcast over the CBS television network, February 6, 1983.

2. James C. Dobson, Excerpt from "Gaps in Communication", troubledwith.com, a website of Focus on the Family, © 2009 Focus on the Family, http://www.troubledwith.com/Relationships/A000000664.cfm? topic=relationships%3A%20communication%20gaps

3. Atwood & Schwartz, *Journal of Couple & Relationship Therapy* (2002),

as quoted in Infidelity Statistics, Menstuff, © 1996-2011 Gordon Clay, Actual survey results were 45-55% of married women and 50-60% of married men. http://www.menstuff.org/issues/byissue/infidelitystats. html

4. *Australopithecus afarensis* translates to "southern ape from the Afar tri-angle of Ethiopia," believed by some evolutionists, paleontologists, and archaeologists to be a 2-million year old extinct origin species of Homo genus, and here used symbolically to refer to a semi-controversial ori-gin and connection between anger and bitterness.

*Chapter 12*

1. Charles Montaldo, "Top Ten List of Dumbest Criminals in 2011", About.com Crime/Punishment, © 2012 About.com, http://crime. about.com/od/stupidcriminals/tp/Dumb-Criminals-2011.html

2. Eric Platt, "How a Tenacious Summer Analyst Applicant Got Laughed At By Goldman, Morgan, And Everyone Else On Wall Street", YAHOO! Finance, Business Insider, February 9, 2012, © 2012 Yahoo! Inc., http://finance.yahoo.com/news/tenacious-summer-analyst-appli-cant-got-laughed-at-by-everyone-else-on-wall-street.html

3. Ibid.

4. Andrew Knox, "Albert Pujols: A Hero's Worship", The 700 Club, CBN.com, © 2012 The Christian Broadcasting Network, Inc., http://www.cbn.com/entertainment/sports/700club_albertpu-jols080206.aspx

5. Ibid.

6. "Tebow laughs at Hurricanes bounty report", FloridaToday.com, Aug. 18, 2011, © 2012 www.floridaytoday.com, http://www.floridatoday. com/article/20110818/BREAKINGNEWS/110818020/1002/ SPORTS/Tebow-laughs-Hurricanes-bounty-report

7. See Genesis 35:22b-26 for a list of Jacob's wives *[and/or mistresses]*, and children.

8. Charles Lowery, "A Box of Chocolates", *SBC Life*, (Nashville, TN: SBC Executive Committee, January, 2007).

9. "Laughs", Reader's Digest, © 2012 The Reader's Digest Association, Inc., http://www.rd.com/laughs/years-of-romance-joke/

10. Randy Raysbrook, "Resisting Group Pressure", *Discipleship Journal*, Issue 33, (Colorado Springs, CO: NavPress, 1986), *[page unknown]*.

11. Bear Grilles is a British adventurer and international TV personality, famous for his *Man vs. Wild* wilderness survival series. Bear is a man who has always loved adventure. After breaking his back in three places in a parachuting accident, he fought his way to recovery, and two years later, at the age of 23, entered the Guinness Book of Records as the

youngest Brit to climb Mount Everest.

12. Improvised Explosive Devices were homemade bombs used in the Iraq and Afghanistan Wars against coalition forces and usually hidden by a roadside for maximum destruction.

13. Boldness for God's name and truth is also linked to the power of the Spirit living in a believer (see Acts 4:8).

## Chapter 13

1. Steve Henson, "As Real As It Gets: Bullying Victims Can Fight Back With Help From Brazilian Jiu-Jitsu Royalty", The Post-Game, August 21, 2011, © 2012 Sports Media Ventures, Inc., http://www.thepost game.com/features/201108/real-it-gets-victims-schoolyard-bullying-can-fight-back-help-ufc-royalty

2. Ibid.

3. Bill O'Reilly and Martin Dugard, *Killing Lincoln: The Shocking Assassination That Changed America Forever*, (New York: Henry Holt and Company, LLC, © 2011), 3.

4. Ibid., 5.

5. Quoted from a November 9, 2007 *London Daily Mail* interview.

6. John McCain, *Faith of My Fathers*, (New York: Random House, © 1999), 228.

7. Timothy Stenovec, "Youcef Nadarkhani, Iranian Pastor, May Face Execution For 'Apostasy From Islam'", HUFF POST RELIGION, *The Huffington Post*, February 23, 2012, © 2012, TheHuffingtonPost.com, Inc., http://www.huffingtonpost.com/2012/02/23/youcef-nadarkhani-iranian-pastor-death-execution_n_1297262.html

8. Ibid.

9. "Full Story of Youcef Nadarkhani", PresentTruth Ministries, http://presenttruthmn.com/the-ministry/youcef-nadarkhani/

10. "Lara Logan Breaks Silence on Cairo Assault", *60 Minutes*, April 28, 2011, Produced by Robert Anderson, cbsnews.com, © 2012 CBS Interactive Inc., http://www.cbsnews.com/stories/2011/04/28/60minutes/main 20058368_page2.shtml?tag=contentMain;contentBody

11. Ibid.

## Chapter 14

1. Albert Pujols, "My Testimony", pujolsfamilyfoundation.org, © 2012 Pujols Family Foundation, http://www.pujolsfamilyfoundation.org/faith/testimony.htm

2. Seth Godin, "10,000 hours", Seth Godin's Blog, December, 2008, http://sethgodin.typepad.com/seths_blog/2008/12/10000-hours.html

3. Seth Godin, *The Dip: A Little Book That Teaches You When To Quit (and*

*When To Stick)*, (New York: The Penguin Group, Do You Zoom, Inc., © 2007), Back Cover.

4. *American HUNTER Magazine*, May, 2011, (Palm Coast, FL: National Rifle Association), 23.

5. Excerpted from *Pure Excitement* by Joe White, as quoted in Real Life Stories, premaritalsex.info, Marty D, © 2009, http://www.premarital sex. info/stories.htm

6. Consider the scenario of God's decision to destroy all life on the planet in Noah's generation—a scheduled judgment—even personally closing the door on the Ark. See Genesis 6:1-6, 12-13; 7:16.

7. Us Weekly Staff, *Video: Jesse: "I Wanted to Get Caught" Cheating on Sandra Bullock*, UsMagazine.com, May 24, 2010, © 2012 US Weekly, http://www.usmagazine.com/celebritynews/news/jesse-james-i-wanted-to-get-caught-cheating-on-sandra-bullock-2010245

8. From Proverbs 5:9-23, 6:24-35, and 7:21-27.

*Chapter 15*

1. "Russell Brand's Jokes During Detention", Contactmusic.com, May 23, 2011, © 2012 Contactmusic.com Ltd, http://www.contactmusic .com/news.nsf/story/russell-brands-jokes-during-japan-detention_ 1220780

2. "Brad Pitt Says He Was 'Trying To Pretend' Marriage With Jennifer Aniston Was 'Something That It Wasn't'", Excerpted from interview in *PARADE Magazine*, gossip.com. September 15, 2011, © 2012 Gossip Cop Media, http://www.gossipcop.com/brad-pitt-parade-magazine-interview-september-2011-jennifer-aniston-pretend-pretending-marriage-pathetic/

3. Yael Danieli, Editor, *International Handbook of Multigenerational Legacies of Trauma*, (New York: Plenum Press, 1998), 194.

4. Robert McNamara, "Mary Todd Lincoln Saw Ghosts In the White House and Held a Séance", *Supernatural and Spooky Events of the 1800's*, About.com, New York Times, © 2012 About.com., New York Times Company. http://history1800s.about.com/od/entertainment sport/ss/ supernatural-19th-century_5.htm

5. Ibid.

6. "Mary Todd Lincoln and Clairvoyance", forbiddentruth.com, http://www.theforbiddenknowledge.com/hardtruth/mary_todd_lin-coln.htm

7. Ibid.

8. J.G. Randall and Richard N. Current, *Lincoln The President: Last Full Measure*, Volume 4, (Chicago, IL: University of Illinois Press, © 1955, 1983), 374.

9. Dennis William Hauck, "White House Ghosts", Haunted-Places.com,

http://www.haunted-places.com/WhiteHouseGhosts.htm

10. Ibid.

11. Ibid.

12. Ibid.

13. A sample of background references include: Job 1-2, Daniel 10:1-2; Matthew 8:28-34 / Mark 5:1-13 / Acts 5:3; 16:16-18; 19:13-16 / 2 Corinthians 11:13-15; 12:7 / Colossians 1:15-20 / 2 Thessalonians 2:9-10 / Luke 4:41; 9:37-35; 11:24-26; 13:16; 16:19-31; 22:3 / 1 Timothy 4:1-3 / James 2:19 / Jude 1:9 / Revelation 7:1; 8:5; 12:9; 15:1,16.

*Chapter 16*

1. "Elizabeth Smart Recalls Rape After 'Marriage' In Trial Testimony", *Fox News*, foxnews.com, November 9, 2010, © 2012 FOX News Network, LLC. http://www.foxnews.com/us/2010/11/09/elizabeth-smart-recalls -rape-marriage-trial-testimony/

2. Elizabeth Tumposky, "Elizabeth Smart Confronts Her Tormentor In Utah Sentencing", *ABC News*, abcnews.go.com, May 26, 2011, http://abcnews.go.com/US/elizabeth-smart-confront-tormentor-sen-tencing-today/story?id=13683810

3. Ibid.

4. Meredith Lepore, "JFK's Affair With An Intern Should Be Looked At As A Tale Of Caution For Young Women", The Thread, The GRIND-STONE, February 7, 2012, B5Media Lifestyle Network, http:// thegrindstone.com/office-politics/jfks-affair-with-an-intern-should-be-looked-at-as-a-tale-of-caution-for-young-women-717/

5. Brandon Dutcher, "For Adolph Coors IV, Money Couldn't Fill the Emptiness Inside", Dutch Reformed Blog, From an April, 1994 Interview with Adolph Coors IV, November 8, 2005, http:// brandondutcher.blogspot.com/2005/11/for-adolph-coors-iv-money-couldnt-fill.html

6. "February 5, 1960: Coors Brewery Heir Is Kidnapped", This Day in History: Crime, History.com, © 1996-2012, A&E Television Networks, LLC, http://www.history.com/this-day-in-history/coors-brewery-heir-is-kidnapped

7. Lee Strobel, *God's Outrageous Claims*, (Grand Rapids, MI: Zondervan, 1997), *[page unknown]*.

8. Sue Shellenbarger, "Before They Were Titans, Moguls and Newsmakers, These People Were...Rejected", *The Wall Street Journal Online*, March 24, 2010, © Dow Jones & Company, Inc., http://online. wsj.com/article/SB1000142405274870421170457513989139059596 2.html

9. Ibid.

10. Jud Wilhite, *TORN: Trusting God When Life Leaves You In Pieces*, (Colorado Springs, CO: Multnomah Books, © 2011), 38.
11. Ibid., 40.
12. Ibid., 42-43.
13. "Ted Turner Was Suicidal After Breakup", *Associated Press*, April 16, 2001, © 2011 The New York Times Co., www.nytimes.com/aponline/ arts/AP-People-Turner.html
14. Tommy Mitchell, "Why Does God's Creation Include Death and Suffering?", *The New Answers Book*, answersingenesis.org, January 31, 2008, © 2012 Answers in Genesis, http://www.answersingene sis.org/articles/ nab/why-does-creation-include-suffering
15. A. Desmond and J. Moore, *Darwin: The Life of a Tormented Evolutionist*, (New York: W.W. Norton & Company, 1991), 387.
16. "NATO Unaware Qaddafi Was in Convoy at Time of Strike, Officials Say", *FOX News*, foxnews.com / October 21, 2011, © 2012 FOX News Network, LLC, http://www.foxnews.com/world/2011/10/21/ libyans-qaddafi-to-be-buried-in-islamic-tradition/

### Chapter 17

1. Bill Gates, "Microsoft's Bill Gates: Harvard commencement speech transcript", From the transcript published on NetworkWorld.com, © 1994-2012 Network World, Inc., http://www.network world.com/news/2007/ 060807-gates-commencement.html
2. Bill O'Reilly groups newsmakers into two categories, "Pinheads" (those who do dishonorable things) or "Patriots" (those who do what is right) for his nightly polls on FOX News' *The O'Reilly Factor*.
3. Luis Palau, *SAY YES! How to Renew Your Spiritual Passion*, (Grand Rapids, MI: Discovery House, © 1995), *[page unknown]*.
4. Natalie Angier, "If Anger Ruins Your Day, It Can Shrink Your Life", *New York Times*, nytimes.com, June 19, 2008, © 2012 The New York Times Company.
5. Ibid.
6. "Elderly Man Returns Cash Stolen From Sears in '40's", *Associated Press*, November 29, 2011, © 2012 Yahoo! Inc., http://news.yahoo.com/ elderly-man-returns-cash-stolen-sears-40s-031332055.html

### Chapter 18

1. Bethany Kandel, "The Wedding Couple Depart In Good Humor", *The New York Times*, July 15, 2011, nytimes.com, © 2011 The New York Times Company, http://www.nytimes.com/2011/07/17/fashion/wed dings/wed ding-couples-make-memorable-entrances-and-exits.html?_r=2
2. Ibid.

3.  Lev Grossman, "Outliers: Malcolm Gladwell's Success Story", *TIME Magazine* / ARTS, time.com, November 13, 2008, © 2012 Time Inc., http://www.time.com/time/magazine/article/0,9171,1858880-2,00. html
4.  Ibid.
5.  Ibid.
6.  Quoted from a live interview during the FOX News coverage of the Florida Republican Primary on January 31, 2012.
7.  Denny Coates, "The 10,000-Hour Rule", Building Personal Strength Blog, October 25, 2010, http://www.buildingpersonalstrength.com/ 2010/10/10000-hour-rule-in-malcolm-gladwells.html
8.  Ibid.
9.  "Abraham and Mary Lincoln: A House Divided", Part Four: The Dearest of All Things, Transcript, The American Experience, pbs.org, PBS Broadcast, © 1996-2010 WGBH Educational Foundation, 4. http://www.pbs.org/wgbh/americanexperience/features/transcript/lin-colns-transcript/4/
10. Ibid.
11. Ibid.
12. Donald Miller, "A Response To Pat Robertson's Comments About Haiti", Donald Miller's Blog, January 13, 2010, http://donmilleris .com/ 2010/01/13/1513/

### Chapter 19

1.  David Gergen, "Mitt Romney: Family Man", *PARADE Magazine*, December 4, 2011, © 2012 Parade Publications, 10-16.
2.  Eric Pape, "Mitt Romney's Life as a Missionary: Nearly Killed in a Car Accident", *THE DAILY BEAST*, thedailybeast.com, January 15, 2012, © 2011 The Newsweek/Daily Beast Company LLC, http://www. thedailybeast.com/articles/2012/01/14/mitt-romney-s-life-as-a-mis-sionary-nearly-killed-in-a-car-accident.html
3.  Ibid., 11.
4.  Lee Strobel, *God's Outrageous Claims*, (Grand Rapids, MI: Zondervan, 1997), *[page unknown]*.
5.  "The Weekly Thought from Breakfast With Fred", BWF Project, Inc., July 27, 2010, © 2010.

### Chapter 20

1.  Internet Movie Database, *The Fades*, Plot Summary, © 1990-2012 IMDb.com, Inc., http://www.imdb.com/title/tt1772379/
2.  John is thought to have been exiled to the isle of Patmos (a Greek island in the Aegean Sea) during the reign of Emperor Domitian (see Revelation 1:9), when the persecution of Christians reached a peak (81-96 C.E.).
3.  David Jeremiah, *Prayer: The Great Adventure*, (Colorado Springs, CO:

Multnomah Books, © 1997), 111-113. The story was originally taken from an InterVarsity Christian Fellowship mailing.

4.  Ibid., 113.
5.  Ellen Tumposky, "Husband Combs Florida Landfill to Find Wife's Engagement Ring", *ABC News*, abcnews.com, Nov 11, 2011, http://abcnews.go.com/blogs/headlines/2011/11/husband-combs-landfill-to-find-wifes-diamond-ring/
6.  "Relationship Reasons For Divorce", PsychPage, Psychpage.com, http://www.psychpage.com/family/mod_couples_thx/divorce.html (Sourced 3-06-12).

*Chapter 21*

1.  Erwin Raphael McManus, *An Unstoppable Force: Daring To Become The Church God Had In Mind*, (Loveland, CO: Group Publishing, Inc., © 2001), 39.
2.  Ibid.
3.  Ibid., 40.
4.  Romans 8:28-29, 31.
5.  *Our Daily Bread*, March 22, 1994.
6.  2 Corinthians 4:5-12 explains all suffering for Christ in particular has a purpose and is always controlled by God.
7.  Romans 2:13-15.
8.  1 John 2:15-17 (see also 2 Corinthians 1:12 and 1 Timothy 1:19-20).
9.  1 Samuel 16:14 / 1 Thessalonians 5:19 (see also Acts 4:31; 16:5-8).
10. 1 John 3:20-21 / 1 Corinthians 11:27.
11. Ecclesiastes 2:1-11 / Romans 1:28 (see 1:18-32).
12. Genesis 13:10-11; 19:16-26. Lot's conscience killed him daily according to 2 Peter 2:7-9.
13. Jonah 1:15-17.
14. Joshua 7:1-12.
15. 2 Samuel 12:1-19; 13:14, 29; 14:30.
16. James 5:14-16 / 1 Corinthians 11:29-32.
17. Acts 5:1-5. There actually is a "sin that leads to death" (see 1 John 5:16-17).
18. Hebrews 12:10-13.

CPSIA information can be obtained at www.ICGtesting.com
Printed in the USA
LVOW10s2258160813

348308LV00003B/11/P